BLOOD
and
HISTORY
in CHINA

BLOOD
and
HISTORY
in CHINA

*The Donglin Faction
and Its Repression, 1620–1627*

John W. Dardess

University of Hawai'i Press

Honolulu

07 06 05 04 03 02   6 5 4 3 2 1

Library of Congress Cataloging-in-Publication Data

Dardess, John W.
    Blood and history in China : the Donglin faction and its repression,
1620–1627 / John W. Dardess.
        p. cm.
    Includes bibliographical references and index.
    ISBN 0–8248–2475–X (alk. paper) — ISBN 0–8248–2516–0 (paper : alk.
paper)
    1. China—History—Ming dynasty, 1368–1644. 2. Dong lin shu yuan (China)
3. Political parties—China.   I. Title: Donglin faction and its repression,
1620–1627. II. Title.

DS753.2 .D37 2002
951'.026—dc21

                                                                2001053063

Designed by David Ford

Printed by The Maple-Vail Book Manufacturing Group

Contents

◀

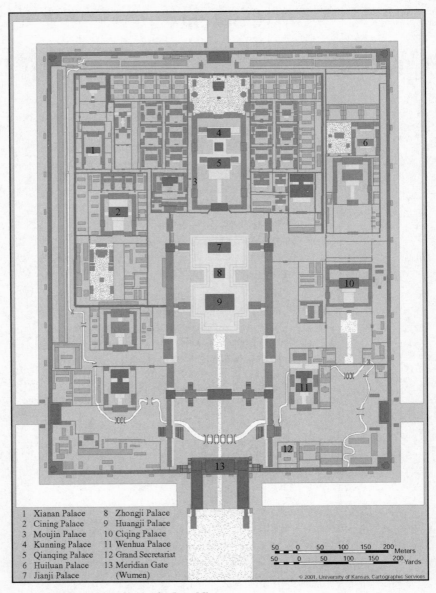

1	Xianan Palace	8	Zhongji Palace
2	Cining Palace	9	Huangji Palace
3	Moujin Palace	10	Ciqing Palace
4	Kunning Palace	11	Wenhua Palace
5	Qianqing Palace	12	Grand Secretariat
6	Huiluan Palace	13	Meridian Gate
7	Jianji Palace		(Wumen)

50   0   50   100   150   200 Meters
50   0   50   100   150   200 Yards

© 2001, University of Kansas, Cartographic Services

Map 1. The Forbidden City in the Late Ming

Acknowledgments

◀

I FIRST WISH to thank Samuel Chu and the ACLS-sponsored conference he organized at the University of Hawai'i in 1993. That conference, whose theme was "The Continuing Relevance of Traditional Chinese Institutions in the Context of Modern China," prompted me to revisit the Donglin affair and to discover how much of that story had never been told. I also thank Wei Sheng, Peter Bol, Susan Naquin, Chün-fang Yü, and Carolyn Nelson for providing me the opportunity to present some of the ideas developed in this book to small but knowledgeable groups at Harvard, Princeton, Rutgers, and the University of Kansas. Sabbatical leave from the University of Kansas in the fall of 1998 gave me time to draft most of the chapters. It has been a pleasure to work with Patricia Crosby of the University of Hawai'i Press; and I also thank the readers for their helpful and constructive comments.

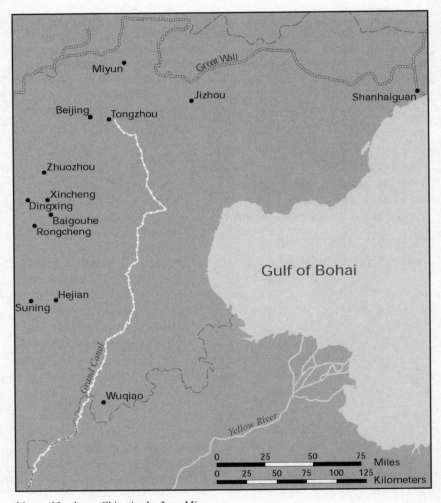

Map 2. Northeast China in the Late Ming

BLOOD
and
HISTORY
in CHINA

Introduction

◀

IN SEVENTEENTH-century China, the name "Donglin" meant three different but partly overlapping things. It stood for an ethical revitalization movement; it referred to a national Confucian moral fellowship; and it also labeled a Beijing political faction, whose activities are the main focus of this book. The name comes from the Donglin ("East Forest") academy of Wuxi county, located about fifty miles west of Shanghai, in what is now Jiangsu province. The heyday of the Donglin in all of its dimensions were the early decades of the seventeenth century.

The Donglin academy, from its refounding in 1604, disseminated through its widely attended lecture sessions, open to officials and students from all over China, an ethically intense and militant Confucianism, according to which, in the words of Heinrich Busch, everyone was "urged to form convictions on the basis of truth and adhere to them uncompromisingly without regard to the consequences."[1] Important for our story is the fact that the Donglin leaders also labored to place their adherents and sympathizers in key offices of the central government and, through them, to achieve nothing less than the remaking of a troubled Ming China starved, they believed, of morally right-guided leadership.

In 1620 and 1621, after the death of the Wanli emperor, who had long been hostile to the Donglin, it appeared that the movement had triumphed at last. But over the next several years its pretensions were challenged and its power curtailed, and from 1625 to 1627 the young Tianqi emperor and his favorite eunuch, Wei Zhongxian, purged and destroyed the Donglin movement in one of the most spectacularly gruesome political repressions perpetrated in the history of China to that point.

It all makes for gripping drama. Normally the story finds its place as an episode in the longer history of late Ming partisan struggle and dynastic decline and collapse.[2] Long ago, Charles O. Hucker published an excellent chapter-length study of the Donglin movement, the conclusions of which still strike me as valid. But when I first read that paper in the

1

early 1960s, I was left puzzled and bewildered by the affair, and I found it inexplicable why so many should have sacrificed even their lives for what seemed to be no important or useful or even definable purpose.[3]

Until 1989, that is. The Tiananmen demonstrations of spring 1989 offered several compelling clues to a satisfactory rereading of the events of the 1620s, which also had their epicenter in Beijing. Whatever it was that kept so many of us who were not in China in 1989 glued to our television sets while the demonstrations were under way, it had something to do with loving good and hating evil; with vilifying the corrupt and cheering for the selfless and the brave; with the play of hope against despair; and, in the end, with the smashing of beautiful, fragile ideals on the ugly rocks of entrenched power. And all those things were searing and memorable because they were visceral, and it all ended, appropriately enough, awash in blood and martyrdom.

From what happened in 1989 it became evident that, in China, a political-moral confrontation was not necessarily aimed at achieving practical reforms or concrete results. The point was not to achieve victory in the usual sense. Rather, the intention was to communicate sincere moral feelings to the rulers and to the public at large. The agenda was imprecise, symbolic, unrealistic. The protesters did not venture beyond spontaneous or ad hoc organization as a matter of principle rather than oversight. Their mood became so vehement as to be intolerant of negotiation and compromise. In the end, the protesters (both the Donglin and the students in 1989) did achieve something through their elitist storm of absolute self-righteousness: glorious commemoration for the dead and imprisoned participants, and eternal infamy for those who unleashed the dogs of repression upon them. Repression and memory; blood and history. Hence the title of this book.

With perhaps very few exceptions, the protesters of 1989 were not knowledgeable about China's past or aware of what had taken place in the 1620s on the same ground now occupied by Tiananmen Square.[4] Even so, scholarly commentary has called attention to the place of China's national self-obsession and persistent traditionalism in the story of Tiananmen in 1989. It has been said that Tiananmen was "ritual or 'ritualized' political theater" in which an educated elite, articulating ideals on behalf of the entire nation, demanded "a greater voice" in the affairs of government.[5] It has also been said that, like the students and scholar-officials *(shi)* of imperial times, the intellectuals and students who protested in

1989 were an "achievement-based elite—or at least an aspiring elite" who had proved themselves, or were in the process of proving themselves, through academic competition.[6]

At center stage, then, ready for suffering and death, converged the nation's brightest and best. By a display of total sincerity, they hoped to "move" (gandong) the holders of power. Compelling public statements were composed. On May 18, 1989, a dozen student leaders actually gained the opportunity to meet with Premier Li Peng in a moral showdown, a meeting of feverish emotional intensity of which excerpts were later televised. As is usual in such cases, authority proved resistant to the ethical reawakening that the protesters demanded of it.

Meanwhile, confined as always to the sides of the stage, the common people enlarged the unfolding drama by offering from the sidelines their sympathy and moral support. In 1625, there had been crowds of tradesmen and commoners who wept and offered sacrifices and donated cash to the Donglin hero Yang Lian as imperial police escorted him north to Beijing. There were shopkeepers and laborers and commoners who surged in riot in the rain-soaked streets of Suzhou in 1626 when the police came to arrest Zhou Shunchang. There was also an outpouring of public support for the Beijing protesters of 1989, when, thanks to television, the sideline chorus swelled to include the whole globe. The last act of 1989 was a crackdown, as authority in the end retaliated against the protesters with spectacular cruelty.

There seems to be something psychologically askew about the idea that political authority should somehow yield to collective displays of selfless sincerity. Government, Ming and modern, assumes and acts upon the assumption that protesters have hidden agendas, that what they are demanding is not what they really have in mind. The effort to "move" authority fails, and everything ends in bloody retaliation. Given their constant talk of blood, the protesters themselves half expect this. One suspects it all ends this way because, in part, the more radical of the protesters underestimate the force of their rhetoric and fail to gauge the effect their unlimited and unconditional claims to moral righteousness may have upon those in power whom they are addressing. Grand Secretary Ye Xianggao, as a man caught in the middle, noted this phenomenon at work in 1624. In 1989, foreign television viewers could see for themselves how effectively the protesters managed to transform Deng Xiaoping from a hero of liberalization into a vicious, corrupt autocrat, or Li Peng from a faceless party functionary into a personification of evil, a kind of latter-day Wei Zhongxian.

Bloody crackdown, evidently, is a requirement of the script. The protesters are the nation's moral and intellectual elite. They cannot be maneuvered or finessed or bought off, and so it all ends in blood and beatings and arrests and torture-murders and machine guns. Blood and history. As student leader Chai Ling suggested, it is through the periodic reenactment of this compelling public drama that China seems to reaffirm its moral and spiritual oneness as a civilization and as a nation.

In the speeches and placards and protest literature of 1989, "blood" and "history" are two words that stand out through constant repetition. By "history," the protesters sometimes meant history-as-past, and in that (for them) negative sense of the word, they construed the current regime as a recrudescence of the oppressive imperial dragon of olden times. But, more often, the protesters meant by "history" not past but future history, because their actions would ensure remembrance by future generations of what the protesters were doing now. As exhausted but ecstatic student demonstrators returned to their campuses on April 27, "history wept and history also smiled."[7] "Let the son call you once more, 'Mama!' You will not understand your son, but history will," read a big-character poster of April 23.[8] "History will remember this historic time, these historic lives, these historic heroes!" read another, in mid-May.[9] "With the spirit of the sacrifice of our lives," said student leader Chai Ling in an emotional mid-May interview, "we fight for life. Death is not what we seek but we contemplate death knowing that the eternal, broad echoes [of our cries] and the cause that we write with our lives will float in the air of the Republic."[10]

Blood, of course, was the ink of this future history. "Even if ahead lies the end of our lives / Our blood and our unconquerable souls, / shall forever be in the annals of our nation!" stated a small-character poster of the week of April 20.[11] "My students, history's heavy burden rests heavy on your shoulders. . . . [And] if there are people who force us to shed blood, then let our blood flow!" cried intellectual Ren Wanding in a speech of late April.[12] In the words of Chai Ling, late in May, "only when the government descends to the depths of depravity and decides to deal with us by slaughtering us, only when rivers of blood flow in the Square, will the eyes of our country's people truly be opened, and only then will they unite. . . ."[13] And when the end came, on June 3, she said: "Everybody sat there quietly, awaiting with calm expressions the butcher knives of the slaughterers. We were carrying out a war of love and hate, not a battle of military force. . . . The students just sat there quietly, lying down to await [the moment of] sacrifice."[14]

Here, one striking difference between the Tiananmen affair and the Donglin protests of the 1620s can be noted. The Donglin radicals were themselves central government officials, men of mature age, who voluntarily surrendered themselves to the very authority whose moral credentials they had challenged, and then suffered martyrdoms of a most cruel and gruesome kind. By contrast, the Tiananmen radicals were young students who, for all their rhetoric of blood and sacrifice, escaped the regime's violent crackdown, the brunt of which fell on workers and others.[15]

In one essential respect, however, the Donglin hero-martyrs of the 1620s beg to be understood in the same light as the leaders in Tiananmen in 1989—that is, not as insurrectionaries, but as uncompromising champions of a moral point of view, a national ethical vanguard proposing to use its very blood to write that point of view in such a way as to seize the attention of present and future generations.

The available sources for the events of 1620–1627 are many and rich, and they have not been much used by modern researchers. There are personal letters that participants wrote describing their thoughts and feelings to friends and family; there are personal diaries and autobiographical accounts; there are prison letters of victims, some of them written in blood; and there are eyewitness records, like that of the pseudonymous "Beijing guest" who worked under cover as an orderly in the Decree Prison in Beijing and left a detailed description of the sufferings inflicted on six of the Donglin heroes in 1625. There are publications of private copies of imperial edicts and rescripts, and of extracts from memorials that came out in the so-called "Beijing Gazette" *(Dibao)*. There are original memorials to the throne, unedited by official court historians and bearing the original dates of submission and rescript. Beginning right after the suicide of eunuch Wei Zhongxian in 1628, there began to be published compilations of personal accounts and official documents, such as the *Bixue lu* (Jade blood record), as well as topical histories written to satisfy an evident public appetite for reading material devoted to recent events. Probably no earlier event in China's long history has available for modern retelling anything like the archive available for the Donglin affair.

The seventeenth century in China was in many ways an age that licensed the unleashing of romantic passions. It was a time when many

people, in literature and in drama as well as in real life, felt somehow compelled to pursue emotional commitments to their often lethal conclusions. The protean term for such passionate commitment was *qing*, which
usually attached itself to sensual impulses, such as love affairs, but could
as well be harnessed to the pursuit of moral ideals. And suffering and
death in pursuit of one's moral ideals, far from being invalidated, might
actually be "authenticated" by the failure of one's efforts to affect and
move the object of one's moral struggle.[16] The Donglin martyrs failed in
their stated purpose, which was to encourage the Tianqi emperor, inadequate figure as he was, to step forward and behave as an ideal Confucian
ruler should; yet although they failed, they died in the attempt, and so
won eternal remembrance from an understanding public for their hero-
ism and steadfastness.

Seventeenth-century China was also a society suffering from chronic
and worrisome crises, particularly its inability to stop the steady advancement of Nurhaci's Jurchens (after 1635, Manchus) upon what official circles considered to be Ming ancestral territory in Liaodong, just a few
hundred miles northeast of Beijing. A catastrophic collapse of Ming
armies there in 1619 was followed by further major reverses in 1621 and
again in 1622.[17] Somehow the dynasty had to be rallied to reverse that situation. Moderates among the Donglin argued that it was time for everyone to put other concerns aside and work together to solve the crisis.
However, radicals among the Donglin insisted that the crisis could not be
solved unless Ming China first undertook national moral rearmament under the personal auspices of its ultimate authority, the Tianqi emperor.
The radicals relentlessly pushed their agenda. Deceptively trivial issues,
especially the so-called Three Cases, were elevated by them into centerpieces of life-and-death political struggle. The radicals lost this battle.
Donglin opponents rallied behind Palace eunuch Wei Zhongxian and in
1626 managed, temporarily at least, to impose a first-ever military defeat
upon Nurhaci's Jurchens. Unfortunately, the Donglin opposition fatally
degraded the quality of Ming political life with their frightening arrests
and horrible tortures of the leading Donglin partisans, and their purge of
the rest, a process that raged through two years, 1625 and 1626, and indeed was still going on when the Tianqi emperor died in September 1627
and the whole effort collapsed. The aftereffects of that partisan violence
were more than the last Ming emperor, Chongzhen, could cope with,
though he tried. Internal rebellions broke out and soon grew uncon-

tainable. Seventeen years later, in 1644, the Manchus seized Beijing and commenced the conquest of all the rest of China.[18]

Many people in the Manchu Qing dynasty looked back with fear and horror at the Donglin encounter with "blood and history" because, as will be noted in Chapter 6, they believed the Ming collapse to have been brought about in some major way by the political provocations of the Donglin heroes' moral extremism. The Manchu rulers worked, with better success than the Chongzhen emperor was able to achieve, to ensure that weak imperial leadership and other conditions favorable to a renewal of all-out factional confrontation should never arise again.

But something of a cultural predilection for political-moral "struggles to the death" (sizheng) lived on to resurface in times of crisis in the modern era. Tang Tsou has noted a spirit of "final confrontation" and "settlement of accounts" in which not just Tiananmen but much of twentieth-century politics in China has been enacted.[19] It is evident from what happened in the 1620s, and again in 1989, that the absolute moral certitude the radicals espoused marginalized as corrupt all efforts toward negotiation and compromise. And, in both cases, the extreme personalization of the issues of engagement so demonized the opposition that it was left with little alternative other than to agree to do battle on the protesters' terms and crush them in the same high spirit of rectitude that they themselves had been forced to confront.

The Donglin affair was no harbinger of some possible future parliamentary democracy.[20] Donglin Confucian thought was monarchical and authoritarian to the core.[21] However, the arrangement of political institutions in Beijing in the 1620s was already in some ways closer to a parliamentary system than the party-driven regime of 1989, at least insofar as the Ming state included a corps of some 170 "speaking officials," that is, members of the Censorate and Offices of Scrutiny (often jointly referred to as the kedao), whose duties included criticism of mistaken or inappropriate imperial acts.[22] The Donglin martyrs were mainly, though not exclusively, kedao who conducted their protests against the imperial government both as a political duty formally required by their offices and as an ethical obligation stemming from their extracurricular understanding of Confucian doctrine.

But that is about as far as parliamentarism went. The whole tragedy and pathos of the Donglin protests was a function of the protesters' unshakable belief in the ultimate decision-making power of the emperor. Not one of them entertained even for a moment the thought of challenging that power. Even as they were unjustly arrested and abused and tortured, even when they could have joined the rioters in the streets of their home cities of Suzhou, or De'anfu, or Tongcheng, or Jiangyin, or Changzhou, and opposed Tianqi's grotesque tyranny with popular force, the Donglin martyrs resolutely refused to seize the opportunity. They obeyed the imperial orders. They voluntarily delivered themselves into the hands of murderers, and their blood made history.

The Ming Throne Imperiled
The Three Cases

◀

IN THE SUMMER of 1620, Ming government at its highest level came close to a point of meltdown. Many opinion makers of the time asserted that the ultimate blame for that lay with Zhu Yijun, better known as the Wanli emperor (r. 1573–1620).

For decades, Wanli liked to do things, or not to do things, in his own way. He hated being pressured. Ming house law, the Ancestral Instructions *(Zu xun)*, clearly required that oldest sons be designated as successors to the throne. Wanli had an oldest son, Zhu Changluo. Formally installing him as heir apparent should have been a routine matter. Somehow it was not. For fifteen years Wanli made excuses about it, and his delay became the focal point of dark speculations and fervent protests among Beijing officialdom. Sequestered inside the Forbidden City as he kept himself, no one knew for certain what Wanli's procrastination meant. A protracted standoff, indeed a national crisis, resulted and earned its own rubric: the "struggle over the root of the state" *(zheng guoben)*. In October 1601, the emperor angrily gave in to the pressure and had the nineteen-year-old Zhu Changluo formally designated heir to the throne of Ming China.[1]

But the struggle over the root of the state, far from quieting down, soon intensified. Rumors about family matters inside the Forbidden City caused many officials to suspect that the emperor did not care for Zhu Changluo and was maneuvering to replace him with Zhu Changxun, a younger son by his favorite concubine, the notorious Zheng Guifei.

In 1614, after many years of official protest, Wanli again yielded to pressure and sent Zhu Changxun (Prince of Fu) away from the Forbidden City and out to a lavish residence built especially for him in Henan province.

Zhu Changluo's position as heir apparent, once again, seemed secure. But, once again, it was not. The first of the sensational Three Cases happened in the very next year, 1615. It involved an alleged attempt to murder Zhu Changluo. It is known as the Stick Case *(tingji zhi an)*. Overnight, it became a major issue of dispute between the Donglin party and its opponents in late Ming China's steadily intensifying intrabureaucratic struggle.

◀

A few facts about the convoluted Stick Case everyone agreed upon. There was no doubt that in the early evening of May 30, 1615, a lone assailant armed with a stick somehow managed to enter the Forbidden City and proceeded to the lightly guarded Ciqing palace, where Zhu Changluo lived as heir-designate to the Ming throne. The assailant struck an elderly eunuch by the name of Liu Jian to the ground. Then he went up the steps of the palace. Eunuch Han Benyang cried for help. Six or seven other eunuchs came running. They seized, disarmed, and tied up the intruder. Then they took him to the office of the security guards at the Donghua gate. Meanwhile, Han Benyang told Zhu Changluo what had happened, and Zhu Changluo sent him to tell Wanli.

At the Donghua gate, squad leader Zhao Guozhong interrogated the suspect. His superior, Commander Zhu Xiong, wrote up a report that, on the following day, May 31, was incorporated into a formal memorial by Censor Liu Tingyuan, on duty as imperial city patrolling inspector. According to Censor Liu's memorial, the assailant's name was Zhang Chai; he was a commoner, thirty-five years *(sui)* old; his home village was Jingeryu in Jizhou prefecture (some fifty miles east of Beijing); and he was a religious sectarian of some sort. Little else of his testimony made sense, however. It appeared he might be mentally deranged *(fengmo),* but his demeanor also suggested some possible deceit. Censor Liu recommended that Zhang Chai be interrogated further, and then be severely punished for his violent intrusion upon the imperial security.[2]

However, the Stick Case exploded within a matter of days into an irresolvable national political dispute. Was Zhang Chai merely a deranged loner? Or was he part of some sinister plot to kill Zhu Changluo? Those in the upper echelons of the bureaucracy who believed that Zhang Chai was unquestionably involved in an assassination plot were the so-called Donglin faction of moral absolutists.

Prisoner Zhang Chai was moved from the guardhouse at the Donghua gate to the custody of the Ministry of Justice. On June 5, Acting Vice

Minister Zhang Wenda ordered Bureau Director Hu Shixiang, Vice Directors Yue Junsheng and Zhao Huizhen, and Secretary Lao Yongjia to reexamine the prisoner under torture about the motive for what he had done. The four interrogators were from Zhejiang province, Hu and Liu Tingyuan were related by marriage, and the Donglin people considered them all to be members of a nefarious regional clique.

Under torture, Zhang Chai stated that back in Jizhou two men named Li Ziqiang and Li Wencang had set fire to his fuel pile. In anger, he had come to Beijing. He wanted redress from the imperial court for the wrong done him. He was unfamiliar with the gates and streets of Beijing. Outside Beijing he met two men who told him he could not enter the city unless he equipped himself with a stick to show his intent to raise a formal complaint. He followed their advice. He got a jujube stick and entered the Donghua gate and beat at a guard who tried to bar his way. It was at this point that he was arrested.[3]

Wang Zhicai, secretary in charge of the ministry's prison office, did not believe Zhang Chai's testimony. He decided to reinterrogate the prisoner. On June 6, he placed a meal in viewing range of the prisoner, who must not have eaten for some time. Two guards hauled Zhang Chai to his feet, and Wang threatened to let him starve unless he talked. With the meal before him but beyond his reach, Zhang gave a story completely at odds with the one he had given the day before. He now said that two men, Ma Sanjiu and Liu Waifu, had introduced him to a certain eunuch, who in turn recruited him for a mysterious mission. On May 30, Zhang Chai followed this eunuch to Beijing. They came to a residence, where another eunuch gave Zhang Chai a meal and told him to go strike and kill anyone he might encounter, that he would be rescued if he did that.

"Strike whom?" asked Secretary Wang. "I was to hit anyone I saw," answered Zhang. "The eunuchs gave me a jujube stick and had me go through the Houzai gate to the palace gate. The gate guard [Liu Jian] struck me with his hand, so I knocked him over with the stick. Once inside I waved the stick around but a bunch of eunuchs overpowered me. That was lucky for the young master [i.e., Zhu Changluo, the heir apparent]."[4]

Zhang Chai further alleged that there were other assailants involved, armed with cedar and other kinds of sticks, but he refused to name their names. All this was copied down in the local dialect that Zhang spoke.

So there *was* a plot! Wang Zhicai reported by memorial to the emperor this sensational new testimony. He demanded that Wanli authorize a full-dress reinterrogation of Zhang Chai in open court. It was Wanli's long-standing habit not to respond to contentious matters sent up from the bureaucracy, and he was silent now.

Wang Zhicai could not prevail unaided with his new testimony, and so other Ministry of Justice officials rallied to help him. A low-ranking official by the name of Fu Mei rushed to the home of Vice Director Lu Menglong and urged him to convene a larger group to reinterrogate the prisoner. Lu called together a group of seven, including himself, Fu Mei, and Wang Zhicai, plus the four who had already questioned Zhang Chai on June 5 and had agreed that he was mentally disturbed. The four were averse to a new grilling, but they agreed to it provided that the questioning would be limited and no torture used.

On June 11, the reinterrogation was held. To everyone's surprise, Lu pounded the table and demanded that torture appliances be placed at hand. Prisoner Zhang Chai no longer appeared deranged, but stood erect and spoke confidently. Lu gave him a pen and a sheet of paper and asked him to sketch his route into the Forbidden City. "Are you mad? How can a madman draw a map?" laughed one of the doubters. But Zhang went ahead and made the map. "How did you know the way?" asked Fu Mei. "I'm from Jizhou," the prisoner replied, "and I couldn't have gotten in without guides." "Who were the guides?" asked Lu. Zhang said they were two eunuchs named Pang and Liu, and he added that they had given him gifts and that he'd known them for three years. Lu demanded to know the eunuchs' personal names. But Hu Shixiang and the others, determined to limit the investigation, objected to the question on the ground that Zhang Chai could not be expected to know the eunuchs' personal names. Lu then went on to ask Zhang what the eunuchs wanted him to do. "Strike the young master," said Zhang. "Who do you mean by 'young master?'" asked Lu. At this point, Bureau Director Hu Shixiang rose from his seat and objected to the question as out of bounds, and the interrogation came to an end.[5]

However, Acting Vice Minister Zhang Wenda was persuaded that there was more to be learned of this new testimony, and so on June 15 he ordered yet another interrogation before a plenary session of eighteen Ministry of Justice officials. The prisoner now identified the eunuch who had recruited him as old, tall, pale-faced, and named Pang Bao. He could not identify or locate the house in Beijing he was taken to, except to note that it had a black gate. But he now identified as Liu Cheng the thirty-five- or thirty-six-year-old, thin, dark-complexioned eunuch who fed him the meal at the house with the black gate and gave him the stick made of jujube wood. Ma Sanjiu and Liu Waifu were Jizhou charcoal makers. They were supplying charcoal to the eunuch Pang Bao (Pang Bao was in charge of building the Tiewadian, or "Iron-tile Palace," a Jizhou Buddhist temple, for Wanli's favorite concubine, Zheng Guifei).[6] Prisoner Zhang Chai then stated that there took place a meeting at a local temple, at which Ma, Liu, and the two eunuchs promised him food and clothing if he would "fight his way into the palace, hitting anyone he met, until he hit the young master." The prisoner also stated that Ma Sanjiu brought him a "red enfeoffment ticket," which conferred upon him the title "perfect man" (zhenren), understood to be a position in a sectarian group of some sort.

This confession added sensational new details to the story first coaxed out of Zhang Chai by Wang Zhicai. Some of the sixteen officials who heard this version for the first time refused to endorse it. However, all agreed to fetch Ma Sanjiu and Liu Waifu from Jizhou to Beijing for interrogation, and to ask the emperor's permission to arrest the two eunuchs Pang Bao and Liu Cheng.[7]

The case riveted the attention of Beijing officialdom and further polarized the existing factions. Everyone sought out more information to corroborate his preferred story. Censor Guo Tingxun (from Zhejiang) contacted Qi Yanling, prefect at Jizhou, and asked him to investigate. Prefect Qi's detailed report stated that Zhang Chai was a woodcutter and occasional hired laborer who had been driven to frenzy by business associates and others who repeatedly cheated him, and that it was in such a fit of depression and rage that, according to informants, Zhang Chai departed Jizhou on April 29 with two catties of beans and an axe-handle, not telling anyone where he was going.[8]

By now, many days had passed since the arrest. Wanli maintained his silence. Urgent memorials from the grand secretaries, supervising secretaries, and censors begged the emperor to act to allay all the suspicions and resolve the case once and for all. Zhang Chai had confessed in open court to an attempt on the life of the crown prince! Who was behind this? He Zongyan (acting vice minister of the Ministry of Rites) directly accused Wanli of a lack of concern for his son. "The realm suspects you of having long mistreated the heir designate. His position is not secure.

Only two [eunuchs] were on guard on the day of Zhang Chai's attack, and one of them was over seventy, and the other over sixty," he asserted.[9]

There were further suspicions. Lu Dashou, bureau director in the Ministry of Revenue, all but directly accused Zheng Guotai (Zheng Guifei's brother) of having masterminded a plot to assassinate Zhu Changluo. Zheng Guotai at once issued a statement denying the imputation. He Shijin, supervising secretary of the Office of Scrutiny for Works, then weighed in with a scathing reply to Zheng Guotai, impugning his veracity and linking him, not just to this recent incident, but to a number of other unexplained events in the long history of the "root of the state" struggle. The only way to get to the bottom of the matter, insisted He Shijin, was to turn the two named eunuchs over to the Ministry of Justice for interrogation under torture.[10]

Emperor Wanli had not seen or spoken with anyone in the outer bureaucracy since the year 1602.[11] In the mid-morning of June 23, 1615, he surprised everyone by sending eunuchs out to invite all the civil and military officials to a general meeting in the Cining palace, residence of his recently deceased mother. One after another, the officials rushed in. They found Wanli seated on a platform, a table in front of him. Zhu Changluo, the heir apparent, stood at his right. Three imperial grandsons stood at his left, below the platform. "Come up, come up!" ordered the emperor to the officials as they arrived. They all inched forward on their knees until the closest of them were only a few paces away. "I've been in deep mourning since my mother died [on March 18, 1614]," explained the emperor. "Since spring I've had no strength in my legs. Even so, on the first and fifteenth of every month and on her death anniversary I've unfailingly come to the Cining palace to do the rites. I've never dared neglect that."

Then Wanli scolded the kneeling mass of officials for using rumors about the crazy intruder Zhang Chai to divide him from his own son, Zhu Changluo. "You all have fathers and sons, so why are you trying to split me from mine?" He grasped the hand of the thirty-two-year-old heir apparent, and said: "This boy is completely filial. I love him very much."

After a commotion in the rear ranks of the assembled officials, the emperor continued his extraordinary public performance. He patted Zhu Changluo on the head. "He's been taken care of since his mother died, and now he's an adult. Wouldn't I have deposed him long ago, if I'd wanted to? Why are you so suspicious, seeing that he's grown up? The

Prince of Fu [Zhu Changxun] is at his fief, thousands of *li* away, and do you think he has wings and can fly here?"

The emperor then called for his three grandsons to come up to the platform where everyone could see them. In a sharp voice he insisted that the heir apparent was kindly, and that all those officials who were recklessly manufacturing rumors about the imperial family were evil. Evil!

Wanli turned to Zhu Changluo. "Is there anything you want to say?" he asked. For the first time, the target of the alleged assassination attempt spoke up. "It appears that fellow [Zhang Chai] was crazy, that's all there is to it. No wide-scale investigation will be allowed." He went on to echo his father's scolding. "I and my father are very close and affectionate. There is all that talk in the outer court. You're all subjects who recognize no ruler. You make me out to be an unfilial son. That is deeply hateful."

"Did you all hear that?" Wanli asked the kneeling officials. He urged the latecomers to come up and have a closer look. "Has everyone had a look?" he asked.

Wanli then authorized three prosecutions only: of Zhang Chai and of the two eunuchs Pang Bao and Liu Cheng. With that, one of the most unusual meetings in the imperial history of China was concluded.[12]

The hapless Zhang Chai, his inconsistent testimony unresolved, was executed on the next day, June 24. Wanli did not hand over the two eunuchs to the Ministry of Justice. Rather, on the day after Zhang Chai's execution, they were interrogated on neutral ground, in front of the Wenhua gate, with the palace eunuch office retaining custody of them. The ministry officials could question the two eunuchs but could not apply torture to them. Repeatedly, the two eunuchs denied any involvement with Zhang Chai. While these proceedings were in progress, a message arrived from Zhu Changluo, stating to the officials that the deranged Zhang Chai had acted alone and that the two eunuchs had at worst cheated him in transacting for fuel, so causing his derangement.[13]

The Ministry of Justice still demanded full custody of the eunuchs, but Wanli refused. Then, on June 27, the emperor announced that he had ordered the palace eunuch office to conduct its own interrogation under torture of the two eunuchs; that five times the eunuchs denied knowing Zhang Chai, or giving him a meal, or a stick; and that the two were now dead—of the effects of the torture and the extreme heat of the June climate.[14]

And so the case was laid to rest, for the time being. Officials, mainly those in the Donglin camp, who had been certain that Zhang Chai was in fact a hired assassin, were removed from their positions. But beginning in 1620, when Wanli died, those officials were recalled to duty, and the whole case was reopened and reargued in the cause of partisan struggle.[15] It was now linked to two later incidents, which the Donglin officials interpreted as conclusive evidence of a conspiracy of long standing against the throne of Ming China.

◄

In the troubled summer and fall of 1620, three emperors ruled Ming China, one after the other. Wanli, seriously ill for months, died on August 18, a few months short of his fifty-seventh birthday. Zhu Changluo succeeded him as the Taichang emperor, but he died unexpectedly under perplexing circumstances on September 26, at the age of thirty-eight. The third emperor was Tianqi, Taichang's oldest son, who assumed the throne on October 1, at the age of fourteen.

The second of the Three Cases was the so-called Red Pill Case, which stemmed from the medications Taichang was given just before he died. Did the pills cause his death? And if they did, was Taichang poisoned by accident or deliberately?

For years, Zhu Changluo had been a model heir apparent. Stories filtering from behind the walls of the Forbidden City described how, despite his father's neglect and the insecurity of his position, he comported himself as a paragon of unwavering filial respect and stoic dedication to his studies. When Zhu Changluo became the Taichang emperor, he reversed many of his father's policies and endorsed the recall of many central-level officials whom Wanli had dismissed for defying him. Many of those recalled were Donglin men. They included some of the brightest and most famous lights of the realm.

The new emperor was in the prime of his life. Everyone comfortably assumed that he had a long reign ahead of him. There was wide rejoicing at his enthronement. Then, barely a month later, he was dead. People were thunderstruck! There was shock and grief. Had he been assassinated? Had dark forces finally accomplished what Zhang Chai had failed to accomplish five years earlier?

On August 28, the day of his formal enthronement, Taichang had looked perfectly healthy. Three days later it was reported that he was slightly ill. On September 5, he failed to attend court. On the day following, imperial physician Chen Xi was called in to read his pulse. The emperor attended court on September 8 and 9, but Yang Lian (then supervising secretary of the Office of Scrutiny for War) thought that he did not look well. Censor Zhang Po thought he looked exhausted. On September 12, a delegation of officials visited the ailing emperor, who complained of dizziness and weakness and an inability to walk. "We were shocked," stated Yang Lian, "and we could not understand what had caused this."[16]

The next day, physician Chen Xi and a small group of officials visited the emperor, who now complained of insomnia and lack of appetite. "I don't know what to do," he wailed. The officials were alarmed. Word leaked from the palace that eunuch Cui Wensheng, superintendent of the palace clinic, had administered a purgative to the emperor when what he actually needed was a tonic. On September 16, Yang Lian impeached Cui Wensheng for incompetence. The emperor refused to endorse the impeachment, but he stopped taking any more medicine.[17]

Days passed. On September 25, a delegation of thirteen high-level officials visited the emperor's bedside in the Qianqing palace. The mood was somber but intimate. Yang Lian wrote that it was like a family of sons gathered around their dying father. It was during this visit that the first of the infamous red pills entered the picture. Somehow the emperor had been told that a certain Li Keshao, an assistant director in the Court of State Ceremonial, had in his possession a red pill that was certain to effect a cure. In the presence of the thirteen officials, Taichang demanded the pill.

While under arrest two years later, Li Keshao wrote a detailed statement of his side of the whole matter. Li presented himself as a simple, good-hearted citizen, distressed as everyone else was by reports of the emperor's failing health. "So I thought," wrote Li, "that I have this 'elixir of the three primary vitalities' *(sanyuan dan)* which always works." On September 21, Li told chief Grand Secretary Fang Congzhe that he had this medicine and was willing to give some of it to the emperor. But it appears that the emperor had somehow already heard of the pill. "On [September 25]," continued Li, "I was in my office when several eunuchs and guardsmen came in and said that the emperor wanted my medicine. In alarm I fetched it." Li was then rushed off with his pill to the Qianqing palace and the emperor's bedside. "The emperor was thin and looked lifeless," Li reported. "His breathing was rapid and he couldn't talk intelligibly. A eunuch had to interpret for him. 'Save me, save me!' he said. He extended a hand and I took his pulse. 'What is your medicine?' he asked. I said: 'It's called *sanyuan dan*. It's compounded of lead, autumn mineral, human milk, and cinnabar.' The emperor said: 'Those are all tonic medicines. I want it now. If I get better, I'll give you a big reward and promotion.' I said, 'Please just don't punish me for my daring.' He said, 'Just bring it, I won't hurt you.' So I had no choice."

Li Keshao and the thirteen officials then left the emperor's bedside, while eunuchs hunted up a palace wet nurse to provide the human milk. Li mixed the ingredients himself, to achieve an exact balance between the yin and yang components. Soon the pill was ready. Li gave it to the emperor. Then he left to join the officials who were keeping vigil just outside the palace. Presently word came that the emperor was feeling better. Warmth was returning to his hands. He was resting comfortably.

Li and the thirteen officials were called back to the ruler's bedside. "That's magic medicine, magic medicine," said Taichang. "I feel much better. My heart has stopped throbbing. My sore throat has gone. My body feels warm. Maybe my color is better too." Everyone agreed that the emperor looked better. "What makes that medicine so effective?" he asked. Li Keshao replied: "Your primary *qi (yuanqi)* was depleted. The red lead is a young girl's *yuanqi*. The autumn mineral is a young boy's *yuanqi*. The milk is a woman's *yuanqi*. Only the true *yuanqi* from the human body can repair a [sick] person's true *qi*. When the upright *qi* grows, it dispels the deviant heat. That's why it's effective." "Why didn't you come see me before this?" asked the emperor. "I'm just a small official, and I didn't dare," replied Li. The emperor told Li he was a "true loyal official." Then he turned to the officials and said to them: "You're all true loyal officials. For seven days I couldn't sleep, so now I'll take a nap." He wanted another pill, but Li cautioned him that one pill a day was enough.

Again, Li and the officials left the emperor's bedside. After a while word came that the emperor was hungry. Li said: "Don't feed him! He should only take human milk." Then word came that the emperor was weakening. With the thirteen officials present as witnesses, Li relented and prepared another pill. He also directed that the emperor could have plain rice without meat. By now it was early evening on September 25, and Li was sent home and asked to come back the next morning.

Very early in the morning of September 26, palace eunuchs called an emergency meeting of the officials. When they arrived at the palace, they were given shocking news. The emperor was dead.[18]

◄

Now, among the thirteen high officials whom Li Keshao cited as eyewitnesses to the Pill Case were three who were, or soon became, prominent in the "pure-current" Donglin faction. They were Grand Secretaries Liu Yijing and Han Kuang, and Supervising Secretary Yang Lian. Because they were right there on the scene, they could not become the wholehearted partisans of the conspiracy theory that other adherents of the Donglin, who were not there, rapidly became. Yang Lian's detailed statements defending his own behavior omit all mention of Li Keshao and his red pills. But Grand Secretary Han Kuang issued a long statement in 1622 that corroborated Li Keshao's account but admitted his own guilt in failing to stand in the way of the emperor's demand for Li's medicine. Thus, while Han Kuang endorsed the Donglin belief that the red pills had caused, or helped to cause, Taichang's death, he did not venture to suggest that the emperor had been deliberately poisoned.[19]

Minister of Rites Sun Shenxing was the spear carrier for the "pure-current" view that the emperor had in fact been assassinated, and that the immediate engineers of his death were pill maker Li Keshao and chief Grand Secretary Fang Congzhe, the senior official among the group at the emperor's bedside.

"I was living at home," wrote Sun in a memorial of May 25, 1622, "when the two imperial deaths occurred in quick succession. I later read in the *Capital Gazette* how Li Keshao, an official in the Court of Imperial Entertainment, had prepared two pills, the giving of which was allowed by former Grand Secretary Fang Congzhe. Li was not a medical official, and it is not known whether the medicine in the pills was really meant to cure the sickness at hand. Yet someone allowed that medicine to be administered [to the emperor]! [Nor was the medicine pretasted], and that the classics, the *Chunqiu* and *Shangshu,* call regicide!"[20]

Wei Dazhong (supervising secretary of the Office of Scrutiny for Works) went even further than Minister Sun. He asserted that the failed Stick Case of 1615 had made every loyal and righteous person in the realm fear for Zhu Changluo's life, and plots to harm him continued! Li Keshao's pills were preceded by Cui Wensheng's purgative, and Cui's purgative followed a deliberate attempt to weaken the emperor by having palace maids exhaust him sexually! Thus it was not Li's pills alone that had killed the emperor; it was their part in a deliberate sequence of sexual and medical abuse![21]

It is not known for sure whether Zhu Changluo ever had an exhausting session with palace maids, or, if he did, whether the maids were part of a planned assault on his health. A few days before his death, Taichang had denied outright Yang Lian's assertion that something of the sort had occurred.[22] Even so, later that same year, Yang Lian raised the same allegation. He wrote that "it was reported in Chang'an [street] that on a certain day Lady Zheng presented eight singing girls to him, but the emperor was ill, so she visited him, and then she ordered the eunuch physician Cui Wensheng to give him medicine, but it wasn't effective, as the emperor got up thirty or forty times [with diarrhea]."[23]

Censor Zhang Po's long statement in support of Yang Lian has it that on September 3, Lady Zheng had Cui Wensheng give the emperor a purgative. Yang Lian alleged that on September 10, the imperial in-laws Guo Jiazhen and Wang Tianrui had come weeping to the outer offices of government, stating that the situation in the palace was dangerous, that Lady Zheng and Lady Li were in charge of things, and that Taichang's young heir (the soon-to-be Tianqi emperor) could not understand why "daddy" (diedie) was sick, what "those slaves" were doing to him, and wondered how we could stop this? "My innards cracked when I heard this," wrote Yang.

Censor Zhang Po wrote that on that same day, September 10, Director of Studies Li Tengfang told Yang Lian that those two in-laws had said to him that Lady Zheng had sent maids to Zhu Changluo, and that it was through them that Cui Wensheng's purgative was administered, and that this was no accident, but all by plan.[24] Thus imperial in-laws hostile to Lady Zheng were the source of the story of the maids, for which there is no other confirming testimony.

◄

The third of the Three Cases was the Moving out of the Palace Case, which unfolded in tandem with the Pill Case and cannot be disentangled from it. As in the Stick and Pill cases, so here again an assemblage of ambiguous, incomplete, and conflicting testimony was read as evidence of conspiracy by the Donglin, and in a perfectly innocent way by those who opposed the Donglin (including especially the so-called Zhejiang or Zhe faction).

The Donglin belief was that, as the Taichang emperor's health deteriorated during the month of September 1620, the Ming dynasty fell under the effective control of two women: Wanli's favorite concubine, Zheng Guifei, and her ally, Taichang's own favorite concubine, Lady Li (known as "Western Li").

Wanli's dying request was that Zheng Guifei be promoted to the rank of empress. In an act of filial respect for his father's wishes, on September 2 Taichang directed the Grand Secretariat to confer the title of empress on Zheng Guifei. A court conference gathered to discuss the matter. Chief Grand Secretary Fang Congzhe (of the Zhe faction) asked Vice Minister of Rites Sun Ruyou to draft the formal request. But Donglin partisan Yang Lian had acting charge of the seal of the Office of Scrutiny for Rites, and he refused to let the memorial go forward.[25]

On September 12, following an urgent suggestion from Censor Zuo Guangdou, a general court conference was held to discuss the issue of a new title for Zheng Guifei. Lady Zheng's oldest surviving male relative, her nephew Zheng Yangxing, was also in attendance. Minister of Personnel Zhou Jiamo confronted Zheng Yangxing in the presence of everyone and gave him a stern warning. "The former court failed to settle the 'root of the state' matter early on, and the blame for that fell on your aunt. . . . Everyone thought the succession would be changed, until your aunt agreed to forgo promotion to empress. So why does she stay on in the Qianqing palace, giving jewels and girls to the emperor, thinking strange thoughts, and making inordinate demands? This is a serious matter, and all you Zhengs could end up exterminated!"[26] Zheng Yangxing blanched with fright. "Your aunt probably just wants to keep her present status," continued Minister Zhou. "If you cooperate with us, we'll help you, and if not, you'll be in trouble. Lady Zheng is smart; she knows she must move to the Cining palace."

Ladies Li and Zheng and Taichang's young heir (the soon-to-be Tianqi emperor) were all living together in the various apartments of the emperor's palace, the Qianqing. At some point over the next several days, Lady Zheng indeed moved out. Debate among the officials continued over the ritual-political question of whether or not the dying emperor's young heir should move from his father's palace and into the Ciqing, the regular palace of the heir apparent. Because the emperor himself was too sick to manage these things, Yang Lian argued that it was therefore the duty of the Grand Secretariat and the officials of the outer court to intervene.

The Grand Secretariat, long abused and neglected by Wanli, had consisted of the sole grand secretary, Fang Congzhe. Taichang aimed to revive it. He had made six new appointments, two of whom were already in Beijing. They were Liu Yijing and Han Kuang, both identified with the Donglin faction. They had introduced themselves to the new emperor at his sickbed on September 18. The emperor let it be known that he wanted his son to stay in the palace with him. He also wanted Lady Li to be given a title. "She's served me a long time," he said. He gestured toward his son. "I'm worried that she won't get a title, except through me."

A week later, on September 25, came the dramatic incident that set the Palace Case in motion. The delegation of high-level officials were all eyewitnesses to what happened. The emperor sensed that he had little time left to live. "I'm at the end," he said. "Take care of the dynasty, help my son be a good ruler. My tomb must be prepared." The officials protested. "You'll live," one of them said. "Why do you speak of that?" All sobbed.

At that moment, a young eunuch emerged from behind the curtains and whispered something into the ear of Taichang's young son. The boy nodded. Then entered the "woman dressed in red"—Lady Li. She took the young heir up to his father's bedside. There was some whispered conversation between her and the dying emperor. The officials could not make out what was being said. Then Lady Li forcibly brought the boy up closer to his father. The young heir appeared flushed and angry. Then the officials heard him say, "Imperial daddy wants to give her the title of empress." Censor Zhang Po thought his voice sounded strained.

Vice Minister of Rites Sun Ruyou replied on behalf of the gathered officials. "If the emperor wants to give Lady Li the [lesser] title *huang guifei*, we will obey." He had the regulations for such a conferment with him. "Bring the regulations here," said the emperor. Then he gestured toward the rest of the officials standing by. "It's essential that you help him." He meant his young son.

As the officials withdrew from this awkward and disturbing meeting, Censor Gu Zao said: "The emperor is very sick, and his cleaving to us shows that he's unwilling to die in the arms of a woman, and he hopes for the security of the dynasty. He is a great ruler. But there was something shocking and brazen about what Lady Li did." Grand Secretary Liu Yijing made some similar remarks.

Early in the morning of the next day, September 26, the emperor died.

The officials, hastily summoned to the Qianqing palace to hear the announcement, began a worried discussion of the succession and the security of the Ming throne.

Several years earlier, Lady Li had prevailed upon Lady Zheng to have Wanli authorize the placing under her care of Zhu Changluo's two sons (the future Tianqi and Chongzhen emperors), plus her own daughter by Zhu Changluo, together with three wet nurses.[27] This made Lady Li, in effect, Tianqi's guardian and stepmother, because his birth mother had died. Ming house law did not provide for regencies for child emperors. The heir to the throne was no longer exactly a child, yet not an adult either. Born on December 23, 1605, he was not quite fifteen years old in September 1620. Could he serve in his own right as ruler of Ming China, effective immediately?

Some of the officials thought that Lady Li should act as regent for him. There is unanimous testimony that Supervising Secretary Yang Lian, despite his low rank, objected violently and took charge of matters from that point on by the sheer force of his personality. "That cannot be allowed to happen," he shouted. "There are no grounds for entrusting an emperor to a woman." Everyone had seen Lady Li push Tianqi around on the previous day. "What sort of scene was that?" asked Yang. "The former emperor was forty years of age *(sui)*. The present emperor [is too young to] stand up to that."

Yang Lian continued his argument, to the effect that Ladies Li and Zheng were conspiring with each other to capture and sequester the emperor and rule China in his name, and that it was now up to the officials led by the three grand secretaries present to fetch the boy from his father's palace and personally escort him from there to the Ciqing palace (the palace of the heir apparent).

After some discussion, the officials agreed and walked up to the Qianqing palace. Eunuch guards wielding sticks barred the entrance. The officials milled about. Yang Lian urged the three grand secretaries to enter. The guards stopped them. Yang waved his arms and yelled at the guards. The guards stood aside. All the officials filed in. They made weeping sounds in honor of the dead emperor. They called out three or four times for the imperial son. At length he appeared. *"Wansui!"* shouted the officials. The boy made the appropriate reply: "I dare not accept," he repeated three times. The officials asked that the formal enthronement take place on October 1, and that Lady Li be given her title on that same day. The boy was slow to respond to these proposals, but he agreed.

At this point the officials demanded that the future emperor accompany them to the Wenhua palace to show himself to all the other officials and accept their acclamation. Palace eunuch Wang An brought the boy forward and delivered him bodily. Grand Secretary Liu Yijing took him by the left arm, and a hereditary duke, representing the military, took him by the right. The other officials gathered around. Just as the entourage was about to exit the palace, eunuchs came running from one of the interior apartments, shouting and wanting to know what was going on. "Where are you dragging the young master? Give him right back! He's afraid!" Some of the eunuchs grasped the boy's robe. Yang Lian yelled at them: "You're talking nonsense! He's our ruler! We're his officials! The realm is his! What should he be afraid of? You survivors of castration, who are you to order him back to the palace?" The eunuchs backed away.

The procession marched out the gate of the Qianqing palace. The soon-to-be emperor was placed in a sedan chair. At the Wenhua palace, an assembly of lower-ranking officials bowed five times and kowtowed three times and shouted in acclamation. Then the procession left the Wenhua palace and made its way to the Ciqing palace, where Grand Secretary Liu Yijing asked the ruler-to-be to stay while the main palace was "cleaned up" and Lady Li moved out. Minister of Personnel Zhou Jiamo warned Tianqi not to go back to the Qianqing palace alone. Tianqi nodded his agreement and went inside.

The officials then began arguing about the enthronement date. Some urged that the date be moved up to September 28, or even to noon that very day, the twenty-sixth. Yang Lian told Censor Gu Zao that there was no need to hurry things; others echoed Gu Zao's point, that matters were perilous and the ceremony had to be completed quickly. Reports came in from outside the Forbidden City that the people were worried about the succession. Officials on the spot thought the security of the state mattered more than strict ritual observance. A eunuch was sent to convey these concerns to Tianqi. Presently the eunuch returned and reported, "The young master didn't say much—any day would do, but the sixth [October 1] has already been agreed on, so we shouldn't change it."

Meanwhile there was confusion among the officials who had gathered at the Wenhua palace. Many had rushed to dress in formal ceremonial costume only to discover that they had gathered at the wrong place at the wrong time. They milled about the Wenhua palace, looking angry and upset. Yang Lian came by and tried to explain. Xu Yangliang (vice minister of the Court of the Imperial Stud) and Censor Zuo Guangdou sprayed saliva in Yang Lian's face as they screamed at him that delaying the enthronement was a stupid mistake. Matters were too uncertain! Yang Lian deserved to die for that! "I felt," recalled Yang Lian, "that a knife had been stabbed in my back. There was no hole for me to hide in. I was ashamed for what I had said."

The enthronement date could not be changed now, but police protection had to be enhanced. Yang Lian at once directed the Embroidered-uniform Guard to form a special detail of mounted police to control traffic in and out of the Forbidden City. Li Ruogui, supervising secretary in charge of inspecting the military training divisions of the capital, placed additional armed guards at all the main city gates. Yang and Zuo visited Minister of Personnel Zhou Jiamo and got him to write a memorial that the others could cosign demanding that Lady Li not be allowed to share the same palace as Tianqi. Zuo also wrote a memorial of his own, insisting that, since Lady Li was not Tianqi's mother, she had no right to stay in the Qianqing palace and act as though she were empress of the realm, like Empress Wu of the Tang.[28]

After the hectic events of September 26, the next two days were tense, but quiet. At some point, Tianqi slipped unobtrusively back into the Qianqing palace. On the twenty-ninth, as the officials gathered at the Qianqing palace to wait for Tianqi to appear, one of Lady Li's eunuchs came out. Yang Lian accosted him and demanded to know if Lady Li had moved out yet. "Don't talk about moving out," replied the eunuch. "Mother and son are getting along very well, so why should they live in two separate places? Lady Li is very upset. Today she got the young master to agree they should live together. And she wants to know what Censor Zuo means by his talk of Empress Wu." Yang swore at the eunuch, who then went back inside.

On September 30, the day before the scheduled enthronement, word came from the Palace that Lady Li had backed down. She now agreed to vacate the Qianqing palace on October 7.

This was unacceptable to Yang Lian. At a meeting of officials and palace eunuchs, he demanded that chief Grand Secretary Fang Congzhe inform the Palace that Lady Li had to move out immediately. No compromise was possible. There were rumors that one or more of Lady Li's eunuchs were stealing palace valuables. The officials argued. The eunuchs argued back. Yang Lian put the issue in terms that anyone in China could easily grasp. "In the families of common people, a maid serves her master, but when he sickens and dies, his son moves into his quarters, and the maid must of course move out. That's because roles and statuses can't be mixed. You eunuchs eat the food of the Zheng and Li families, and you'll have to kill us to get your way!" Voices were loud. Faces reddened. Inside the palace, the young ruler heard the commotion. He ordered Lady Li to move quarters immediately. Three of her eunuchs were arrested for theft. The officials were so notified. Yang Lian had won.

On October 1, the young heir, Zhu Youjiao, two months short of his fifteenth birthday, took up formal residence in the Qianqing palace under the reign-title Tianqi, as emperor of Ming China. Overnight there had been a rainstorm. As the dawn broke, the skies were clear and blue, all except for a purple vapor encircling the newly risen sun. It was a felicitous sign. Everywhere, officials and people rejoiced that the succession had been properly secured. Unfortunately, Lady Li was almost immediately to become the center of a white-hot controversy.

◀

As he lay dying, Taichang had, in the presence of some dozen officials, indicated that he wanted Lady Li to be given the title "empress"—or at least that of "imperial honored consort" *(huang guifei)*. Surely he also wanted her to be well cared for. However, during the night of September 30–October 1, she had been hurriedly evicted from the Qianqing palace. Censor Jia Jichun noted that in all the turmoil of ensuring Tianqi's succession, the welfare of Lady Li had been forgotten. In a letter of October 19 to chief Grand Secretary Fang Congzhe, made public immediately, Censor Jia asserted that Taichang had for thirty years exhibited his filial respect for Wanli by showing care and concern for Lady Zheng; but now Tianqi's own filial respect for his father had been damaged! The new ruler had been forced to abuse Lady Li, in defiance of his father's wish that she be well cared for! (It was irrelevant to the core of the issue that neither Lady Zheng nor Lady Li was a woman of good character.) Jia asked Fang Congzhe to intervene to ensure that Lady Li and her little daughter be secure and comfortable.[29]

Censor Jia's letter prompted the issuance of a sensational public edict from the Palace. The language seemed to be that of Tianqi himself. The document divulged intimate revelations of a troubled family life inside the Forbidden City. Tianqi openly accused Lady Li of having slapped his mother in anger, causing her illness and death (in 1619)! Then she humiliated Tianqi when, in the infamous scene at Taichang's deathbed, she had made him beg the officials for the title of empress. Then, when his father died, and Tianqi was moved to the Ciqing palace to avoid her, official memorials were sent, not to him, but to the Qianqing palace, where her eunuchs vetted them before relaying them to him. So Lady Li was indeed intending to "lower the curtain and listen to government" *(chuilian tingzheng)* in the style of Empress Wu, just as Censor Zuo Guangdou had charged! The young ruler also stated that he hated Lady Li for the above reasons and so forced her to vacate the Qianqing palace. But now he wished to reassure the world that Lady Li was being well looked after; she was living in the Huiluan palace with the full subsidy that Taichang had earlier authorized. Tianqi ordered "Lady Li's clique" in the outer court henceforth to cease their agitations in her behalf.[30]

Chief Grand Secretary Fang Congzhe read the draft of this edict, which had been written somewhere in the palace, in shock, and tried to stop it from being issued. It was good to inform the world that Lady Li was being well treated, he argued, but the emperor should not divulge such details about her. Fang was sternly rebuked by the Palace, so let the edict go through. Tianqi followed with another edict reassuring everyone that Lady Li's little charges had been reassigned: the eighth younger sister to the Xuqin palace and a different consort Li; the fifth younger brother (the future Chongzhen emperor) to the Zhaojian palace, in the care of consort Fu.[31]

These edicts, however, did not still the controversy. In November and December the case rekindled. Supervising Secretary Zhou Chaorui accused Jia Jichun of deliberately creating trouble with his letter of October 19 to Grand Secretary Fang. Why did he care more for Lady Li than for the security of the dynastic succession? Jia denied that he cared more for Lady Li, arguing that the succession was secure, the dynasty was safe, and there was no need to force the poor woman out of the palace in the middle of the night. She had been denied a title; her father was under arrest; and, think of it, if her little daughter fell into a well, would anyone care? If the poor widow, Lady Li, committed suicide, would anyone air her grievance? Don't we officials have human feeling enough to help even one concubine and one daughter of the dead emperor? The whole world weeps in anguish over this matter![32]

This was a compelling argument. Officials weighed in on either side of it. Donglin adherents like Zhou Zongjian and Fang Zhenru emphasized the danger that had been dispelled by the resolute action taken by Yang Lian and the others on September 30. It was better to have offended Lady

Li, they argued, than to have delayed her removal and allowed her to rule "from behind the screen" on Tianqi's behalf.[33]

On December 29, Supervising Secretary Yang Lian made public his detailed account of his own role in the Palace Case, in the vain hope that full disclosure would put the controversy to rest.[34] The Palace replied with a fervent endorsement of Yang Lian's every word. It then issued, on January 1, 1621, another sensational edict. This one purported to give Tianqi's own eyewitness testimony in much greater detail than had the October 22 edict. It aimed to justify Lady Li's abrupt nocturnal eviction. The emperor described how, on September 26, Lady Li had tried to confine him to his apartment and prevent his meeting with the officials; and how, on September 27, she had tried to intercept him as he was returning to the Ciqing palace from the Renzhi palace, where his father's coffin lay. "All the officials witnessed that," stated Tianqi. "Clearly she was manipulating me, hoping to rule from behind the curtain." The edict went on to make further revelations about how Lady Li had struck his mother, causing her death; about how Taichang realized that it had been a mistake to put Tianqi under Lady Li's care; about how Lady Li forbade Tianqi any contact with his dead mother's eunuchs; about how she had her own eunuchs spy on him; and about how, at one point, Tianqi had cried night and day for a whole week because of her abuse of him! The edict concluded by announcing that, out of filial respect for his dead mother, the emperor would not grant Lady Li any title, but that, out of filial respect for his dead father, he was treating her liberally. "The officials must understand this and stop being partial to Lady Li," he ordered. "Everyone must work together and not create factions."[35]

The young emperor (or the Palace, who could be sure?) was furious with Jia Jichun for suggesting that he was unconcerned for Lady Li's welfare and for raising the rumor that Lady Li had committed suicide, or might be driven to it. The emperor did not believe Jia's explanations or accept his apology. He suspected that Jia had ulterior motives for his behavior and dismissed him from the civil service.[36]

Meanwhile, Yang Lian had entered the spotlight of controversy himself. Donglin partisans held him up as a major hero for his leadership in forcing Lady Li from the Qianqing palace and eliminating the threat to the Ming dynastic order that she seemed to have posed. But some voices accused him of taking sole credit for what had been a major effort involving others in key roles: Li Ruogui, Liu Yijing, Zhang Wenda, Zuo

Guangdou, Zhang Po, and several more. Censor Ma Fenggao criticized Tianqi for overpraising Yang Lian's detailed account of his actions, causing suspicion and uneasiness in the outer court.[37] Yet others defended Jia Jichun, agreeing that there had been no need to force Lady Li out in the middle of the night and doubting that she had any intention of ruling from behind the screen.

All this prompted Supervising Secretary Yang Lian to resign his position. He was uneasy that his role had been blown out of proportion, and that others were accusing him of ignoring the well-being of Lady Li. He thought it best to leave.[38] In January 1621, the Palace reluctantly agreed to let him go home on the ground of illness.

◀

Thus the infamous Three Cases and the profoundly politicized disagreements surrounding their meaning. Donglin officials and intellectuals read the Stick Case as an attempted assassination, the masterminds of which (Lady Zheng and her family) were never exposed and punished. The Pill Case they read as, at best, negligent homicide, with the many culpable parties (Grand Secretary Fang Congzhe, eunuch Cui Wensheng, pill maker Li Keshao, and, again, Lady Zheng) also unexposed and unpunished. The Palace Case they read as an attempted usurpation of monarchical authority. Evil forces had for many years threatened the Ming throne, and through it the very political security and moral order of China.

Donglin opponents read the Three Cases very differently. The Stick Case, they argued, was simply a case of a lone assailant who was mentally deranged. The Pill Case was just a well-meaning but unfortunately unavailing attempt to effect a last-minute miracle cure of a dying emperor. The Palace Case was a chimera, based upon nothing but groundless suspicions about Lady Li.[39] The Donglin partisans who made "cases" of these events, placing filial relations among the members of the imperial family in jeopardy, surely harbored dark ulterior motives of their own.

Over the next several years, the Three Cases, singly and together, were argued and counterargued with ever greater ferocity. Partisan lines were drawn tighter and tighter, as new officials, upon arriving in Beijing, were questioned as to which side they supported.[40] In 1621, Tianqi fully supported the Donglin, as had his father, who had only just begun recalling them to office when he died. But Tianqi—and/or the Palace, acting in his name—soon began to undergo a change of heart. The Donglin partisans found their newly won dominance at court gradually eroding. In 1625–1627, the Donglin were thoroughly purged, and their leaders, in unspeakable acts of cruelty, were put to death after slow torture in prison.

CHAPTER 2

Beijing, 1620–1624

The Storm Clouds Gather

◀

THE DEATH OF their patron Taichang in September 1620, after a reign of just one month, gave a severe jolt to the Donglin partisans' hopes for political and moral dominance over the affairs of Ming China. However, Yang Lian and the other Donglin men had played so forceful a role in guarding the succession of his young son, the Tianqi emperor, through the "removal from the palace" crisis that they seem to have assumed that the unsteady new ruler would favor and rely on them as much as his father had. They acted as though they thought it possible to educate the new ruler and, under his auspices, reverse the waning fortunes of Ming China. The Donglin were disappointed in this expectation, as the years 1620–1624 showed.

For all his undisguised physical and psychological handicaps, Tianqi managed to win battle after battle in the face of violent Donglin challenge. He retained the companionship of his wet nurse, Madame Ke, despite the sociomoral objections and the contemptuous insults the Donglin hurled at him. From the outset of his reign, he shifted the rescript-drafting function from the Grand Secretariat to the eunuchs of the inner palace, and he seized personal control over all new appointments to the Grand Secretariat. He secured a personally congenial palace eunuch staff headed by the controversial Wei Zhongxian, and he protected Wei Zhongxian against a series of withering Donglin assaults launched from the outer court.

Up until the summer of 1624, the Palace cooperated with chief Grand Secretary Ye Xianggao in a strategy of compromise with the Donglin in the outer court. But as the rift in the outer court between the Donglin partisans and their opponents grew increasingly unmanageable, the Palace by degrees gave its support to the anti-Donglin forces.

The Donglin program for Ming China consisted of three main elements. First was their insistence upon scrutinizing all high-level official appointments with a view to supporting the "good species" and rejecting the morally unfit. Second was their nationwide effort at Confucian moral rearmament, revolving around the organization of lecture meetings and academies, with the Shoushan academy, which they set up in Beijing in 1622, as the center. And third was their claim to a right on moral grounds to interfere in the affairs of the Ming imperial family and its inner palace staff. The opponents of the Donglin readily accepted the Palace and the imperial family as they were, rejected Donglin assertions of absolute moral and judgmental certitude, and accused them of using moral arguments as a cloak for partisan mobilization.

The worrisome external event of Tianqi's first four years of rule was military defeat and the loss of yet more Manchurian territory in 1622 to Nurhaci and his emerging Manchu state. Given the already heated political climate in Beijing, it proved impossible for either the Palace or the outer court to prevent the personal disagreements between the two commanders responsible for that loss from becoming engulfed in the partisan battles. The Donglin—with some reluctance—rallied behind Xiong Tingbi, while their opponents energetically vilified him and protected (also with some reluctance) Xiong's enemy Wang Huazhen.

Then, in the summer of 1624, the Donglin camp itself began to unravel over the issue of official appointments. Secret decision making by Minister of Personnel Zhao Nanxing and his agent, the controversial broker of recommendations Wang Wenyan, created disappointment, suspicion, and anger among men who had hitherto been friendly to the Donglin and drove them into the arms of Tianqi's surrogate, the palace eunuch Wei Zhongxian. That set the stage for Yang Lian's sensational but desperate "Twenty-four Crimes" memorial against Wei Zhongxian in July 1624, and for the retaliatory political murders that so darkened the later years of Tianqi's rule, 1625–1627.

The Palace, 1620–1624

One of the Taichang emperor's key aides in identifying and recalling Donglin officials was the palace eunuch Wang An. He had been for many years a tutor *(bandu)* and personal aide to Taichang (i.e., Zhu Changluo) when he was heir apparent. Wang An suffered from various infirmities and spent much of his time after around 1601 in his private home in Beijing, where he lived well off the proceeds of house and shop rents. There he practiced longevity techniques, played chess, studied, and, most important, welcomed visits from "upright men" and inscribed fans for his friends in officialdom.[1] It was through the unofficial personal contacts that Wang An had long cultivated that Taichang, as emperor, was able to identify and restore to office so many Donglin men.

Confined as he was to home, Wang An himself needed help in building a network among the officials in disfavor. Here his principal operative was a man named Wang Wenyan, whose arrest in 1625 would initiate the repression of the Donglin that so damaged the political and moral climate of the late Ming.

Wang Wenyan was a fixer and a network builder, a fringe member of officialdom who had a talent for bringing people together. He was affable and sincere in manner, a perceptive observer of character, and a keen political strategist. He lived modestly, as befitted a camp follower of the Donglin. He knew personally many of the principal Donglin men.[2] He came from Xiuning county, Huizhou prefecture, home of some of China's richest merchants. Through his patron, mentor, and county compatriot Huang Zhengbin, a secretariat drafter with a purchased degree, he was introduced to eunuch Wang An. This was in 1613–1614.

It was said of Wang Wenyan that he loved to put his fingers together and discuss high political strategy. The capital evaluations of 1617 had been ruinous for the Donglin men. Wang Wenyan correctly saw that the winners of 1617 were a loose coalition of provincial factions led by Zhejiang. Wang Wenyan made contacts among some of the coalition partners and succeeded in detaching the Huguang provincial faction and bringing it over to the Donglin side. In the "palace" crisis of 1620, Wang Wenyan played a role behind the scenes as a contact maker for Wang An.[3]

When Taichang died after his short reign, the recall of the Donglin men to office had scarcely begun. Although it was Ming political tradition that any new enthronement should entail major policy revisions and personnel changes, eunuch Wang An aimed to have Tianqi continue his father's legacy and not preside over any major changes in it.

During the hectic days of September 26–October 1, 1620, Wang An appears to have done much to support Yang Lian and the others who were clamoring for Lady Li to vacate the Qianqing palace. Wang An personally hated Lady Li, and he did not treat her with courtesy.[4] There is testimony that, as Tianqi cowered in Lady Li's clutches in a private apartment in the Qianqing palace on September 26 while the officials outside demanded that he show himself, it was Wang An who extricated him. "Good tutor has come to save me!" cried Tianqi in his palace baby talk.[5]

But after Tianqi's enthronement, Wang An spent less time with Tianqi than some thought he should. According to palace eunuch Liu Ruoyu's insider's account, from September 1620 until the summer of 1621 Wang An set up an office in the southwestern arcade inside the Qianqing gate, about 100 meters south of the palace. Then he moved to a small office near the Longdao pavilion, about 100 meters west of his old office. He was in bad health and needed assistance walking. He spoke in hoarse whispers, which few besides his own personal eunuchs could understand. Often he communicated by wordless gestures. His eunuchs ran documents back and forth between himself and Tianqi. On one occasion, Tianqi inscribed a fan with the words "Helping Me to Become a Benevolent and Enlightened Ruler" and sent it over to Wang An. In summer 1621, Tianqi offered Wang An the top eunuch post, that of Director of Ceremonial. Wang An politely declined. He wanted a more fervent expression of support from the boy emperor before accepting.[6]

There would be no such expression. As Grand Secretary Ye Xianggao later explained, Wang An wanted restraints placed upon Tianqi's private life, and he was conducting a purge of those in the palace eunuch corps who seemed to be leading the young ruler astray. Aggrieved eunuchs pleaded with Tianqi. "The emperor was willful and wanted things his own way," wrote Ye. "He detested Wang An's hard sternness and chafed under his restraints. He wasn't free to act. So when Wang An asked to retire, the emperor exiled him to the eunuch army at Nanhaizi and rehired all [the eunuchs] he had squeezed out."[7]

What actually happened was a bit more complex than that. Huo Weihua, supervising secretary for the Office of Scrutiny for War, was informed by his brother-in-law, who was himself a palace eunuch, of the eunuchs' opposition to Wang An. Huo Weihua, an opponent of the Donglin faction, then sent up a memorial opposing the appointment of Wang An, on the grounds that he was too eager for the position and was not trustworthy.[8] So the position was denied Wang An and given instead to another senior eunuch, Wang Tiqian. Wang An was then demoted and exiled to Nanhaizi, where he was imprisoned and abused, and, at Wang Tiqian's urging, killed on November 27, 1621.[9] The loss of Wang An was a major blow to the political fortunes of the Donglin men, because he had been their main channel to the throne.

The political future of Ming China indeed hung on the question of who had personal access to young Tianqi. Tianqi, orphaned and isolated in a position of awesome responsibility, clung tenaciously to people he believed loved and cared for him. The Donglin partisans never fully understood this fact. It is clear that Tianqi hated Lady Li. But he did cling to his wet nurse, the formidable Madame Ke, a widow about forty years old. A later Palace source described her as having been "alluring, slightly ruddy in complexion, and bodily well endowed."[10] It is not known precisely when Madame Ke became a widow, or exactly when she entered palace service, but to the end of her life she preserved in a tiny box Tianqi's baby teeth, baby hair, nail parings, and scabs, and so may have nursed Tianqi from the time of his birth in 1605.[11]

Any male of the upper class owed certain filial obligations to his wet nurse, and so Tianqi was obliged to Madame Ke, a woman whose milk had nurtured him; still, the expectation was that she should be sent from the Forbidden City with a modest pension now that her charge had no further need of her services. But Tianqi loved her and was exceptionally generous to her. He gave her a title in October 1620 and some months later assigned her the Xian'an palace, about 250 meters west of his own. (She could no longer live with Tianqi in the Qianqing palace now that Tianqi was emperor and steps were being taken to select for him a young girl as his empress).[12]

Madame Ke loved Tianqi and protected him, and so she was in a position to determine the choice of which palace eunuchs would have access to his person. That of course made her central to the whole question of what direction the Ming government would take in the Tianqi era, 1620–1627. Of this the Donglin faction were fully aware. This is where the infamous palace eunuch Wei Zongxian enters the picture.

◀

Who was Wei Zhongxian? An illiterate and a street rowdy, his early life is the stuff of fiction. The presumed facts are that he was born in 1568 in Suning county, about 100 miles south of Beijing; he was married at some point to a girl of the Feng surname and had one daughter by that marriage. Then he had himself castrated. He entered palace service in 1589, at the age of twenty-one.[13]

Why would a grown man have himself castrated? The Ming dynastic history simply says it was because he was "angered" when pressed to pay gambling debts. But another source has it that it was because he had con-

tracted a skin disease that affected his private parts.[14] Stories vie with each
other in depicting Wei Zhongxian's raffish youth. Was he a poor boy who
found excitement in gambling, sport, drunkenness, and riotous debauch-
ery? Had he and Madame Ke been lovers from the streets long ago,
and did he cheat on her, and did she then have herself selected as a palace
wet nurse out of anger at his philandering, and did he then repent and
have himself castrated so that he could be with her again inside the Forbidden City, and did she love him all the more for that?[15] The story con-
flicts with "known" dates and other evidence, but little of it rests on sure
foundations.

If Wei Zhongxian entered palace service in 1589, then he subsequently
spent thirty-one years very quietly as a menial of low rank, which in light
of his later behavior is hard to believe. But palace eunuch Liu Ruoyu in
his memoirs asserts that Wei involved himself in several risky misadven-
tures during those years.[16] Popular chronicler Zhu Changzuo, whose
book was published right after Wei Zhongxian's death, has it that as a
eunuch Wei turned over a new leaf, or showed a new side, and won everyone's favor and good opinion by his outgoing friendliness, self-denying
generosity, and engaging little acts of honesty and loyalty.[17]

When Tianqi was an infant, Wei somehow got a job serving meals to
the baby and his mother, Lady Wang. In that capacity, he got to meet the
baby's wet nurse, Madame Ke—perhaps for the first time, perhaps not. As
a waiter, Wei sought to please, and knew where to find out-of-season
fruits and other delicacies.

It appears that by 1620, Wei Zhongxian had become an adept player of
the palace power game. Wanli was dying. Zhu Changluo was heir apparent. Wang An was Zhu Changluo's closest adviser. So Wei established a
connection to Wang An. He did so by inviting one of Wang An's favorite
eunuchs, Wei Zhao, to help him in serving young Tianqi. It seems that
he chose Wei Zhao also because Wei Zhao and Madame Ke were already
friendly with each other. Wei Zhao was flattered by Wei Zhongxian's pro-
fessions of friendship, and he convinced his patron, Wang An, of the ex-
cellence and trustworthiness of Wei and Madame Ke.

After Tianqi's mother died in 1619, Wei Zhongxian and wet nurse
Madame Ke were placed under the supervision of Lady Li, whom Tianqi
hated. Tianqi dearly loved Wei Zhongxian and Madame Ke. So thanks in
good part to Wang An's firm relationship via Wei Zhao with Wei Zhongxian and Madame Ke, the "palace" crisis of 1620 ended in defeat for Lady
Li and triumph for Wang An—as well as for Yang Lian and Zuo Guang-

dou and the whole Donglin faction in the outer court. Almost to the end of his life, Wang An thought that Wei Zhongxian and Madame Ke were on his side.

They were not on his side. According to Liu Ruoyu, Madame Ke felt constrained by Wang An. She also came to find Wei Zhao ungenerous and timid. Clearly Wei Zhao was acting in Wang An's behalf. She told Tianqi of her dislike of Wei Zhao and made him promise her to get rid of him.

Madame Ke's coolness distressed Wei Zhao. He became increasingly jealous of Wei Zhongxian. One night the two eunuchs got into a screaming fight in one of the apartments of the Qianqing palace. The emperor, Wang An, Wang Tiqian, and other eunuchs were startled from their sleep. Wang An was unaware of the reason for the fight and his fury fell on Wei Zhao. He slapped him and ordered him to leave the imperial presence. It was a fatal political blunder for Wang An and a crucial move up the power ladder for Wei Zhongxian.

Wei Zhongxian could neither read nor write, but he was a skilled manipulator of personal relationships. To the end he remained in Madame Ke's good graces. She loved him for his "childlike demeanor," his "good looks," and his "martial ferocity." They at times acted as though they were husband and wife. Aside from their palace quarters, both maintained private residences near each other just west of the Imperial City. It was a stable and affectionate arrangement. To the end of his short life, Tianqi clung to the two of them; they indulged his needs and desires, and extended a parent-like protection to him.[18]

◀

Tianqi appeared to suffer from some sort of learning disability. Though he liked some of his tutors, he was a slow pupil. Occasionally he made efforts to learn. His tutors tried to figure out how best to engage him. His eunuch tutor Gao Shiming had taught him parts of the *Great Learning*. Tianqi delighted in some of its phrases. But when he became emperor in 1620 and began formal schooling under court officials, he seemed wholly lost. Court official Sun Chengzong conferred with Wang An and Gao Shiming. "In family schools among the people, the pupils all sit together and help each other, which is how they learn," explained Sun. "But the emperor comes to the teaching sessions and just sits there and doesn't ask any questions.... How can he learn that way?" The three agreed that they should develop a discussion format in which the young ruler would be encouraged to ask questions about what he failed to grasp. Then the teachers could explain things to him in detail in the spoken language.[19]

Tianqi liked Sun Chengzong. Sun reports that when he explained to him the "Canon of Yao" chapter from the *Book of Documents,* Tianqi paid close attention. "When I explained how rulers preside over the realm, [Tianqi] sat up and listened . . . and his expression changed and he became grave, like a true sage ruler," stated Sun.[20] That class was held on November 11, 1620, and was the first of many "discussion and reading" *(jiang-du)* sessions Tianqi attended with some regularity at the Wenhua palace until his final illness in 1627.

But Tianqi never quite seemed to make the expected progress with his studies. Liu Ruoyu says, "he could understand the main idea" but did not like to sit still and concentrate. He learned to write standard characters but was never able to master the cursive script.[21] He fished for praise for his calligraphy. In February 1621, he sent an example of his calligraphy via a eunuch messenger to Grand Secretary Liu Yijing. The characters were "upright." How admirable of Tianqi to have done this, at a time when he had canceled his classes because of cold weather! (Tianqi had practiced his writing in his heated apartment in the Qianqing palace, using as models the draft rescripts prepared in the Grand Secretariat.) Liu Yijing showed Tianqi's handiwork to the other grand secretaries, who were amazed at the improvement it showed. Tianqi promised to send more in the spring, when the weather was warmer.[22] Grand Secretary Zhu Guozuo preserved at home three rescripts dealing with routine ceremonial matters that were written in Tianqi's own "inept" hand.[23]

But Tianqi's tolerance for study remained limited. According to chief Grand Secretary Ye Xianggao, who arrived in Beijing and took up his duties in December 1621, the young ruler "stubbornly refused to study, was petulant, and willful."[24] In September 1622, Ye Xianggao proposed something easier for Tianqi to read: the *Dijian tushuo,* an illustrated children's book about the good and bad rulers of China's past that Zhang Juzheng had put together for Tianqi's grandfather Wanli when he was a child. That seemed to work. Five months later, Tianqi was still being tutored in it, and he rejected a suggestion to begin reading Sima Guang's *Zizhi tongjian* (Comprehensive mirror for aid in government), a standard history of China for adults, because he wanted to finish the picture book first.[25]

What was wrong with Tianqi? The outer court was exasperated by his

extreme passivity. Wen Zhenmeng decided it was up to him to let the outer court's feelings about this be known. On November 20, 1622, he sent
up a scathing memorial that created a brief sensation in the capital. Wen
was already a national celebrity; he had just achieved the number-one
ranking in the Palace examinations, was appointed senior compiler in the
Hanlin Academy, and was informal leader of all the other new degree
winners. Why, asked Wen in his memorial, was the emperor not standing
forth to lead the realm in the face of a national crisis and military threat?
Why, when the emperor attended court, did he just sit there in lifeless
silence while the officials trooped up and down "like puppets on stage"
to introduce the day's business to him? Why were the lessons given at his
tutorials pitched at a level fit only for children?

The memorial was long and impassioned.[26] Days went by. The Palace
made no response. Rumor had it that Wei Zhongxian had Wen's ugly line
about puppets acted out, with puppets, so that Tianqi would get the
point and get angry.[27] Wen Zhenmeng later remarked, probably on the
basis of some friendly palace source, that a puppet show indeed did take
place on November 27, in celebration of the birth of Tianqi's first child,
a girl. After the show, Wei Zhongxian told Tianqi that in his memorial
Wen had likened the emperor himself to a puppet! "Why did he do such
a hateful thing?" Tianqi reportedly asked. "He saw how tiny you are, and
how the palace servants have to help you get up and down the gold platform," replied Wei. "You must kill him, to show the realm [you can't be
trifled with]!"

After an imperial tutorial on November 30, a eunuch conveyed Tianqi's
oral directive that Wen Zhenmeng was to be flogged eighty times for ex-
ceeding his station and demeaning the ruler personally. One of the tutors,
Grand Secretary Han Kuang, argued with Wei Zhongxian over the meaning of Wen's reference to puppets. Other imperial tutors protested the directive: Wen Zhenmeng was a descendant of the Song martyr Wen Tian-
xiang, a god! Others threatened to plead Wen's case directly to Tianqi.
"If you do that," threatened Wei, "I'll order the Embroidered-uniform
Guard to arrest you!" That frightened everyone. When Tianqi next appeared, no one dared say anything about the matter to him. No official
rescript was issued until the celebration of Tianqi's daughter's birth was
completed.[28]

After twelve days had passed, a colleague of Wen Zhenmeng sent up
a memorial sharply protesting the delay. It is said that Wei Zhongxian
then stormed into the Grand Secretariat, waving his arms and cursing,

and demanding that both offenders be flogged. But, in the end, the Palace softened its position and directed that the two be demoted and sent home pending reassignment elsewhere. Ye Xianggao protested even that as too harsh. He reminded the Palace of the stature of Wen as the nation's highest-ranking degree holder and argued that, although Wen's memorial was severe and impassioned, it was not wholly wrong. Grand Secretary Han Kuang also defended Wen. But the Palace stood fast. The demotions and transfers home prevailed.[29]

◀

Although eunuch Wei Zhongxian had become the power behind the throne, the Forbidden City never fell completely under the control of himself and Madame Ke. The ultimate authority was always Tianqi's. There always loomed the threat that Tianqi's affections might be won away by any of several palace women, including especially his new bride, the thirteen-year-old Zhang Ma (1608–1644), or Empress Zhang.

If the Qing litterateur Ji Yun is to be believed, Zhang Ma was a foundling, abandoned as an infant along a roadside, where she was picked up and adopted by Zhang Guoji, an impoverished government Confucian student *(shengyuan)* from Henan province. She may well have grown up to be as demure and graceful as Ji Yun claims, because she won what might be described as a national beauty contest.

Tianqi came of marriageable age in December 1620, and eunuch Liu Kejing of the Palace Directorate of Ceremonial, in conjunction with the outer court Ministry of Rites, launched a national search for an imperial mate. A pool of five thousand girls came to Beijing for inspection and vetting. A thousand passed muster and were admitted into the Forbidden City for intimate poking and prodding by older palace women. Three hundred were kept for a month's further observation, and of these a final fifty were accepted as palace maids and concubines. Eunuch Liu Kejing was especially impressed by candidate Zhang Ma. She and two other beauties, Duan and Wang, were given a final review by a concubine of the late Wanli emperor, and she agreed with Liu that Zhang Ma was the best choice.

The marriage rites were conducted during May and June of 1621. Many people caught a glimpse of the newlyweds when they went together to pay their respects at the imperial ancestral temple just south of the Imperial City. Observers were struck by the contrast between the graceful and elegant Empress Zhang and, beside her, the tiny *(duanxiao)* emperor Tianqi, who looked to them to be three or four years younger than his real age.[30]

For some unknown reason, Wei Zhongxian and Madame Ke had not had any part in selecting the empress. An immediate hostility developed between the beautiful new empress and Madame Ke. Empress Zhang was surely capable of alienating Tianqi's affections, perhaps even turning him against her and Wei Zhongxian. Something had to be done.

In late July 1621, the empress's father (or stepfather), Zhang Guoji, informed the Palace that an impostor in Beijing was falsely claiming to be the real father of the empress. He urgently demanded that the man be arrested and punished. To what extent Wei and Ke were involved in this plot to depose the empress by questioning her paternity is not clear. Perhaps others acted without their knowledge. The impostor was one Sun Er, already in prison for crime. The Palace reaction to Zhang Guoji's memorial reflected the empress's anger. Sun Er and his co-plotters, including three palace eunuchs, were seized and interrogated. Confessions were obtained. The case was sent to the outer court for adjudication. Sun Er was executed. The Palace protected the three eunuchs.[31]

Many in Beijing officialdom suspected that Madame Ke was somehow behind the plot to unseat Empress Zhang and demanded that she be banished from the Forbidden City. Grand Secretary Liu Yijing supported that demand. A Palace rescript explained that Madame Ke was staying temporarily because Empress Zhang was so very young, but that soon a day would be chosen for her departure.[32]

The day turned out to be a day in late October 1621. Madame Ke moved from her palace in the Forbidden City to her private residence not far away. Every day at noon, however, she returned to the Forbidden City and stayed with Tianqi until dark. Then, early in November, she brazenly moved back into the Forbidden City. A Palace edict explained that Tianqi missed her terribly and needed her to stay close by him at night, and it cautioned the outer court not to start trouble by protesting her return.[33]

Immediately, the outer court protested Ke's return. Officials could not abide the publicly acknowledged infantilism of the emperor. Censor Zhou Zongjian's memorial was particularly scathing. He reminded Tianqi that Madame Ke was a servant, not a high dignitary. Had she whined, cajoled, flattered, or used her sexual allure to ensnare the emperor? But such favors were cheap! Any palace woman could supply them. Everyone in Beijing, from high officials at court to common people in the streets, had rejoiced at Madame Ke's departure and felt dismay at her return. The emperor's decision making was that of a child! Even common people could recognize the problem: here was an aggressive servant threatening the family order. Yet now the emperor had shown that he could not control his own servants![34]

There was no response from the Palace. Some days later, Supervising Secretary Hou Zhenyang sent a follow-up memorial. Surely the edict authorizing Madame Ke's return had been forged! Tianqi was not an infant! What need had he for Madame Ke, a common woman from the streets? It was the moral duty of the outer court to help Tianqi be an ideal ruler like Yao or Shun by protesting Madame Ke's presence in the Forbidden City in the strongest terms. The Palace condemned Hou's memorial as "disruptive." It accused Hou of reputation seeking.[35]

Two more supervising secretaries replied in Hou's behalf. One of them, Zhu Qinxiang, raised a cosmic argument. Madame Ke, he said, personified the negative cosmic force *(yinqi)*. So did the "slave miasma" *(nufen)*, by which he meant the war in Manchuria being waged by Nurhaci and the future Manchus. "China" and the "gentleman" *(junzi)* manifest the positive cosmic force *(yang)*, while women and barbarians are *yin*. Dark and evil things attract each other. Eventually the *yinqi* will bring on a "killing cycle" *(shayun)*. To Zhu's memorial, the Palace response was punitive. Zhu was demoted and sent home pending reassignment elsewhere.[36]

It took a long time for Supervising Secretary Jiang Xikong's memorial to arrive from the auxiliary capital at Nanjing, but he protested from a systemic perspective the demotions of his Beijing colleagues. He said that they had spoken out justly; punishing them had created paranoia *(caicun)*; silencing the mouths of the world now would just ensure a greater outburst in the future. Not many officials were brave enough to "enter the abyss"; most would prefer henceforth to be "cold crickets," the "avenue of speech" would close, and China's family state *(guojia)* would then surely face its ruin.[37]

Although no one in the outer court ventured to defend her, the attacks on Madame Ke were of course the work of the Donglin faction. Zou Yuanbiao, recently appointed vice minister of justice, and a celebrated philosopher who was aligned with the Donglin faction, sought to calm things by reminding Tianqi that, despite his great appointive and penal powers, the world was likely to oppose his decision in the Madame Ke matter and honor those whom he had punished in connection with it.

The Palace acknowledged receipt of Zou's remarks but did nothing about them.[38]

The storm over Madame Ke was not yet quite over. A major figure, philosopher Liu Zongzhou, arrived in Beijing on November 28, 1621, to take up an appointment as a bureau secretary in the Ministry of Rites. On December 7, he sent up a memorial criticizing Tianqi for protecting Madame Ke. But he aimed his heavy verbal artillery at eunuch Wei Zhongxian as the villain ultimately responsible for ruining the government. Eunuch Wei was distracting Tianqi from his duties by staging dramatic performances and military parades for his amusement! And he had seized the initiative of drafting palace rescripts *(piaoni)* from the grand secretaries!

Ye Xianggao arrived in Beijing on December 3, and on December 7 he took up his appointment as chief grand secretary. Advising the Palace about how to respond to Liu Zongzhou's troubling memorial was his first piece of business. The Palace demanded at least a demotion. Ye objected. In a memorial of December 8, he advised that indeed Liu was seeking a reputation for himself; but because he was loyal in intent and orthodox in his views, to punish him harshly would simply enhance his reputation. So the Palace backed down and settled for a scolding and a fine of half a year's salary.

"Liu was from Zhejiang," noted Ye in his memoirs, "and strictly pure and fond of disputation. He was pro-Donglin, and his coprovincials hated him. When I passed through Zhejiang [en route to Beijing], he spoke to me gravely about the current situation and advised me that it would be disastrous if [as chief grand secretary] I tried to negotiate compromises *(tiaoting)*. He was impolite to me. I laughed and didn't argue with him."[39]

Thus Tianqi won an important victory in defending the continued residence in the Forbidden City of his wet nurse. The outer court did not protest her presence again. This victory no doubt encouraged Tianqi in his later defense of Wei Zhongxian.

◀

From at least late in 1621, Beijing officialdom was aware of the extraordinary power inside the Forbidden City of the one-time street ruffian Wei Zhongxian. His illiteracy was only a minor handicap. There is no question that he possessed imaginative daring as well as exceptional energy.

It was as a procurer and caterer that he first made his mark in palace service. He soon became an impresario. At Wei's direction, flowers appeared in abundance inside the Forbidden City. In the summer, Wei would festoon himself with jasmine and gardenias. In winter and spring, peonies put forth a spectacular display.[40] Madame Ke favored morning glories, with which she decorated herself and her maids. Empress Zhang forbade her own maids to wear them.[41] There were palace theatricals, including puppet shows, as noted. There were imperial meals to supervise; these now were major productions requiring the efforts of several hundred eunuch cooks and waiters working both inside and outside the Forbidden City.[42]

Tianqi loved watching horse races, so in 1622 Wei had trees removed near the imperial stables (west of the Ciqing palace) to make an open space for racing.[43] The emperor was also fond of Western firearms and military ceremony. In the wake of the panic occasioned by the rout of the Ming armies in Manchuria in 1619, eunuch Liu Chao had organized a Palace Army (Neicao) of some three thousand soldiers, garrisoned at Nanhaizi south of Beijing but regularly assembled for ceremonies and exercises inside the Forbidden City. Tianqi enjoyed the displays of horsemanship, swordsmanship, and the mesmerizing military drum dances. There were frequent firings of guns and cannon. In 1621, a eunuch fired a gun while standing right in front of Tianqi; the gun exploded and blew off the eunuch's left hand, and nearly wounded Tianqi as well.[44] Deafening reverberations from cannon and guns could often be heard well beyond the Forbidden City. Officials complained vehemently, but to little avail.

◀

But not all was fun and games in the Forbidden City. Like it or not, the emperor was China's ultimate decision maker, and as such he was positioned in the very center of a brewing national political storm. The obvious and unfortunate fact was that Tianqi was in no way equipped to handle a job that would have taxed the powers of even a capable and experienced politician. There is no question that the Palace had to shield Tianqi and assume many of his political responsibilities as emperor.

Yet the encroachments of Wang An, Wei Zhongxian, and others upon the formulation and issuance of imperial rescripts and edicts were understandably viewed with deep suspicion in the outer court. The Ming "constitution" as bequeathed by the dynasty's founder required the monarch's open and personal involvement in government. Tianqi's personal needs and his personal limitations did not cancel that requirement.

From the very beginning of Tianqi's reign, Beijing officialdom complained that it did not know exactly how Tianqi's edicts and rescripts were arrived at. As early as October 1620, Censor Zheng Zongzhou protested that Palace edicts were being issued in the middle of the night without giving the Grand Secretariat an opportunity either to draft or to vet them.[45]

In November 1620, chief Grand Secretary Fang Congzhe devised a system designed to solve everything. He would gradually ease the new emperor into the business of government. Imperial tutorials would begin on November 11. Six senior officials were designated to serve as tutors. They would all meet with the emperor at the Wenhua palace, where they would study the *Great Learning* and the *Book of Documents* for a time. Then there would be a rest break. Tianqi would retire to a private apartment, where the eunuch Director of Ceremonial would give him the most important of the day's memorials to read. Meanwhile the grand secretaries would wait in a side room, on call in case the emperor needed their help. "We'll then go in and explain matters carefully, so that gradually the ruler will become adept," suggested Fang. Then, when it came time for the ruler to write rescripts, the grand secretaries would all troop in and stand by to help. The tutorial would resume. A Palace rescript approved this procedure.[46] Things looked promising.

On November 12, Lü Bangyao (a minor official in the Office of Transmission) advised the ruler that he should discuss whatever the eunuchs told him with the grand secretaries, to obtain their broader view; and he urged that, because the emperor could not hope to read all of the daily deluge of memorials, nor could the eunuchs explain each of them line by line, he should therefore have his tutors scan them and underline the important parts for him. Again, a Palace rescript approved the suggestion.[47]

These procedures seem to have worked for about a week. Between November 11 and November 20, Tianqi attended four tutorials. Then he gave notice that he was suspending them due to the chilly weather. The Wenhua palace was in bad repair; the classroom let in cold drafts of air. Chief Grand Secretary Fang Congzhe protested, to no avail. The directive stood.[48]

The outer court continued the protest. Officials argued that memorials needed to be referred to the appropriate ministries for discussion before the emperor rescripted them. The authority to draft rescripts must be restored to the Grand Secretariat, where by established procedure it lay. Why were eunuchs delivering peremptory "inside directives" *(zhong zhi)*? Who knew whose hand had actually written them and affixed the imperial seal? Why couldn't the emperor meet face-to-face with the grand secretaries and make the important decisions with them at hand?[49]

A Palace rescript of December 18 informed the outer court that its fears and suspicions about procedures were groundless. The emperor was receiving effective help from the eunuchs of the Directorate of Ceremonial, and he was doing business with them in his own private apartment in the Qianqing palace.[50]

The outer court was unconvinced. Censor Fang Zhenru doubted the reliability of the palace eunuchs. Censor Zhang Jie reminded Tianqi that eunuchs were menials who, by Ming house law, should not be taking part in government. Supervising Secretary Chen Yincong insisted that the ruler consult his officials and not run government through oral instructions delivered by the eunuchs.[51] The Palace was unmoved by these protests, but on February 2, 1621, Tianqi resumed his tutorials in the Wenhua palace.[52]

◀

A power struggle between the Palace and the bureaucracy began over the question of appointing new grand secretaries. Could the Palace pack the Grand Secretariat with appointees of its own choosing, ignoring the customary ranked listing of nominees as presented by the outer court?

A Palace edict of November 12, 1620, announced the elevation of Minister of Rites Sun Ruyou to the Grand Secretariat in recognition of his role in siding with Yang Lian and the others in the "palace" case. Four censors and supervising secretaries who were anti-Donglin partisans expressed shock that this appointment should have come by way of Palace fiat. They urged Tianqi to rescind the appointment. The Palace refused to do so. A rescript of November 15 informed the court that "the appointment was decided by me personally; the speaking officials may not question the directive."[53]

Sun Ruyou asked to be allowed to decline the appointment. His request was denied. On November 29, he entered the Grand Secretariat. Protests continued. Pro-Donglin officials joined in. Supervising Secretary He Tugao pointed out that "the emperor's personal decision" *(qincai)* lacked valid historical precedent. Tianqi's grandfather Wanli had begun its use "as a habit in his late years, when he became lazy and remiss." It was bad procedure. "If you make the wrong decision, the disaster will be beyond imagining. Even if you make the right decision, you [in effect] usurp the function of the high officials . . . and you may as well close down the Grand Secretariat! The Palace is a closed-off place. Your eunuchs can take advantage of that without the knowledge of you or the outer court."[54]

On December 28, Supervising Secretary Cheng Zhu (pro-Donglin) attacked both Sun Ruyou and chief Grand Secretary Fang Congzhe. The Palace replied with a rescript of reprimand.[55] On January 19, 1621, an edict came down in which the emperor demanded to know why he could not reward Sun Ruyou with promotion to grand secretary; there were precedents for doing that; the obstreperous protests of the officials violated decorum; they were taking advantage of the ruler's youth to defy his commands; they were using specious arguments to imperil and befoul government and disturb people's minds. "I cannot just sit by and listen while this contumely wrecks government," concluded the edict. "I hereby state again that promotions and demotions of high officials are decided by the emperor. Those of lesser officials will be decided on the basis of outer court discussion." The edict threatened retaliatory punishment if the protests continued.[56]

The protests did continue. On February 3, the Palace "noted" the receipt of a memorial from Censor Yi Yingchang arguing that the emperor should not compose his own rescripts and issue them as "inside directives." Censor Yi argued that the device was opaque; no one could be sure who had really authored them, and, as a result, a sense of doubt and insecurity was spreading through the realm and national affairs were being put in danger. Everyone would feel safer when the Palace restored the rescript-drafting prerogative to the Grand Secretariat.[57]

On the same day, the Palace scolded pro-Donglin Censor Zuo Guangdou for his impeachment of Sun Ruyou and his denunciation of the use of an "inside directive" to appoint him. "For the past several months," Zuo asserted, "there have been many protests against the use of inside directives; as their use began when Sun Ruyou was appointed, their use will end when he is dismissed."[58] Later in the month, Sun Ruyou defended himself by noting a long list of grand secretaries who, ever since the Jiajing reign (1521–1566), had been personal selections of the Ming emperors. He concluded that it was just because Tianqi was very young that the officials were challenging his judgment.[59] But Supervising Secretary Wang Zhidao found earlier precedents that he believed overrode the later ones.[60]

Sun Ruyou did not desire to continue the fight. In May 1621, his fourteenth request to resign was granted, and he went home to Yuyao in Zhejiang province, where he died four years later. Contrary to Zuo Guangdou's prediction, the Palace's use of "internal directives" had only just begun.

◄

The fight over the Grand Secretariat shifted ground, however. For the moment, the procedural question of appointment making faded, because the new men had already been appointed by Wanli and Taichang and were only now arriving in Beijing to take up their duties. The Donglin had the upper hand in these personality-centered struggles, and it succeeded in forcing the Palace to agree to the removal of several grand secretarial appointees who were unacceptable to them.[61]

Among the new grand secretaries was Ye Xianggao. Some Donglin adherents, like Liu Zongzhou, had misgivings about him, but most Beijing officials found him acceptable. He was an experienced statesman. He had served Wanli as a grand secretary in 1607–1614 and was chief grand secretary during the last two of those years. His arrival in Beijing and his assumption of duties as chief grand secretary in December 1621 were widely welcomed.[62] Ye Xianggao hoped to do what probably no one else could—develop an effective working relationship with the Palace, harmonize the struggle between pro- and anti-Donglin officials in the bureaucracy, and ameliorate somehow the chronic security crisis in Manchuria.

More than many of his colleagues, Ye had a sense of the big picture. He could speak clearly and effectively about matters of high policy. But he was confessedly a conciliator, not a domineering figure in the style of Zhang Juzheng, the grand secretary who had been virtual dictator of China during Wanli's youth. Indeed, Ye insisted that the Grand Secretariat, for all its eminence, occupied a modest place in the Ming power structure. It could not force or compel. Its purpose was simply to help the Palace draft rescripts (*piaoni*). Real leverage (*quan*), he said, lay with the Six Ministries. Enforcement of rescripts through the power of impeachment belonged to the supervising secretaries of the Offices of Scrutiny attached to each ministry. The Grand Secretariat could not order or compel anything.[63]

By the time Ye Xianggao arrived in Beijing after a five-month's journey from his native Fujian, pro-Donglin eunuch Wang An had already been purged and destroyed, and it was Wei Zhongxian whom Ye found "very much in charge" in the palace. Ye hoped to develop a good working relationship with Tianqi through Wei. An opportunity to do that arose in June 1622.

Censor Zhou Zongjian had earlier been one of those who tried, but failed, to force Madame Ke's removal from the Forbidden City. Now, on June 7, 1622, Censor Zhou impeached Wei Zhongxian. He accused him of moral and political ignorance, usurpation of power, and illiteracy. He implored Tianqi to get rid of him.[64]

Zhou's attack upset Wei Zhongxian. "I really am illiterate," he wailed to Ye. "What's to become of me?" Ye soothed him. He reminded Wei that on an earlier occasion Wei himself had said, "Doing what is good for the people is how to do good for the dynasty." Admirable! "I praised [Wei] highly for saying that," recalled Ye in his memoirs. "I said, 'What you said couldn't have been said better even by someone with a stomach full of *Odes* and *Documents*. Why be ashamed of your illiteracy?' Wei was very pleased and we chatted for a while, and Tianqi was in a pavilion close by, and he heard everything we said." Ye went on to explain to Wei Zhongxian that he preferred not to deal with Tianqi directly. "If we grand secretaries speak face-to-face with the emperor, then he has to heed us; and if he disagrees, then we have to argue with him. That puts high and low in contention, and the appropriate decorum *(timian)* between ruler and subject disappears. But you eunuchs serve the emperor daily, you can plead and cajole until he changes his mind, whereas it would not do if we grand secretaries were to try that."[65]

Wei Zhongxian was happy with such an approach and, until 1624, he and Ye Xianggao managed to cooperate fairly well. Ye was often able to make his views prevail by contesting edicts and rescripts that had been shown to the Grand Secretariat after having been first drafted in the palace.

Defeat in Manchuria

Many thought that what Ming China needed was a strong hand. The realm was in crisis on several fronts in the 1620s. There were revolts in Sichuan and Guizhou, far in the southwest, and a major upheaval closer to home—the sectarian revolt of Xu Hongru in 1622, which affected northeast China and was prompted in part by an influx of refugees from what everyone recognized as the major theater of crisis, Manchuria.

There had been a collapse of the Ming armies in Manchuria in 1619, followed by the loss of yet more Ming territory east of the Liao River in 1621. These losses sparked the national territory *(fengqiang)* controversy, which achieved a prominence at least equal to that of the Three Cases in the increasingly violent partisan struggle that was developing in Beijing. It was essential to rally and strengthen the Ming military defenses west of the Liao River. This task the Tianqi government placed in the hands of two men, both of them civil officials, who held conflicting strategic views and hated each other personally. They were Wang Huazhen and Xiong Tingbi.

A forward position was established at Guangning, some three hundred miles east-northeast of Beijing. Wang Huazhen was posted there as governor *(xunfu)*. Wang's aim was to carry out a swift reconquest of the territory east of the Liao River with the help of Mongol mercenaries. Simultaneously, Xiong Tingbi was posted as military commissioner *(jinglue)* rearward of Wang, at Shanhaiguan, a hundred miles southwest of Guangning and two hundred miles east of Beijing. Xiong's strategy was longer-range and defensive, with emphasis on making common cause with the ethnic Chinese inhabitants of Manchuria.

Wang and Xiong jealously worked at cross-purposes. While some officials ardently championed Wang Huazhen, others, including especially those in the Donglin faction, supported Xiong Tingbi. Court conferences deadlocked over Manchurian strategy. The Palace ordered the two commanders to cooperate, to no avail. Then, in March 1622, Wang's forces were routed in a skirmish east of the Liao. Guangning was inadequately defended; the future Manchus advanced and seized it. Wang Huazhen and a large mob of civilians and defeated soldiers fled west in disarray and overwhelmed Xiong Tingbi's position at Shanhaiguan. Appearing magnanimous in his personal victory over his failed rival, Xiong Tingbi escorted Wang and the mob accompanying him westward to safety through the narrow Shanhaiguan gateway.[66]

Panic developed in Beijing as the refugees reached the suburbs. There was fear of their starting a rebellion. The Beijing bureaucracy struggled to reorganize the defenses outside Shanhaiguan and to determine appropriate punishments for both Wang and Xiong. At first it was decided to arrest Wang Huazhen and to order Xiong Tingbi to stand down pending further investigation.[67] Some inhabitants of Beijing reacted angrily to this decision. Crowds wept at the sight of Wang under arrest. They flung stones and tiles at Xiong Tingbi, striking his head and causing blood to flow. Supervising Secretary Zhou Hongmo thought the people's rage was genuine, but Censor Huang Zunsu surmised that the stone throwers had been paid by Wang Huazhen's partisans.[68]

In May 1622, two months after the disaster, a joint public meeting of the *fasi* (the Censorate, Ministry of Justice, and Court of Judicial Review) was held to recommend just punishments for both failed commanders. Minister of Justice Wang Ji, Censor-in-chief Zou Yuanbiao (both Donglin men), and Zhou Yingqiu (chief minister of the Court of Judicial Review, and anti-Donglin) met and agreed that both Wang and Xiong should be executed—Wang for incompetence, Xiong for obstructionism and arrogance. Their verdict was severe, but at least it was bipartisan. The Palace endorsed it.[69]

This, however, did not end the matter. The loss of territory *(feng-qiang)* issue was too complex; there were too many unresolved questions as well as suspicions and charges of espionage and treachery. Liao natives in Ming service were accused of pro-Manchu activity. There were charges of gross peculations of military funds and that Donglin partisans had abetted Xiong Tingbi in his obstructionism and must also be prosecuted. Countercharges were brought against those officials who had championed Wang Huazhen. And the heat of the summer of 1622 was further raised by intense partisan debates over the Three Cases.

The temperature rose further still. While Wang and Xiong awaited their fates in the prison of the Ministry of Justice, an ugly confrontation took place between Minister of Justice Wang Ji (pro-Donglin) and Grand Secretary Shen Que (anti-Donglin).

Shen Que had recruited several hundred troops from his home province of Zhejiang to assist, he argued, in the Ming defense of Manchuria. In April 1622 these troops arrived in Beijing. Shen grandly presented them to Tianqi. But rumor had it that Shen Que was in secret collusion with palace eunuch Liu Chao to use those troops, plus ten thousand more he had promised, in support of the controversial palace army that Liu Chao was then organizing. Supervising Secretary Hui Shiyang detailed those rumors in an impeachment of Shen Que. Shen protested the impeachment as wholly unfounded, insisting that he had recruited the troops out of the devotion of his "red heart" to the Ming cause!

Yet his detractors were calling him a villain and a bandit, and sought his death, so he must resign. The Palace consoled him and kept him on duty.[70]

The "speaking officials" (censors and supervising secretaries) then increased the pressure. They now accused Shen Que of bribing Madame Ke and Wei Zhongxian! By accepted custom, Shen Que should have secluded himself at home while the Palace considered this latest impeachment charge. But he did not. He continued to appear at court. Minister of Justice Wang Ji was angered. He told Ye Xianggao that he was going to curse Shen Que publicly if he attended another court assembly. Ye tried to calm him down. Wang Ji sent up two impeachments of Shen Que. These the Palace rejected; it warned that high officials should act to preserve the "national body" (*guoti*) and not assault each other.[71]

Shen Que did not take these impeachments quietly. He accused Wang Ji of deliberately delaying an investigation of the role of double agents in the fall of Guangning. Moreover, he accused Wang Ji of protecting the archvillain, Xiong Tingbi. Again, the Palace asked that high officials cease making such accusations.[72]

Then, suddenly and shockingly, on August 17, 1622, the Palace dismissed Wang Ji from his post as minister of justice and removed him from civil service altogether. Several days later, Shen Que was granted retirement with full honors. No one protested Shen's departure, but the inexplicably harsh treatment of Wang Ji was challenged by the grand secretaries jointly and individually, by joint memorial from the top officials of the ministries, and by various speaking officials. It was all to no avail; the Palace declined to change its mind about Wang Ji. Its tilt against the Donglin partisans was evident.[73]

The agreed-upon executions of Wang Huazhen and Xiong Tingbi were placed on indefinite hold, pending a more thorough investigation of the role played by the accused double agents. Then, in November 1622, Censor Yang Weiyuan laid the groundwork for the 1625 torture-murders of Donglin partisans by making the charge that Gu Dazhang, a top assistant to former Minister of Justice Wang Ji, had, early after the fall of Guangning, argued that Xiong Tingbi's guilt was less than that of Wang Huazhen, and that whereas Wang should be executed, Xiong should be given a lighter penalty and a chance to redeem himself. Yang Weiyuan further charged that Gu had accepted 40,000 taels of silver from Xiong as a bribe to help him win acquittal.

Gu denied the charge. He had been but one of twenty-eight officials at the *fasi* meeting in May and had agreed with the execution verdict proposed on that occasion, so how, he asked, could he be a protector of Xiong Tingbi? Gu's protest was unconvincing. What of the alleged bribe? Besides, Gu had argued that the accused double agents were innocent. Clearly he was protecting Xiong.[74]

Thus the question of blame for the loss of Guangning became hopelessly entangled in partisan infighting. The original bipartisan solution—to execute both Wang and Xiong—could not be sustained. Ye Xianggao rather favored Wang. Anti-Donglin partisans protected Wang Huazhen by ignoring him while they vented their wrath on Xiong Tingbi, making it necessary for the Donglin to defend Xiong. No one was allowed to remain impartial in the dispute. All this would come to a head in 1625.

The Shoushan Academy

The year 1622 featured yet another matter of partisan controversy, this one of a very different kind. It centered on the foundation by Donglin sympathizers of the Shoushan academy in Beijing. The trouble with this academy was that it was not so much a school as a headquarters and gathering place for intellectual exchange, spiritual renewal, and making contacts for officials and students in Beijing.

The leaders in this risky venture were Feng Congwu and Zou Yuanbiao, two senior officials and eminent Confucian philosophers who had spent decades in political exile and were recalled to service after the death of Wanli in 1620. Feng was a northerner, from Shaanxi. In 1622 he was sixty-five years old. Zou was a southerner, from Jiangxi, seventy-one years old. Zou was appointed censor-in-chief. Feng was vice censor-in-chief and the main organizer of the Shoushan academy.

Feng Congwu might best be described as a Confucian evangelist. By his own confession, he "lived, ate, and breathed" the activity called *jiangxue* (literally, "discussing study"). This meant the gathering together of listeners and truth seekers in informal question-and-answer sessions for the purpose of provoking an ethical awakening—the refocusing of minds on the moral foundations of the inherited Confucian tradition.

Although it appeared to be a benign form of extracurricular activity, there is no question that *jiangxue* contributed to the toxicity of political conflict in Beijing. At discussion meetings Feng would hang up a chart showing a fork in a road and explain to his audience how one fork led "good people" and "gentlemen" along a path to humanness and sage-hood, while the other fork led fools away to bestiality and evil. "One instant of thought" at the base of the fork made all the difference. There was no middle path, "no road between the two." Literary cultivation and administrative acumen were irrelevant, he maintained. Either they en-hanced one's villainy, or they embellished one's goodness.[75]

Like his colleagues from the Donglin academy in Wuxi, Feng Congwu placed the common Confucian division of the world into "gentlemen" *(junzi)* and "small men" *(xiaoren)* at the very forefront of his concerns. A listener asked Feng how gentlemen should treat small men who follow the path of self-interested advantage. Feng said it depended upon the sit-uation. You could not befriend such people, but you could welcome them to *jiangxue* meetings, because there was always the hope that they might be morally awakened by the experience. In official life, small men might be tolerated, no more.[76]

Feng agreed with the Donglin academy's revision of Wang Yangming's dictum with regard to good and evil: Wang's error was in trying to tran-scend the distinction and bring about moral change in the world in non-confrontational ways. That was wrong, argued Feng: we must love good and hate evil. But hypostasizing good and evil in this way justified on moral-theoretical grounds a posture of uninhibited ad hominem denun-ciation in bureaucratic life and injected a lethal dose of moral absolutism into the endemic regional and personal rivalries of central-level politics in Ming China.

Thus the founding of the Shoushan academy in Beijing was politically no small matter. Upon their return to official life in 1620–1621, Feng and Zou at first convened *jiangxue* meetings thrice monthly at the city god temple, near Beijing's southwest edge; but the site was too small and far away, so Censor Zhou Zongjian and several of his colleagues found some-thing better inside the Xuanwu gate, about 2,000 meters west of the main complex of offices housing the Ming central bureaucracy. A collection of some several hundred taels of silver was taken up, enough to buy a small building and remodel it so that it housed some ten rooms, including a lecture hall, a library, and a shrine containing an icon of Confucius. Chief Grand Secretary Ye Xianggao composed a dedicatory inscription for the academy. The great artist Dong Qichang calligraphized it and the inscription was cut into stone. A gazetteer was compiled, and notes of what was said at the meetings were regularly recorded. Some were later published. The academy was called the Shoushan. As Feng Congwu explained, the meaning of "Shoushan" was moral-geographical: Beijing was the model for the four quarters of the realm, the "place at the forefront of goodness" *(shoushan zhi di)*, so the new "Forefront of Goodness" academy should rightfully stand nationally in the vanguard of the half-dozen provincial academies, like the Donglin academy in Wuxi, which had been conducting *jiangxue* for many years. Meetings at the Shoushan were held six times a month.[77]

Participants debated the question of whether current political matters should be discussed at the meetings. Lu Shanji, for one, argued that "in these times of crisis, we who are high officials cannot be said to be engaged in 'study' if we don't talk about current government."[78] Feng overruled him. "We don't discuss government, or private matters, or religion," he insisted. "All we talk about is things like father–son, ruler–subject relations, the five virtues, and the Six Injunctions of Ming Taizu."[79] The aim was to revitalize China. *Jiangxue* defined what Ming China was all about. "Today we do *jiangxue,* and to be sure what we're doing is elucidating principles, but really we're sustaining the dynastic fate *(guoyun).* The fate of all of us lies here. It's not idle chat!"[80]

Feng preached that there was no more pressing time than now for "discussions of study." China's officials, burdened by crises in Sichuan and Manchuria, rushing about to mobilize troops and find new sources of supply for them, needed to stop fighting and blaming each other, and rediscover the moral grounds upon which alone they could unite their minds *(tongxin).* The ultimate strategy for resisting the enemy in Manchuria and elsewhere was *jiangxue.*[81] The Ming armies were defeated in Manchuria and the inherited territory *(fengqiang)* was lost there because the nation's understanding of Confucian principles *(lixue)* had not been made clear.[82]

The Shoushan meetings were heavily attended. Feng's exhortations had the ability to reduce sympathizers to tears, and scoffers to shame. However, there were some among the Donglin who doubted the wisdom of holding *jiangxue* meetings in the heated political atmosphere of Beijing. Hanlin academician Yao Ximeng recalled that he had attended a preliminary meeting at the city god's temple late in 1621 and accepted Feng's invitation to one of the first full meetings there. "Some thirty people came," wrote Yao. "They were looking for common ground in their ideas, but there were a few who disagreed, and the differences were left unresolved."

"That night lying in bed," continued Yao, "I thought about how the people of the world have always looked askance at worthy men. [It seemed to me that] to open a venue for discussion right here in the capital would only invite denunciation. At dawn, Zou [Yuanbiao] knocked at my gate and I told him I wasn't going, and I said that, by not going, my hope was to discourage him and Feng.... Then a few days later Feng came by, and I warned him that the state was in trouble, there was a lot of work for the officials to do, and that *jiangxue* was not a priority right now. But Feng said: 'It's exactly because the state is in trouble, and the officials don't realize they must die for it, that they cover their heads and flee like one rat after another. We must resurrect the mind of cleaving to the ruler, and risk our lives for our superiors. How can we lay *jiangxue* aside?' I was silenced, and didn't dare reply."[83]

But Yao Ximeng's misgivings were on target. Some officials viewed the Shoushan as a sinister threat to political order. In October 1622, Supervising Secretary Zhu Tongmeng attacked the institution. He said that there was nothing wrong with "clarifying the Sage's ideas and teaching them to juniors," as the Donglin academy had long ago begun to do, but their lecture meetings had also attracted a motley gathering of deviant men who exploited the Donglin to build a faction, advance friends, and attack rivals. They set up a "camp" *(menhu)*, strengthened the walls, and fought bloody skirmishes with their foes. Those Donglin partisans were eventually defeated (in 1617), but now Feng and Zou had erected a new academy right here in Beijing and were building another camp just like the old one! Zhu Tongmeng urged the emperor to close down the Shoushan. The Palace replied by rescript that it did not believe Feng and Zou were intentionally building a faction, but it asked both men to "reflect" on what they were doing.[84] Feng and Zou at once sent up memorials explaining and defending the meetings. They then offered their resignations, which the Palace did not accept.[85]

Attacks on Feng and Zou intensified. Violent debates about the Three Cases were in progress in which Zou and Feng weighed in with strong briefs on behalf of those who perceived conspiracy in the "stick" and "pill" affairs.[86] In November 1622, Supervising Secretary Guo Yunhou again impeached Zou Yuanbiao for his role in the *jiangxue* meetings, on the ground that those meetings were attended by ambitious elements hoping to obtain official appointments. "The good species are being squeezed out, and disaster threatens the state," he warned.[87]

Inside the palace, the notion had somehow taken hold that *jiangxue* had caused the fall of the Southern Song dynasty some three centuries before. Wei Zhongxian told chief Grand Secretary Ye Xianggao that this was what Tianqi understood. Ye endeavored to refute the idea. The Palace refused to change its mind, but it directed Zou and Feng to stay on the job.[88]

The attacks continued. Supervising Secretary Guo Xingzhi stated in a memorial that Zou Yuanbiao had told one of his subordinates that "right and wrong needn't be made too clear." What on earth sort of statement was that? Did Zou want to close the mouths of the censors and supervising secretaries? Did he want to forbid judging the character and quality of others? Did he want to muddle merit and blame? Yet this is what *jiangxue* had come to! What we need, concluded Guo, is the real study of Confucius and Mencius, not this irresponsible stuff.[89]

In reply, Zou protested that Guo had taken his words out of context. Of course right and wrong are never unclear. It's just that there may be good reasons to soften one's assaults on targeted figures. The Palace's response was to support Zou and scold Guo.[90]

Guo took no heed. Immediately he assailed Zou Yuanbiao as a crypto-Buddhist and not an exponent of "upright learning" at all. Such a person should not be censor-in-chief. He also attacked Ye Xianggao for supporting Zou. Ye asked to resign. The Palace chided Guo Yunhou. "The good species are the primary *qi* of the state," said the Palace. "Why is Guo trying to triumph over the good species?"[91]

Both Zou Yuanbiao and Feng Congwu offered repeatedly to resign in response to these attacks. On November 25, the Palace finally allowed Zou to do so, and it accepted Feng's resignation on December 3. Feng pleaded that the emperor not use the departures of himself and Zou as an excuse to close down the Shoushan academy and prohibit *jiangxue*.[92] Indeed, both continued to function until suppressed in 1625.

Ye Xianggao remarked in his memoirs that, according to his own observation, *jiangxue* was "ninety percent empty discussion," and therefore he never engaged in it himself but harbored no hostile feelings toward those who did. "I always told people that while there was no need to 'discuss study,' there was no need to forbid it either, and that it was no enlightened policy for the court to prohibit it. Zhu Tongmeng and the other [critics] had an ulterior motive, which is why I spoke out so sharply. Thanks to me, the [Shoushan] academy wasn't destroyed ... until after I retired."[93]

Packing the Grand Secretariat

A fear existed that the sexennial official evaluations of 1623 might be exploited for partisan purposes again, as they had been in 1617, when opponents used them to force Donglin adherents out of their positions. (In 1617, it was enough for a person to interpret the Stick Case of 1615 as evidence of a conspiracy to assassinate the heir apparent, Zhu Changluo, to count as "Donglin".) But the 1623 evaluations, conducted in February and March, were not much politicized, as things turned out. Officials were rated on their merits rather than on their political leanings.[94]

It was otherwise with a new set of appointments to the Grand Secretariat. In February 1623, the Palace appointed four new grand secretaries —Zhu Guozhen, Gu Bingqian, Zhu Yanxi, and Wei Guangwei—to join the five already on duty. The disturbing feature of these appointments was not that Tianqi had "personally selected" them out of the blue (as he had done with Sun Ruyou in 1620–1621). In accordance with established procedure, an outer-court conference had met and agreed on a ranked list of nine nominees for grand secretary. The expectation was that the Palace would follow the outer court's rank order. The Palace did not. It rejected the court's top two nominees, Sun Shenxing and Sheng Yihong, selected the third and fourth nominees (Zhu Guozhen and Gu Bingqian), and then went to the bottom of the list and picked the eighth and ninth (Zhu Yanxi and Wei Guangwei).

The Beijing bureaucracy was astounded. Chief Grand Secretary Ye Xianggao remarked that, although he personally saw nothing wrong with the Palace's choices, it was incumbent upon him to make a formal protest in the hope of dampening controversy and paranoia in the outer court. Ye asked the Palace to explain why it had rejected the top two nominees. The Palace replied that Sun Shenxing had discredited himself by his continuing charges of regicide in the Pill Case, while Sheng Yihong was unacceptable because of his thick Shaanxi accent.[95]

That ended the matter. Grand Secretaries Gu Bingqian and Wei Guangwei would soon become major anti-Donglin players. The display of Palace willfulness in appointing the new grand secretaries troubled many, in that it eroded the integrity and prestige of the outer-court bureaucracy and sent a strong signal of support to the opponents of the Donglin.

The Partisan Struggle Escalates

A sense that the Donglin position was being undermined surely inspired the ugly public dispute between Censor Zhou Zongjian and Supervising Secretary Guo Gong that erupted shortly afterward, in March 1623. At the center of the dispute was the imprisoned ex-commander of Ming forces at Shanhaiguan, Xiong Tingbi. When the arrogant and widely hated Xiong Tingbi was appointed commander at Shanhaiguan in 1621, the Palace had acted to reassure him of its backing by demoting his loudest detractor, Supervising Secretary Guo Gong.[96] Then, after Xiong's arrest in 1622, Guo Gong was reinstated. In early 1623, ignoring the pleading of Ye Xianggao and others, who urged him not to, Guo Gong went ahead and sent up an impeachment of Xiong Tingbi's former supporters.[97]

In February 1623, a Nanjing censor by the name of Tu Shiye sent up a memorial accusing Censor Zhou Zongjian of having once referred to Xiong Tingbi as the "savior of Liao." Censor Zhou sent up a rebuttal in which he denied ever having backed Xiong's appointment. Then, gratuitously, he added the allegation that Tu Shiye really had an ulterior motive: he was in league with Supervising Secretary Guo Gong and palace eunuch Wei Zhongxian and was angling to advance his own promotion prospects.

The Palace sent Zhou's rebuttal down to the outer court for its comment. Supervising Secretary Guo Gong exploded in anger at Zhou's allegation. In retaliation, he further linked Zhou to Yang Lian (the main actor in the "palace" case), to the now deceased palace eunuch Wang An, and to the "bandit thicket" of the Shoushan academy. These, he alleged, were all components of one and the same "deviant clique."[98]

Zhou replied to Guo Gong on March 11 with a stinging statement that accused Guo of turning all the facts upside down in "extremely ugly language." "What is Guo's motive, since his reinstatement?" asked Zhou rhetorically. "Why is he alone of all those recalled being so obnoxious? I won't speculate. He is a year-mate of mine. But the emperor should order Guo Gong to rectify himself, to discuss one case at a time, and not concoct conspiracies." To this the Palace's reaction was calm. It said Xiong Tingbi's case was already decided and reminded both disputants that they

should state right and wrong according to principle, and refrain from raising implications.[99]

But on March 28, 1623, Censor Zhou Zongjian sent up a long and sensational bill of new charges, alleging that Guo Gong was the linchpin in
a plot hatched by palace eunuch Wei Zhongxian to create a new political
order for China—at the expense of the "good species"! Zhou wanted the
emperor to know all the vile details of this plot. He wanted Tianqi to
know that when Guo Gong was demoted in 1621 he actually stayed in
Beijing and secretly contacted Wei Zhongxian. Wei, deeply stung by
Zhou's powerful assault on him in June 1622, wanted revenge. Having
already allied himself with Madame Ke, and with eunuch Liu Chao and
his palace army, Wei now extended a tentacle into the outer court
through Supervising Secretary Guo Gong, since reinstated. Guo Gong
then compiled for Wei Zhongxian an enemies list consisting of some fifty
names of Beijing officials. Over the past several months, eleven good men
from that list had already been cashiered: Wang Ji, Zou Yuanbiao, Feng
Congwu, Wen Zhenmeng, Sun Shenxing, and six others. Zhou further
claimed: Guo Gong openly flaunts this enemies list! Right now, I have a
copy of it in my hands. Most people are too fearful to say anything about
it, but Guo Gong cannot be allowed to pursue his evil plan and "gather
more ants and flies" for Wei Zhongxian. Does the ruler know how Wei
killed Wang An? He cut off his head and fed his flesh to crows and his
bones to yellow dogs! The cruelest thing in history! Zhou demanded that
Guo answer these charges. He vowed he would not serve in the same
court with "a sucker of boils and licker of hemorrhoids like Guo Gong!"

To this the Palace replied, again calmly, on March 31. It stated that the
eleven dismissals had all been decided by the emperor personally, and had
been endorsed by the Grand Secretariat. It also demanded that Zhou
Zongjian supply facts to substantiate his other allegations.[100] Zhou replied
immediately by restating his case in further detail, but he explained that
he lacked the powers of arrest and interrogation, and could not substantiate everything. It was simply his duty as a "speaking official" to report
what he heard. To that, the Palace drafted a rescript ordering that Zhou
be flogged eighty times. The Grand Secretariat objected, and argued successfully for reducing the penalty to a fine of three months' salary.[101]

Zhou Zongjian's charges were explosive. By making them, he was vis-
ibly placing himself in a position of leadership on the Donglin battlefront.
It appears, however, that others were not prepared to follow him. Perhaps
he was too recent a convert to the Donglin side.[102] Friends reportedly ad-

vised him that his "righteous demeanor" was evident, and that if he now just kept quiet for a few months, he would not risk being considered a "cold cricket," that is, someone too intimidated to speak out. "I'm ready to be flogged to death here and now," replied Zhou. "How can you suggest such a thing? The emperor gives me life, and I dare not but offer my own life in return."[103]

Supervising Secretary Shen Weibing (pro-Donglin) memorialized that the "tongue battle" between Guo Gong and Zhou was, at bottom, about Xiong Tingbi. He begged the emperor to proceed with Xiong's execution. Delaying it was giving Guo Gong and all the others the opportunity to accuse Yang Lian and others of serving as his protectors! The Palace was unimpressed by Shen's long argument and declined to act on it.[104]

It came to the attention of Supervising Secretary Liu Honghua that his name appeared at the top of Guo Gong's enemies list, and early in April 1623 he complained bitterly about this in a memorial. Did his name appear there because Xiong Tingbi, Yang Lian, and Liu himself were all coprovincials from Huguang? "The talk on the street is that [imprisoned former commander] Wang Huazhen has given out generous bribes, and that Guo Gong is exerting all efforts to get Wang released. . . . Guo hopes to kill Xiong Tingbi, and he has concocted his list to remove everyone who opposes him." Concluded Liu, "the primary *qi* of the dynasty consists of impartial opinion and the good species. Guo Gong with his foul mouth and poisoned hand wants to repress me. I must plead with the ruler." The Palace replied that "impartial opinion" was clear, and that there was no need for Liu's attack.[105]

On April 14, Censor Zhou Zongjian provided his colleagues with a triumphant public statement of his achievement thus far. He said that his fact-based exposure of Guo Gong's collusion with Wei Zhongxian had beaten both malefactors into fear and silence. "I was not wrong to say as I did that I put myself at risk to untangle the nets," stated Zhou. Happily, public opinion has been favorable; thanks to Zhou, the ruler-father will have his rightful powers restored to him; officials will fear denunciation no more; and the palace eunuchs will soon withdraw and "use no longer their authority as city foxes and country rats to spread their strange poisons." Zhou invited Guo Gong to confess his errors publicly and return to the good graces of the realm.[106]

Censor Fang Daren followed Zhou's statement with a memorial to the throne asserting that very few people ever wanted to save Xiong Tingbi. Many made statements about him that tried to be fair, but Guo Gong kept reading wrong messages into them, accusing perfectly innocent people of being "clique bandits." Meanwhile Guo Gong said nothing of his own efforts to save Wang Huazhen! And there was evidence to corroborate Zhou Zongjian's charges against Wei Zhongxian. Fang had seen with his own eyes the imperial-scale sepulcher Wei was having built for himself at the Biyunsi, in the Western Hills! Guo Gong, moreover, has never replied effectively to Zhou's impeachments of him; Guo said nothing of Wei Zhongxian, but simply vowed to have Zhou flogged and exiled, which in itself is clear proof that Guo Gong is in league with Wei Zhongxian! Censor Fang demanded that Guo Gong be severely punished.[107]

The Palace informed the Grand Secretariat that it would not tolerate any further disputes among the speaking officials. It said they had joined into self-interested cliques, battling each other for victory in the loss-of-territory (fengqiang) issue. They cared nothing for the ruler or the dynasty. They all deserved flogging and imprisonment. The ruler had so far been lenient, but (threatened the Palace) he will not forgive those who disobey him in the future.[108]

However, early in May, Guo Gong asked the emperor to authorize a court conference to review the charges and countercharges between himself, Zhou Zongjian, Liu Honghua, and Fang Daren.[109] Accordingly, Minister of Personnel Zhang Wenda convened a discussion and, upon its conclusion, made the recommendation that all the officials mentioned had spoken too recklessly and shown inadequate self-cultivation, but that all had acted in good faith and should be given a chance to reform themselves and do their jobs. The Palace agreed, and it also fined both Zhou and Guo three months' salary for their contumely.[110]

In the fall of 1623, Zhou Zongjian was sent away to serve in a provincial position.[111] Then he took mourning leave. In 1625, he was arrested and tortured to death in the Decree Prison in Beijing. But, for the moment, his radical bid to force change in Ming governance came to nothing; stronger hands and cooler heads had prevailed.

The Donglin Unraveling

Late in 1623, however, Minister of Personnel Zhang Wenda's request to retire from government was granted. He was replaced by another northerner, Zhao Nanxing. As things turned out, it was not a good choice.

Zhao Nanxing, seventy-three years old, had spent many years in private life outside Beijing, in compulsory political exile. In his younger years, Zhao had been a bureaucratic turf fighter and administrative disciplinarian, a man who hated corruption and anyone engaged in it. Although he was not philosophically inclined, his personal ties to Gao Panlong and others in the Donglin camp were close and of long standing.

Anyone who held the office of Minister of Personnel had, not a decisive role, but an important influence upon personnel selection, and therefore upon the partisan struggle in progress in Beijing. Zhao Nanxing was not a conciliator. His style of behavior was dictatorial rather than collegial. In vain his friends warned him about his self-righteous coldness.[112] Without intending it, he helped to widen the rift between the Donglin and their opponents. Indirectly he bears some responsibility for the bloody destruction of the Donglin in 1625–1627.

Take, for instance, his attitude toward palace eunuch Wei Zhongxian. Report has it that Wei was, at the outset, favorably disposed toward Zhao and expedited favorable Palace rescripts to Zhao's memorials.[113] Wei wanted to go further and consolidate a personal relationship. To that end, he sent his nephew Fu Yingxing with a gift to Zhao's house. Zhao curtly refused him admittance. There also came an occasion when Zhao and Wei were seated together at a meeting inside the Forbidden City. Under discussion was a minor appointment. What Wei said is not recorded, but Zhao replied to him with a righteous air, "The emperor is young, and we officials inside the Palace and out must strive to do good." Wei Zhongxian did not reply, but his anger was visible on his face.[114] Zhao had called Wei Zhongxian's ethics into question.

It was also Zhao who provoked the hostility of Wei Guangwei, appointed a grand secretary over the objections of the outer court in February 1623. Wei was the son of a deceased colleague and friend of Zhao's, but for reasons that are not entirely clear (Wei's hatred of Xiong Tingbi may have been partly the cause), Zhao despised Wei Guangwei and said that he was no true son of his father's. Wei went to Minister Zhao's home to pay a courtesy call. Zhao told his gateman to inform Wei that he had gone to bed and would not receive callers. Wei tried two more times to pay a call, but Zhao rebuffed him each time. Understandably, Wei Guangwei was deeply offended.[115] Personal dislike notwithstanding, that was no way to treat a grand secretary. Zhao was also cool toward Ye Xianggao.[116]

As minister of personnel, Zhao Nanxing's self-appointed mission was to purge government of sloth, corruption, and incompetence, and fill vacancies with upright and capable men. Unfortunately, he discharged that task in such a way as needlessly to kindle hatreds.

The trouble began in April 1624, when he peremptorily appointed one Zou Weilian to a vacancy in his own Ministry of Personnel. He ignored the standing procedure of clearing a candidate with his coprovincials among the censors and supervising secretaries before sending his name up to the Palace for confirmation. He also forgot or dismissed the fact that there already was a coprovincial of Zou's—Wu Yuwen—serving in the same bureau. The province in question was Jiangxi. The Jiangxi officials raised a storm of protest, demanding to know why they had not been consulted. Wu Yuwen immediately resigned his position. Zou Weilian soon resigned as well. Zhao Nanxing confessed to the Palace that he had muddled the affair; the Palace consoled Zhao and directed both Wu and Zou to resume their positions. Zhao asked to be allowed to resign. The matter raged on, and in June it took an ominous turn.

Zhao Nanxing's rationale for summarily appointing Zou Weilian was that he knew Zou to have an outstanding reputation for uprightness and competence; that Jiangxi people were well known for their Confucian study *(daoxue)* and their principled righteousness *(jieyi);* and that therefore it came as a complete shock to him when Zou's coprovincials protested his appointment. The coprovincials in question were Supervising Secretaries Zhang Yunru, Chen Liangxun, and Fu Kui. All had good reputations. None was known to be anti-Donglin. They should never have become antagonists. But they were deeply offended at having been ignored; and they also suspected that Zou Weilian had advised Zhao to ignore them. When the Palace disallowed their initial protest, they sensed that, behind the scenes, a conspiracy was making its force felt. This was the atmosphere in which, in June 1624, Supervising Secretary Fu Kui sent up a sensational impeachment that threatened to destroy several key players in the Donglin faction.[117]

That there existed, if not a conspiracy, then at least a suspiciously opaque mechanism for discovering and promoting "good men" is beyond doubt. Fu Kui felt excluded and victimized by it, and he was not alone in that feeling. The situation was this: an opening occurred in the position of chief supervising secretary in the Office of Scrutiny for Personnel, a plum assignment. There was an informal waiting list of candidates for it. The first man on the list had to take emergency leave. Wei Dazhong (Supervising Secretary of the Left in the Office of Scrutiny for Revenue, soon to become a major Donglin figure) understood that he

was the next man in line. Actually he was not. Ruan Dacheng, a supervising secretary of rank slightly lower than Wei's, was next.

Ruan Dacheng (his notoriety as a playwright would develop later) considered himself a member of the "pure current," an alternative label for
the Donglin. He happened to be home on leave, far from Beijing, in
Tongcheng county in modern Anhui province. So his county compatriot,
Assistant Censor-in-Chief Zuo Guangdou, sent him an urgent letter advising him to hurry back to Beijing. Ruan did so.

Ruan hosted a gathering for his pure-current comrades when he returned to Beijing. Supervising Secretary Wei Dazhong, Censor Huang
Zunsu, and the Jiangxi men Zhang Yunru and Chen Liangxun joined
him over rice beer, and, according to Huang, they all vowed to Heaven
that they would cleave together. But not long after this gathering Ruan
found that "outer-court opinion" was against him, in part because of
negative comments (superficiality, carelessness in speech) that had been
placed in his evaluation file. His friend and patron, Zuo Guangdou, suggested that perhaps Ruan should withdraw and make himself available for
another, slightly lesser vacancy in the Office of Scrutiny for Works.

Ruan Dacheng was stung. He felt that Zuo Guangdou had betrayed
him. A clique had formed against him! He turned a cold shoulder toward
Zuo and Wei Dazhong. He would have revenge! Through Fu Kui, the
disaffected supervising secretary from Jiangxi, he made contact with palace eunuch Wei Zhongxian's nephew Fu Jijiao. Then, at some point (the
chronology is not clear), Ruan and Fu Kui met Wei Zhongxian himself at
Zhuozhou, twenty miles south of Beijing, where the eunuch was paying
a ceremonial visit. Reportedly, Ruan paid obeisance to Wei and gave him
a list of his friends and enemies in the bureaucracy. On May 1, 1624, Ruan
got the appointment he coveted.

Ruan's former friends were horrified. Wei Dazhong tried to reason
with him. Censor Li Yingsheng wrote Ruan of his disappointment and
regret, and reminded him that while the *junzi* of the Northern Song had
had their mutual disagreements, they had never sought the help of *xiaoren* in their mutual struggles. "Unfortunately," wrote Li, "schemers have
dragged you into the vines."[118] Censor Huang Zunsu, likewise, chided
Ruan for his behavior. "Why do you stalk off because of a difference of
opinion?" he asked. "The *xiaoren* are pleased to see this. They see a rift
they can exploit. They're doing everything they can to win you over.
They've painted the whole dragon except for the eyes, and they want you
to paint those."[119]

Ruan resigned his new post within days of receiving it and retired home. Perhaps he found the partisan cross-fires too intense. However, before leaving Beijing he reportedly helped Fu Kui to draft a searing memorial of impeachment of his former Donglin friends, a memorial whose verbal pyrotechnics left no doubt but that the Donglin partisans were about to destroy each other.

On June 4, the Palace rescripted and released to the public Fu Kui's sensational memorial. In it, Fu alleged the existence of a dangerous conspiracy of deviant and vile men aiming to dominate Ming government. He asked the ruler to consider that even in good times there are predatory owls among the phoenixes, thorn bushes among the orchids, and *xiaoren* among the *junzi*. As long as the *xiaoren* do not have high position, or form cliques, the evil they can do is minor. But, charged Fu Kui, we now see the ugly faces and predatory heart-minds of Zuo Guangdou and Wei Dazhong! They consider themselves red-blooded males, and others think them intelligent, but in fact they belong to the evil species *(feilei)!* Until lately they kept their weapons hidden, but they could not keep up forever their pretense of being *junzi,* and so now they have openly joined other *xiaoren* and have launched an assault on the *junzi!*

By "other *xiaoren*," Fu Kui had one person specifically in mind. It was none other than Wang Wenyan, last seen as a middleman for eunuch Wang An in the Palace Case of 1620, when he was known as Wang Shoutai. He was now back in Beijing under the new name Wang Wenyan, busily brokering appointments for Minister of Personnel Zhao Nanxing. Fu Kui revealed some awful facts about him:

Wang Shoutai was originally a servant in She county [in Huizhou prefecture, modern Anhui province]. He became a government storehouse clerk there. For embezzlement he was sentenced to a garrison, but he escaped, and came secretly to Beijing where he served Wang An as a son his father. When that collusion was exposed, people thought that was the end of him. But then he changed his name [to Wang Wenyan] and purchased his present post [as Secretariat Drafter]. Instead of prosecuting him, the Censorate official Zuo Guangdou became his intimate friend! Far from eradicating him, Supervising Secretary Wei Dazhong abetted his corruption! Thus were the contacts made, weapons readied, men recruited, and official appointments manipulated. The excuse is opposition to the eunuch [Wei Zhongxian], but the reality is the advantage that has accrued to villainous men, and the disfavor that upright men have been receiving![120]

Fu Kui demanded that the ruler dismiss Zuo Guangdou and Wei Dazhong, and punish Wang Wenyan, for the sake of the security of the dynasty and the well-being of the realm. The Palace rescript ordered that
Wang Wenyan be arrested immediately and interrogated under torture.[121]

Fu Kui's memorial, and the imperial rescript to it, sent shock waves
rolling through Beijing officialdom. Fu Kui used the Donglin's own moral taxonomy (the "good species," the *junzi*) and turned it against the
Donglin itself. The arrest of Wang Wenyan and his consignment to the
Decree Prison was serious business, likely the first step in a sweeping
purge of Donglin men from government.

Chief Grand Secretary Ye Xianggao tried to allay the turmoil by sending a statement to the Palace in which he accepted sole responsibility and
blame for having agreed to the appointment of Wang Wenyan as a secretariat drafter. He offered to resign. Perhaps that would stop an impend-
ing partisan war and prevent "a disaster for officialdom." By rescript of
June 11, the Palace asked Ye to stay on the job.[122]

In his memoirs, Ye gave further details about the shadowy Wang Wenyan and his role as contact man for the Donglin:

> Minister of Personnel Zhao Nanxing, the Censorate officials Yang Lian
> and Zuo Guangdou, and the Supervising Secretary Cheng Zhen were all
> friendly with Wang Shoutai, and when it fell to the Grand Secretariat to se-
> lect imperial college students to serve in the history office [as Secretariat
> Drafters], they all spoke up in Wang's behalf. At this time Wang had
> changed his name to Wenyan.
>
> I said to those gentlemen that Wang was fortunate to have returned
> home alive, and that I couldn't understand why he was now angling to ad-
> vance himself; and that if they liked him, they should tell him to leave at
> once, and not stay in the capital where his life was at risk.
>
> Those gentlemen didn't agree, so I dropped the matter. Soon Zhao
> Nanxing and the others argued forcefully in Wang's behalf, and ten or
> more officials of the Censorate pleaded for him as well. They got their col-
> leagues to join them. There was nothing I could do but write a request for
> his appointment.
>
> And so Wang Wenyan consorted with those gentlemen, and whenever
> they wanted to communicate with Zhao Nanxing about personnel selec-
> tions, they did so through Wang Wenyan. Wang never accepted money for
> this; but he was a small man *(xiaoren)* of limited understanding who
> thought highly of himself for being able to suggest people suitable for ap-
> pointments and promotions. Zhao Nanxing kept aloof from the other

court officials, who resented him for that, but there was no one besides Wang upon whom they could vent their anger. I knew that, and I called Wang in, and I warned him that he should leave at once, and that if he didn't, there would be serious trouble which would involve other people. I also asked Grand Secretary Han Kuang and the others to urge him likewise.[123]

Ye went on to explain that Zhao Nanxing needed the services of Wang Wenyan to help make the controversial appointment of Zou Weilian, and so Wang did not leave but stayed on, and so made himself a ripe target for Fu Kui's frightening exposé.

On June 4, Zuo Guangdou was stunned to read Fu Kui's memorial in the Capital Gazette *(Dibao)*. He replied by memorial at once. Zuo said that Fu Kui was applying labels like "clean path," "possessing the Way," and "good species" to the wrong people. What possible motive could he have? What of his own tie of sworn brotherhood with the vile Fu Jijiao, Director of Punishments in the Eastern Depot? If Fu Kui believed Zuo to be corrupt, why did he fail to substantiate that charge with facts? Zuo offered to resign. The Palace consoled Zuo, praised him, and asked him to stay on the job.[124]

Fu Kui's memorial, meanwhile, placed Donglin firebrand Wei Dazhong in grave difficulty. On June 3, the Palace endorsed his promotion to the contested post of chief supervising secretary of the Office of Scrutiny for Personnel. On June 4, Wei Dazhong, too, read Fu Kui's memorial in the Capital Gazette. Because Fu Kui had impeached him, he could not now assume his new post. He replied by memorial the same day. He denied ever having bribed Wang Wenyan and accused Fu Kui of making life so difficult for Zou Weilian, Wu Yuwen, Zuo Guangdou and various other "gentlemen" that they could not enjoy even a moment of security in their positions. He accused Fu Kui himself of corruption, and of calling people by the wrong labels. He asked the ruler to reject Fu Kui, to preserve the "good species," and to dismiss Wei himself as a sop to Fu Kui's feeling of personal insecurity. On June 8, the Palace directed Wei Dazhong to go ahead and assume his new post.[125]

Wei Dazhong's friends urged him to go ahead and formally assume his new duties. But Wei was still technically under impeachment, and so he hesitated. On June 10, Supervising Secretary Zhen Shu memorialized in his behalf on the matter, and the Palace replied that its directive of June 8 was still valid. So, urged on by his colleagues, Wei assumed the post on June 11. On June 12, the Court of State Ceremonial placed his name in its memorial scheduling a routine ceremony in which new appointees personally thanked the emperor. It therefore came as a complete surprise to Wei to read the Palace rescript of June 13: "The mutual attacks of Wei Dazhong and Fu Kui haven't been clarified yet, so how can he take up the post? The Court of State Ceremonial should not have listed his name." On June 14, a worried Wei Dazhong memorialized that he would not dare to assume the post and was staying home awaiting punishment. The Palace reply of June 15 gave a detailed defense of its own procedures in all this and directed Wei to take the post, though it forbade him to attend the ceremony.[126]

Now Fu Kui reached for his pen. He expressed shock that the Palace had appointed Wei Dazhong but denied him the ceremony. That was unprecedented. Obviously the decision had been taken inside the Palace, bypassing the Grand Secretariat. Evidently favorites inside the Palace had seized power. The dispute between himself and Wei Dazhong was left in doubt and unresolved. And why, moreover, wasn't the Palace interrogating Wang Wenyan more severely?[127]

On or around June 18, Censor Liu Fang echoed Fu Kui's consternation over the Palace's inept handling of Wei Dazhong. "Especially now, when we have a disordered clash of views, when a war of words is in progress, and ugly accusations fly about, the writing and issuing of rescripts from inside the Palace [bypassing the Grand Secretariat] creates bewilderment and paranoia *(caicun)* in the outer court," he stated in his memorial to the emperor. "The court needs consistent orders to quell the paranoia, reduce conflict, and restore harmony.... Yet just when the officials' passions *(xueqi)* have quieted and their verbal assaults have eased, and the disputes have slackened, you stir everything up with these contradictory rescripts. This will only rekindle the controversies, and the national right *(guoshi)* will suffer." The Palace was unimpressed by Liu Fang's argument and stood by its previous rescripts.[128]

Chief Grand Secretary Ye Xianggao did not contest the Palace's right to formulate its own rescripts. He did express anger at Wei Dazhong. Because Wei was under impeachment, he should never have accepted his new appointment under any circumstances. Ye displeased Wei Dazhong by telling him that to his face. "This matter shows," concluded Ye in his memoirs, "that while those fellows [of the Donglin] made a good showing by standing upright and not riding the waves of common custom, they were by no means averse to struggling for their own advancement and reputation. They completely ignored the larger issues in the political crisis of the time. I earnestly spoke about this [to Wei], but he didn't listen, and so he ended up humiliating himself, getting himself killed [in 1625], and ruining the affairs of the realm."[129]

Meanwhile the Donglin appointments broker, Wang Wenyan, languished in the Decree Prison. The main charge against him was accepting a bribe of 2,000 taels of silver from Zou Weilian to plead the case for his promotion to Minister of Personnel Zhao Nanxing. There were further allegations of his having trafficked with Zuo Guangdou and Wei Dazhong.[130]

The Palace ordered Wang interrogated under torture. The Donglin men were extremely worried. Wei Dazhong often visited Censor Huang Zunsu's house to talk about what they should do. One day when he came by in alarm, Huang Zunsu was not at home, and so Wei wrote an urgent note and gave it to Huang's young son Huang Zongxi (the future philosopher) to pass along to his father.[131] The note begged Huang Zunsu to intervene to effect Wang's release. Huang Zunsu knew Liu Qiao, the director of the Decree Prison, and paid him a secret visit. "Wang Wenyan himself is of no account," argued Huang, "but we can't have him be the cause of a disaster for the scholar-officials."[132] Liu Qiao agreed. On his own authority, he made sure that Wang Wenyan was not pressed hard. The Palace was angered by Liu Qiao's noncooperation, and, on or about June 16, it ordered him dismissed and stricken from the official register.[133]

Thus the Palace's case against Wang Wenyan was botched. On August 9, Minister of Personnel Zhao Nanxing memorialized that Wang Wenyan was being detained for no reason in the "black prison" and asked that he be granted a release. On August 11, the Palace replied that Wang Wenyan was a thoroughly bad character who ought to be put in the cangue, but the ruler had decided to be lenient and ordered him to be flogged a hundred times at the Meridian gate, removed from official status, and forbidden to return to the capital ever again.[134]

◀

The Beijing situation was volatile. It was unclear how long the Palace could continue to play the bureaucratic factions against each other, leaning first to one side, then to the other. At some point the Palace would have to choose, because the rhetoric of character assassination had come to a near boil, factional differences were becoming more and more sharply drawn, and some erstwhile Donglin supporters who deserted the ship did so in the same provocative spirit of absolute moral righteousness that the Donglin itself had grown accustomed to enjoying as its unique possession.

It was also unclear who the preeminent Donglin leader or spokesman might be. Zhou Zongjian made a loud bid for that role in 1623, but his timing was premature and he lacked adequate career credentials. However, his effort seemed to show, even in its failure, that in order to march to the front of the corps of Donglin adherents one had to attract public attention; and nothing served that purpose better than the language of moral terrorism—language at its logical extreme, language at its most uncompromising, language heated to the highest possible degree of emotional incandescence. And that was Yang Lian's rhetorical bombshell of July 1624.

CHAPTER 3

Political Murders, 1625

◀

IN MID·JULY 1624, the political stale-
mate in Beijing was blown apart by means of a verbal high explosive: the
shattering "Twenty-four Crimes" memorial submitted by Yang Lian. The
twenty-four crimes were imputed to palace eunuch Wei Zhongxian. The
memorial was addressed to Tianqi, and it asked him, in effect, how he
could continue to protect and abet a national criminal. The repercussions
of this memorial were such as to bring on one of the darkest episodes of
political repression in the long history of China, highlighted by the public arrests and secret murders of twelve leading figures of the Donglin faction, including Yang Lian, and the suicide of a thirteenth, Gao Panlong.

It required uncommon courage—indeed utter recklessness, a willingness to court martyrdom—to send up to the throne an indictment as
sweeping and as damning as the "Twenty-four Crimes" memorial, and
incidents are related of Yang Lian in his youth that suggest a need, or at
least an ability, to reach on occasion the requisite state of mental and spiritual exaltation. For instance, there was the occasion when, as a county
student, on a snowy night he and a friend pledged themselves to become
heroes *(haojie)* and then walked singing all through the county seat, now
and then leaning on pillars and howling crazily, writing words in the
snow, crying bitterly—strange behavior whose meaning onlookers could
not grasp.[1]

Since his voluntary retirement in the wake of the Palace Case of late
1620—the event that secured his national leadership credentials—Yang
Lian lived at home, in Yingshan county, Hubei, where he was active in
local affairs and kept up with developments in Beijing when from time to
time copies of the Capital Gazette *(Dibao)* reached him. People saw him
weep and curse when reading about eunuch Wei Zhongxian's latest out-
rages.

Yang Lian had been right at Taichang's bedside in 1620 when the dying
emperor had laid a deathbed command *(guming)* on the emergency
gathering of officials, begging them personally to help Tianqi be a good
ruler. "If I could see [Tianqi] face-to-face," vowed Yang to his comrades,
"I'd break my head telling him about how his father had entrusted him

to us. I must kill that bandit [Wei Zhongxian] to requite [the Taichang emperor's] friendship!" Two comrades argued with Yang. Power, they said, now lay in enemy hands, and voicing "empty ideas" *(kong yan)* at this juncture would be fruitless and perhaps disastrous. To avoid argument Yang Lian agreed with them.[2]

In May 1622, the Palace endorsed a number of recalls of officials, among them Yang Lian. Earlier chief supervising secretary of the Office of Scrutiny for War, he was now assigned the same position in the Office of Scrutiny for Rites.[3] His young sons were pleased, but Yang Lian set them straight about the matter. "Do you think I'm going back to serve like a horse or an ox?" he shouted at them. "We have a young, isolated ruler, a military crisis on the frontier, a eunuch in charge in the Palace, and all that could well be killing grounds for me. There's no time even to fret. What are you pleased for?"

The partisan struggle in Beijing was hot in 1622. The Three Cases were being reargued with vehemence. Yang Lian had of course been a chief actor in the Palace Case, and his behavior in it was being praised to the skies by his friends and denounced by his enemies.[4] Furthermore, the Ming military collapse in Manchuria had led to the arrest of the commanders Xiong Tingbi and Wang Huazhen, and partisan battles were raging over the question of who was more to blame and what punishments should apply. Yang asked friends to take care of his family. "When old Yang leaves the mountains this time," he laughed, "who knows how the return trip will be?"[5]

In August 1622, Yang Lian was promoted to the post of vice minister of the Court of Imperial Sacrifices. He maintained a low profile. In March 1624 he was promoted again—to vice censor-in-chief, a more responsible, visible, and strategic position.[6] The newly appointed vice censor-in-chief's "Twenty-four Crimes" memorial of July 1624 would, as things turned out, make its author a martyr and a national hero in the eyes of posterity. A number of witnesses, including Yang himself, have attested to the thought and emotions surrounding its composition and submission.

Yang Lian had begun drafting the memorial at home, before his recall to Beijing in 1622. He would get up during the night to work on it, when family members could hear him sobbing. He lied to them about what he was doing. They did not, apparently, find out the truth until the memorial was sent up and the deed was done.[7]

Later in Beijing, however, some colleagues did find out. Someone told Censor Huang Zunsu that Yang Lian would stop at nothing until he had gotten rid of the eunuch, and that he would "win an immortal name for himself." Huang doubted that Yang's plan would work; he needed collaborators inside the palace, and he had none. "If his strike misses, we're all going to be destroyed as a species," said Huang.[8] Huang confronted Yang Lian himself, and Yang showed him the draft of his memorial. "You have no [inside collaborators]. And you must erase the hearsay from your allegations about the palace women," advised Huang, "because if the emperor can't confirm every detail of that, he'll reject even your well-founded allegations." Yang Lian took no heed.[9]

Assistant Censor-in-Chief Zuo Guangdou, Yang's supporter in the Palace Affair of 1620, also knew what Yang Lian was doing, but he encouraged him, and he told his colleague Miao Changqi about it. Miao thought an all-out impeachment of Wei Zhongxian was likely to fail, but Zuo said nothing when Miao told him that.[10] Indeed, Zuo had already prepared an impeachment of his own, charging eunuch Wei with thirty-two crimes, which he planned to submit as a follow-up to Yang's.[11] Censor Li Yingsheng was also privy to what Yang was planning and tried to dissuade him. "If your strike misses, you'll be eaten and you'll harm the national body (*guoti*)," urged Li. "I'm a speaking official, not a high official like you," he continued, "so you should let me do this instead of you." At home, Li had prepared a sixteen-count impeachment of Wei Zhongxian; but his older cousin, an usher in the Court of State Ceremonial, at some point seized it in horror and destroyed it.[12] It is unlikely that Yang Lian would have agreed to Li's proposal in any event.

In fact Yang Lian was not thinking about practical politics in the short term at all. He was thinking about martyrdom and future history. "I know full well this will fail," he is said to have remarked, "but I've about mounted the tiger, and I'll not have posterity say that among the officials there to receive [Taichang's] deathbed instructions, there was not one with the *qi* of a male. I made up my mind long ago; I will sacrifice myself in the name of righteousness."[13]

On July 14, Tianqi was scheduled to make a personal ceremonial appearance before all the assembled officials. It was Yang Lian's intention to use that opportunity to read his memorial of impeachment aloud for maximum effect, "like a clap of thunder that makes people cover their ears." Also, the often secluded emperor would be sure to hear it. But something went wrong. Apparently the Palace caught wind of what was going on. Unexpectedly, the ceremony was canceled.[14]

Yang Lian was stunned. If he waited for a rescheduling of the ceremony, it was likely that the Palace would in the meantime find out more about what he was up to and stop him. He decided, therefore, to preempt that possibility. He went to the Huiji gate and submitted his long impeachment in its written form first. Perhaps there would be an opportunity in the next several days to deliver an oral version of the impeachment directly to Tianqi.

So the deed was done. The impeachment itself was horrific in what it alleged that Wei Zhongxian had done: usurped the powers of the Grand Secretariat; driven a dozen and more excellent men from office; murdered Wang An; murdered two palace women; caused the empress to abort her child; seized control of the palace army; seized control of the secret police of the Eastern Depot; built an imperial-scale tomb for himself; and acted as though he himself were emperor of China, not Tianqi. The memorial, as Hucker has described it, "almost jeers" at Tianqi for allowing Wei Zhongxian to get away with these monstrous acts.[15]

"I nearly died of anguish," wrote Yang to a colleague, explaining what happened on July 14. "But the memorial was already written, and so I had to submit it sealed. I knew it would be of no avail, but it expressed what was in this red heart of mine, and if by any chance fortune smiled, perhaps the spirits of the dynasty would be present and save matters."[16]

When the emperor finally made a ceremonial appearance on July 20, the Palace made sure there would be no oral memorial from anyone on that occasion. Armed guards surrounded Tianqi. The ushers of the Court of State Ceremonial were under orders to allow no one to speak out. Yang Lian attended, but was silent. To onlookers it appeared as though the Palace had managed to cow the outer court.[17]

Some inside source conveyed the story to Yang Lian that his written bill of impeachment had created acute distress inside the palace. Wei Zhongxian went about from room to room wailing. Madame Ke and her eunuch servants stayed up all night figuring out how to prepare Tianqi for the bad news. At lunch the next day, the memorial was brought in and laid before the emperor, who may or may not have attempted to read it. Wei Zhongxian, hat in hand, knelt to one side and lamented about how faithful he had been to Tianqi's dead mother. Tianqi just nodded and said: "You can get up and go. I'll send the memorial to the Grand Secretariat for a draft rescript."[18]

When the memorial arrived at the Grand Secretariat, Ye Xianggao, the

steady hand the situation required, was not on duty. Grand Secretary
Han Kuang looked at it, but backed off. Grand Secretary Wei Guangwei,
angered that Yang's memorial indirectly alluded to him as a "protégé"
of Wei Zhongxian, agreed to write the rescript. The rescript, issued on
July 16, merely acknowledged the receipt of Yang's memorial, announced
Wei Zhongxian's offer to resign, and followed it with a statement from
Tianqi forgiving Wei Zhongxian and retaining him on duty.

This was unheard-of procedure. In a confidential note of the same day,
July 16, Han Kuang and Ye Xianggao protested to the Palace that it must
release Yang Lian's memorial so that it could be publicly discussed in the
outer court, where a climate of paranoia was rapidly growing. The Palace
hotly denied any procedural irregularity.[19]

On July 18, the Palace released Yang Lian's memorial, together with
a rescript directed to the eighth, ninth, and tenth charges, that Wei
Zhongxian had caused the deaths of two imperial concubines plus
Tianqi's own child by empress Zhang. "The memorial is reckless and
without foundation in what it alleges," stated the rescript. "Matters re-
garding imperial concubines and palace women are confidential, and [the
impeachment] provides no facts. How [in any case] would the outer
court know anything about it? This is just deliberate speculation aimed at
dividing me from people close to me, leaving me alone and isolated on
high." The emperor (or, rather, Grand Secretary Wei Guangwei writing
in his behalf) went on to insist that he made all decisions personally and
warned officialdom not to send up any memorials of rejoinder in support
of Yang Lian.[20]

Chief Grand Secretary Ye Xianggao was sick in bed at home when he
received copies of Yang Lian's sensational memorial and the imperial
response to it. These he read in what he described as a state of shock.[21]
"My belief was," he later wrote, "that these matters should not have been
forcefully contested, for fear it would cause a rupture (juelie), and I said
this at the time to people I knew."[22]

At about this time, Miao Changqi paid Ye Xianggao a visit. Another
visitor was there already. They discussed Yang Lian's memorial. Ye said he
thought the memorial too slapdash. He went on to share several anec-
dotes favorable to Wei Zhongxian. "That is how conscientious [Wei
Zhongxian] is," said Ye, "and I'm afraid that if Yang's memorial succeeds
in what it demands, it will be hard to find a replacement as careful and
responsible to serve the emperor." Miao by his own account exploded in
anger. "Whoever said that said it to deceive you, and should be execut-

ed." Ye's face changed color. Miao got up and left. Ye escorted him out. Informed of Ye's favorable remarks about Wei Zhongxian, Yang Lian seethed. Miao calmed him down.[23]

Meanwhile in the days following the release of Yang's sensational memorial, some seventy officials in Beijing and Nanjing defied the Palace's explicit warning and sent up written memorials in Yang Lian's support, imploring the emperor to punish the villainous eunuch Wei Zhongxian. Not one memorialist defended the eunuch. Chief Grand Secretary Ye Xianggao rejected pleas from Yang Lian's friends that he openly lend his weight to the attack. He did, however, write a confidential note to Tianqi urging him to allow Wei Zhongxian to leave the Forbidden City—not because Wei was necessarily guilty as charged, but because the realm was fast descending into turmoil over the issue. On July 25, the Palace rejected that advice and gave notice that it was retaining Wei Zhongxian.[24]

The Palace proposed to place under arrest everyone who had ignored its injunction and had memorialized on Yang Lian's behalf. Ye Xianggao argued against that idea.[25] The Palace backed down, because it was not yet in a position in which it felt strong enough to take severe measures against Yang Lian and his Donglin supporters in the bureaucracy.

◄

Meanwhile, the Palace found two surrogate targets for its wrath. The first was Wan Jing, a mid-level official in the Ministry of Works. In the thick of the turmoil just raised by Yang Lian, Wan Jing resubmitted a request that the Palace had earlier denied, to use scrap copper in the Forbidden City to help defray the cost of building Taichang's tomb.

The trouble with this apparently routine memorial was that, in it, Wan Jing directly accused Wei Zhongxian of usurping Tianqi's authority by diverting Palace funds to finance a pet project—the construction of his own grandiose tomb. With his own eyes Wan Jing had seen the eunuch's magnificent mausoleum being built at the Biyunsi outside Beijing, using funds that should have gone to the construction of Taichang's tomb! On his own authority, Wei Zhongxian was forcing Tianqi to assume the posture of an unfilial son. Surely, Wei Zhongxian must be punished.[26]

Wan Jing's awful memorial was sent up on July 29. The rescript was issued the next day. The Palace denied that there was enough scrap copper with which to accomplish anything. Wan Jing had already been told that. Now comes this contumacious memorial accusing the emperor of filial impiety. And at what a time! The emperor's sick infant son had just died. The Embroidered-uniform Guard was ordered to fetch Wan Jing up to the Meridian gate and there flog him a hundred times. After that, Wan Jing was ordered dismissed from civil service, never to be rehired.[27]

Ye Xianggao, sick in bed at home, was shown the draft of this rescript before it was issued. Stunned, he sent a frantic note back to the Palace, begging the emperor to reduce the punishment to a demotion and a fine. The Palace notified Ye by a rescript dated July 31 that Wan Jing's memorial was exceptionally offensive and therefore it was rejecting Ye's plea.[28]

Ye asked to resign. If he could not dissuade Tianqi from reviving the evil practice of flogging officials, which wounds the national body (*guoti*), then, he argued, his usefulness as grand secretary was over. A Palace rescript of August 5 consoled Ye and denied his request to resign.[29] Later, Ye stated in his memoirs that the Palace's savagery in the Wan Jing matter was owing to the radicalizing effect that Yang Lian's "Twenty-four Crimes" memorial had had upon it.[30]

Wan Jing was flogged on August 1. The scene was horrifying. Wan had a history of conflict with the palace eunuchs, which explains why a squadron of them left the Forbidden City, broke into his home, and kicked and pummeled him as they marched him up to the Meridian gate. Wan Jing was physically frail. A colleague from the Ministry of Works, Peng Qisheng, was right there as the eunuchs dragged him up. Wei Zhongxian was also there, and he yelled for guards to shut the gate. Peng was therefore unable to witness the delivery of the hundred strokes or the stomping and kicking the eunuchs allegedly applied afterward to Wan Jing's prostrate form. When they carried Wan Jing out he was scarcely conscious. "This is why the dynasty has nurtured *shi* for two hundred years," Peng heard him say. Wan Jing's point was not sarcastic. His legs were flayed to a pulp. His friends carried him to a Buddhist temple. Peng Qisheng helped with medication. Colleague Li Banghua brought him food. When colleague Li Mingjun visited him, Wan Jing just stared open-eyed, no longer able to speak. Around August 7, he died.[31]

There was more violence. During the same days when Wan Jing was mauled and flogged and lay dying, Censor Lin Ruzhu, on police duty in Beijing, had a violent confrontation with several palace eunuchs over a local crime case. The eunuchs complained to the Palace, which drafted an edict ordering Lin to be flogged and removed from civil service. The draft was shown to the Grand Secretariat. Han Kuang and Ye Xianggao immediately protested: yet another flogging, within the space of two

days? They warned of dire effects on official morale. In reply to this protest a rescript of August 4 explained that Lin had acted wantonly; that he
had to be punished in order to deter others; that flogging was less severe
a penalty than the arrest and torture he really deserved.[32]

At some point during these days the speaking officials (censors and supervising secretaries) met in the office of the Grand Secretariat to protest
the sentences given Wan Jing and Lin Ruzhu. Censor Huang Zunsu described what happened. "A crowd of several hundred eunuchs massed
outside, shaking their fists and screaming. The grand secretaries were red-
faced and speechless. None dared to stop them. I said [to the eunuchs]:
'The Grand Secretariat is off-limits to the eunuch Directorate of Ceremonial except when an imperial order is being delivered. How dare you act
like this? You're disobeying all the Ming emperors!' The eunuchs then
backed away."[33]

But where was Lin Ruzhu? Several hundred armed eunuchs descended
upon his house, and failed to find him. A citywide search was begun. Lin
was from Fujian, and a county compatriot of Ye Xianggao. Someone
thought he was Ye's nephew. Maybe he was hiding in Ye's house. "A
crowd [of eunuchs] surrounded my house and demanded to come in and
search it," Ye recalled. "I said to the eunuchs that if the court orders the
arrest of a censor and the grand secretary hides him, then the grand secretary's defiance of the emperor is the more serious crime. If you search
my house and you find him, then that's what I'll be guilty of. The eunuchs milled about and then they left."[34]

It turned out that Lin Ruzhu had put on a disguise and taken refuge
with Deng Mei, grand coordinator of Shuntian prefecture. Lin was willing to take the flogging. He had fled because he feared the kicking and
mauling inflicted on Wan Jing might be applied to him as well. Deng Mei
negotiated Lin's surrender. Lin took his hundred lashes, recuperated, and
went home to private life.[35]

But it was the eunuchs' attempted search of his home that compelled
Ye Xianggao to insist upon leaving the Ming government once and for all.
He informed the Palace that never in the two hundred years of Ming history had eunuchs surrounded the house of a grand secretary. He had, he
said, completely lost face and therefore could under no circumstances
continue to serve. He moved out of Beijing. On August 20, the Palace
endorsed his resignation. Tianqi seemed reluctant to see him go.[36] Ye had
tried all along to dampen "paranoia" (caicun), to prevent "rupture"
(juelie), to "negotiate compromises" (tiaoting) between the Palace and

the warring bureaucratic factions, but it had all been unavailing. With Ye gone, the struggle would become even more bitter.

◄

The bureaucracy, through its speaking officials (the censors and supervising secretaries), protested strongly the Palace's abuse of Wan Jing and Lin Ruzhu, and perhaps for that reason the Palace henceforth confined the eunuchs to the Forbidden City and forbade their venturing out as armed gangs again. The battlefront between Palace and bureaucracy shifted back to the issue of appointments.

In the days and weeks after his "Twenty-four Crimes" memorial was made public, Yang Lian lay low and kept quiet, unsure whether to remain in Beijing or submit his resignation and leave. In a letter to his family back in Hubei, he expressed a desire to return home but said he was being pressured by colleagues to stay. "The *junzi* chide me about the great issues at stake, and they tell me that my staying in government so worries the inner court that it doesn't dare act with abandon; but that once I leave, it will relax in the expectation that it will have no more trouble."[37]

Huang Zunsu, however, thought it was useless for Yang to remain in Beijing and urged him to leave for the sake of his own safety; but Yang disagreed, saying to Huang, "No one but me cares about the critical life-and-death issues, and, if my death is beneficial in that respect, then I won't mind death." Then Yang had second thoughts, and he sent Censor Li Yingsheng to ask Huang again to help him decide. Li thought a *junzi* should not have to ask colleagues to decide a question like that for him.[38] But Huang's letter to Yang Lian ignored Li's point, and again he urged Yang to leave Beijing. "They've flogged Wan [Jing] and Lin [Ruzhu] just to show who has the power, and they won't be stopped," counseled Huang. He told Yang that making himself a martyr over the matter would achieve nothing.[39] Yang decided to stay. Assassins tried to force entry into his house in Beijing. Censors on city patrol organized a bodyguard for him.

◄

Ye Xianggao's resignation in August left the "good species" without effective support in the Grand Secretariat. Han Kuang was supportive, but he was not effective. Wei Guangwei had been offended by Yang Lian,

Zhao Nanxing, and other leading members of the Donglin, and was hostile. Some of the Donglin ignored contrary advice and made the reckless decision to attack Wei Guangwei.

In November 1624, Grand Secretary Wei Guangwei showed up very late for a solemn sacrifice at the imperial ancestral temple just south of the Forbidden City. It was so obviously an act of disrespect that everyone noticed it. Although the offense was punishable by law, Censor Huang Zunsu thought impeachment tactically unwise and sent an urgent plea to Supervising Secretary Wei Dazhong not to impeach the grand secretary. He thought Wei Dazhong already had enough of a reputation for righteous daring; there was no need now for him to try to enhance that reputation, and put "our party" in danger.[40]

But Censors Wei Dazhong and Li Yingsheng and several other officials went ahead and on November 17 impeached Wei Guangwei for flagrant disrespect, demanding that the corporal punishment specified in the *Da Ming lü* be applied to him.[41] Wei Guangwei asked to be allowed to step down. The Palace consoled him and on November 20 replied harshly to his attackers. At about this time a thoroughly infuriated Wei Guangwei created an enemies list, marking up his copy of the official roster with three circles for big enemies and two circles or one for lesser enemies. The circled names identified a "deviant clique" *(xiedang)*.[42] His was neither the first nor the last such list. Dismissals of his enemies soon followed.

On November 22, a Palace rescript dismissed Wei Dazhong and two others for having made an inappropriate recommendation for an important vacancy.[43] On December 4, another Palace rescript, released in the middle of the night, targeted Yang Lian, Zuo Guangdou, and Vice Minister of Personnel Chen Yuting for making clique-related recommendations for vacancies. They had been told ahead of time by Grand Secretary Gu Bingqian who the acceptable recommendees were, but Chen and the others had blatantly defied him.[44] Yang and the others were not simply demoted and dismissed; they were reduced to commoner status, and were no longer officials at all. Grand Secretary Han Kuang protested the decision, to no avail.[45]

Yang Lian and Zuo Guangdou left Beijing together on horseback. At Zhuozhou they parted ways; Yang went back to Yingshan in Hubei, and Zuo to Tongcheng in present-day Anhui. Neither man carried much baggage. Miao Changqi ignored warnings to stay away from these dismissed colleagues: "I said of course I'll send off people who have been cashiered! I know informers will report that, but I'll do it anyway."[46]

Censor Li Yingsheng filled his letters to distant colleagues and to family back home with gloom and foreboding. He was certain his own removal was imminent. Over the winter of 1624–1625 several leading officials of the Donglin party resigned: Minister of Personnel Zhao Nanxing; Grand Secretary Han Kuang; Censor-in-Chief of the Left Gao Panlong; and Hanlin Reader-in-Waiting Miao Changqi, among others.

◀

In late December, a sensational incident momentarily upset the Palace. The commander of Ming forces on the Manchurian frontier, Sung Chengzong, decided that he had to come see Tianqi in person. Despite his military position, Sun was a civil official. He and Tianqi had gotten on well when Sun tutored him in the classics for a short while in 1620. He owed his position as commander to recommendations made in his behalf by Donglin men Gao Panlong and Zuo Guangdou. Word had reached him that these and other supporters of his had been cashiered or forced to resign. "The emperor is just a youth and he is being controlled by villains," Sun reportedly said. "He doesn't necessarily read or understand the memorials sent him." That was why he believed a personal meeting with Tianqi was necessary.[47]

A military advisor of Sun's, Cai Ding, tried to dissuade his chief. Sun ignored him.[48] Accompanied only by his civilian aide, Lu Shanji (a bureau director in the Ministry of War), plus personal servants and runners, Sun left his base at Ningyuan and made his way some two hundred miles by cart to Tongzhou just east of Beijing, which he reached on December 20. From there he sent word to the Palace that he would enter Beijing the next day, see Tianqi in three days, congratulate him on his nineteenth birthday, discuss strategy with him, confer with the court officials, and then return to Ningyuan on the Manchurian frontier.

The Palace received Sun's notice that same day, December 20. Grand Secretary Wei Guangwei guessed at once that Sun Chengzong must have a large army with him, and that he had come to "cleanse the ruler's side," that is, forcibly remove Wei Zhongxian and all his adherents. Wei Guangwei also guessed that Sun must have an agent on the scene already—and who would that be? It must be Li Banghua, vice minister of war! Wei Zhongxian panicked and went to Tianqi's bedside and wept. Troops were mobilized inside Beijing. Eunuch guards at the outer gates were instructed to shut them against any attempted entry by Sun. Chief Grand Secretary Gu Bingqian hurriedly wrote a stern edict informing Sun that his unauthorized visit was most unwelcome, and that he must return at once to the frontier. Sun obeyed. His mission failed. The Palace's panic subsided.[49]

The Interrogation of Wang Wenyan

By late December 1624, it was clear that the Palace had decided to purge the Donglin party from the political life of the nation. Discussion of the Three Cases heated up again, and the Donglin interpretation of those controversial events came under fierce challenge. Hostile memorialists fingered one Donglin adherent after the other for falsity, corruption, bribe trafficking, and other political crimes.

More information was needed, however. Censor Liang Menghuan asked the Palace to authorize the rearrest of the former Donglin appointments broker Wang Wenyan. The Palace complied by a rescript of February 1, 1625, ordering mounted police of the Embroidered-uniform Guard to proceed seven hundred miles south to Xiuning county and fetch Wang Wenyan back to Beijing.[50] By April 11, Wang Wenyan had arrived, and a Palace rescript of that day ordered him sent to the Decree Prison run by the Embroidered-uniform Guard, located somewhere among the other military agencies south of the Imperial City. Wang Wenyan was to be interrogated there under "severe torture."[51]

When Wang Wenyan was placed in the same prison a year earlier, Censor Huang Zunsu had interceded with Prison Director Liu Qiao and gotten him to agree not to apply torture. But Liu Qiao was no longer director. He had been replaced by Xu Xianchun. This time there would be torture.[52]

The first round of interrogation under torture did not go well. The Palace already had made up its mind about which officials it wanted Wang Wenyan to name. Tormented to the point of unconsciousness, Wang Wenyan gave Xu Xianchun what he wanted, only to recant the testimony when he revived. Assistant Prison Director Wu Mengming suggested to his chief that, for their own protection in case of a future political reversal, Wang Wenyan be made to testify only to a few names, and that the amounts of all alleged bribes be kept vague.[53] Indeed, Xu Xianchun's long and detailed memorial to the Palace of April 22, though damning, contained unspecified bribery allegations and targeted minor figures more than it did the big game.[54] The Palace reply of April 23 demanded that Xu Xianchun reinterrogate Wang Wenyan and this time make all the details

clear. Complaints having been made about Wu Mengming, the Palace removed him from civil service on May 2. His replacement as assistant
director was Cui Yingyuan, a former street thug who had been serving in
Wei Zhongxian's police agency, the Eastern Depot. This time things
would proceed as the Palace desired.[55]

Rumor had it that Wang Wenyan refused to the end to testify as his tor-
turers wished. It may well be that the Donglin people were correct in
their belief that the confession submitted to the Palace as Wang Wenyan's
was in fact not his at all, but the creation of Prison Director Xu Xianchun.
The confession listed twenty-one names of officials who had either taken
bribes in silver and in return had made recommendations for appointments to vacancies in Beijing bureaucracy; or, worse, had accepted huge
payments in silver from imprisoned commander Xiong Tingbi, in return
for which they had acted in evil ways to mitigate his rightful punishment.
It was important to have Wang Wenyan testify to these corrupt transac-
tions because he was allegedly the middleman for each of them.

The Palace rescripted this confession on May 3. It ordered mounted
police (*guanqi*) of the Embroidered-uniform Guard to go out and arrest
and fetch back to Beijing six of the twenty-one men named in the confession. The six would soon become nationally known as the "Six *junzi*."
They were: Yang Lian; Zuo Guangdou; former Censor Yuan Huazhong;
former Supervising Secretary Wei Dazhong; former Vice Minister of the
Court of the Imperial Stud Zhou Chaorui; and Gu Dazhang, former vice
director in the Ministry of Justice. All were accused of accepting bribes
from Xiong Tingbi. The rescript directed that the six suspects be interrogated in the Decree Prison alongside Wang Wenyan.[56]

The Palace's initial expectation was that under joint interrogation the
true facts would come forth, the full scope of the infamy would be revealed, all the malefactors would be justly punished, and a cleansed Ming
court could then return to the business of renovating the realm and allay-
ing its crises. But then it turned out that Wang Wenyan was not going to
be a cooperative witness, and so the prosecution was going to fail. It
would be preferable, therefore, not to have Wang Wenyan on hand to
contest the charges and ruin the whole case. Sometime between May 3
and May 10, Wang Wenyan's "death due to illness" was reported to the
Palace. On May 10, a Palace rescript to that notification stated: "It was
never reported that Wang Wenyan was ill. How did he die all of a sudden? Henceforth regulations must be observed. If [prisoners] become ill,
they should be medicated."[57]

So Wang Wenyan, the one-time Donglin power broker and chief witness for the prosecution, was dead.[58] Probably he was killed by prison
guards at Xu Xianchun's direction. Despite its statement of shocked
surprise of May 10, the Palace may have been secretly complicit in the
murder.

The Arrest and Ordeal of Yang Lian

To send out squadrons of silk-robed imperial guards to the home prefectures of each of the six accused, publicly arrest them, publicly read out the
charges against them, and bring them back to Beijing riding partway in
special prisoners' carts suggests that the Palace and its supporters in bureaucracy were, or were affecting to be, morally certain of the rightness
of what they were doing. Nothing was going to be done in the dark. Hei-
nous crimes had been disclosed. Villains had been named. All the solemn
moral power of the Ming emperor and his court was being put on display. Surely the realm would be impressed and overawed. Six leading
malefactors were going to be made the targets of national outrage and vil-
ification. Six malefactors! Or, were they six good men wronged? The general public of China was going to be drawn into a national judicial drama
as a kind of ultimate judge of the moral guilt or innocence of the Donglin
faction.

Foremost among the "Six *junzi*" was Yang Lian, leader of the group
that had forced Lady Li to leave the imperial palace in 1620 and, of
course, author of the sensational "Twenty-four Crimes" memorial of
1624. The main charge against him was that he had accepted a bribe of
20,000 taels of silver from Xiong Tingbi.

It is not clear on what day Yang Lian left his home county of Yingshan,
or on what day official proceedings were conducted in the prefectural
capital of De'anfu (now Anlu, in Hubei, about forty miles southwest of
Yingshan). Whatever the day, a near riot developed outside the city wall
of De'anfu. Reportedly, "several thousand braves pressed to get into the
yamen inside and assault the imperial police," but the officials closed the
city gates against them and prevented the mob from entering. On the day
of the public reading of the charges against Yang Lian, "several myriad
literati and people from the prefecture and county gathered outside the
south wall and raised a din that reached to Heaven." The crowd refused
to disperse, until Yang Lian himself appeared in the tower above the wall

and pleaded that his arrest was not necessarily going to lead to his death; that if the crowd rioted in his behalf, they would make a loyal official like himself into a rebel, and would put his entire family in jeopardy. The crowd then went away.[59]

Yang Lian was fettered hand and foot and placed in a prisoner cart for the journey north to Beijing. Besides the imperial police, a procession of local sympathizers accompanied the prisoner. Yang's personal servants (including a kinsman, disguised as a servant) carried along his coffin. Yang persuaded his oldest son and son-in-law to go back home. They had come in the fear that the police might kill the prisoner en route. "My body has already been committed to the court," said Yang. "Sooner or later they'll kill me, what difference does it make if it's in the Decree Prison or on the road?" But son Yang Zhiyi and son-in-law Huang Dengxuan went ahead secretly to Beijing.

The procession made its way through scorching summer heat some two hundred miles northwest to Yunyangfu (now Yunxian), where there was another near riot until Yang Lian spoke to the crowd as he had done at De'anfu. Vegetable merchants and hawkers passed a sack and took up a cash collection for him. "In village after village, men and women came up weeping to the prisoner cart and peered in to see what a 'loyal official' looked like."

As the procession crossed Henan province, men and women in the villages along the way held up tablets reading "loyal official" and burned incense and offered rituals on Yang Lian's behalf. At length the prisoner and his escort reached Zhuxianzhen, a commercial town some 250 miles northeast of Yunyangfu. There his guards let Yang Lian visit a shrine to Yue Fei, the twelfth-century loyalist hero and martyr; there Yang gave the hero's shade a long account of his own career and of his hatred of eunuch Wei Zhongxian, who needed to be reminded of the "master–servant distinction."[60] Somewhere along the journey there was a ten-day layover while Yang recuperated from a fever.[61] By July 31, Yang Lian had arrived in Beijing. The Palace ordered him sent to the Decree Prison for interrogation under torture.[62]

Zuo Guangdou

Meanwhile another unit of imperial police approached Tongcheng county to arrest Zuo Guangdou. (For some unknown reason, proceedings were conducted there and not in Anqingfu, the prefectural capital.) As in De'anfu, so also in Tongcheng the people refused to share the Palace's moral vision of the situation. Many of the county people "acted crazed, as though it were their own parent who was under arrest." Handbills distributed at the four gates of the county seat reminded everyone that Zuo was a local benefactor, an "upright spirit" *(zhengqi)* at court, a behavioral model to the official class, that his arrest orders were "false," and that the imperial police should be prevented from making the arrest, violently if need be.[63] As Yang did, so did Zuo. He pleaded with the mob: "You're hastening my death! If you want to keep me alive, why do this?" The edict of arrest, though "forged" by palace eunuch Wei Zhongxian, was still an edict issued in the name of the "ruler-father" and was therefore "valid" *(zhen)*.[64]

So the police made the arrest. The charges were read out. Like Yang, Zuo was accused of receiving a bribe of 20,000 taels of silver from Xiong Tingbi, the imprisoned former Ming commander at Shanhaiguan.

Someone then drafted a memorial to the throne in behalf of the people *(renmin)* of Tongcheng. The memorial described the reaction the news of Zuo's arrest created: "Officials wept in the yamen, the clerks wept in their offices, the peasants wept in the fields, the merchants wept in the market, travelers wept on the roads, and the womenfolk wept in their homes." The memorial reminded the emperor of Mencius' dictum that killing an official was not a prerogative of the throne. "The right *(quan)* to kill people lies not in the ruler's entourage, nor among the high officials, nor even in the Son of Heaven. It lies with the people of the state *(guoren)*." The memorial expressed disbelief that native son Zuo had ever accepted 20,000 taels from Xiong Tingbi to exonerate him from the charge of losing ancestral territory *(fengqiang)* in Manchuria. After twenty years in office, Zuo owned nothing but a bare house of a few rafters and a few mou of land. Where would he have put 20,000 taels? Surely the charges were false, and Zuo should be exonerated at once.

Armed with this memorial, a wailing crowd of local "fathers, sons, and brothers" escorted prisoner Zuo from Tongcheng north for some thirty miles, at which point a delegation of a hundred was selected and provisioned to complete the rest of the trek to Beijing. Zuo dissuaded them: the memorial they were carrying would accomplish nothing, and might even get the presenters killed. He urged the crowd to go home. Most did. A few followed surreptitiously as far as the Yellow River, and turned back there.[65]

Wei Dazhong

Far to the east of De'anfu and Tongcheng, in Jiashan county in Zhejiang province, former Supervising Secretary Wei Dazhong chose to live in strict poverty, his demeanor "stern and cold," his clothing threadbare, his diet vegetarian, "beyond what was normal."[66] He barred his gate and refused visitors, and found no peace of mind in the disturbing news he read in the Capital Gazette. He ended his personal diary on May 29, 1625, the day the imperial police arrived and arrested him. His elder son, Wei Xueyi, continued the diary from the point where his father left off.

"A myriad" gentry and common people (shimin) wailed in the streets as the police escorted Wei from Jiashan. The prisoner and his guards proceeded north by water through Suzhou, where they stopped for three days. There Zhou Shunchang, vice director of the Ministry of Personnel, on home leave, cast all caution to the winds and flamboyantly paid Wei a visit. "He is truly one of ours," said Zhou, and then and there he betrothed his youngest daughter to Wei's grandson.[67] (Zhou's own sensational arrest, provoked by this defiant gesture, would come in 1626.)

◄

The exact route and the timing of Yang Lian's journey to Beijing are not clear. The paths of Zuo Guangdou and Wei Dazhong, however, converged nearly simultaneously at Dingxing and Rongcheng, two counties about fifty miles southwest of Beijing, where several colleagues, friends, and protégés of theirs lived. At Dingxing resided Lu Zheng, father of Lu Shanji, an official in the Ministry of War, who was at the time on duty at Shanhaiguan as an aide to commander Sun Chengzong. From Suzhou, Wei Dazhong's friend Zhou Shunchang had sent a letter by special courier to Lu Shanji at Dingxing, asking for help for Wei. Wei Dazhong himself had sent his son Wei Xueyi ahead to Rongcheng with a similar request for help from Sun Qifeng. A support network for the prisoners sprang into action.

Sun Qifeng sent his brother with a letter for Sun Chengzong (no relation), begging him to intercede in Wei's behalf.[68] Nothing came of that venture. But at Baigouhe, a market town about ten miles south of the Xincheng county seat, and very near Dingxing, lived Zhang Guozhong— a student of Lu Shanji, a son-in-law of Sun Qifeng, a protégé of Zuo Guangdou, and an acquaintance of Wei Dazhong. While Lu Zheng let the prisoners' emissaries stay at his house in Dingxing, Zhang Guozhong and his brother ran errands on the prisoners' behalf and mobilized their comrades *(tongzhi)* to collect donations of silver to help pay the prisoners' fines. It was dangerous to do this, because Xincheng, Dingxing, and Rongcheng lay so close to Beijing that the volunteers' activities were certain to attract the attention of spies and informers. Palace eunuch Li Zhaoqin owned an estate right next to Lu Zheng, and Li was Wei Zhongxian's personal secretary. (Allegedly, Li received reports of what the volunteers were up to, but he said nothing to Wei Zhongxian because, long before, Zhang Guozhong had helped his parents when they were destitute!)[69]

Zuo Guangdou and his police escort arrived at the market town of Baigouhe sometime during the month of July 1625. There Zhang Guozhong greeted him. Zuo wanted to talk to Sun Qifeng. Zhang delivered the message. Sun and another comrade came at once to Baigouhe and met with Zuo, surrounded by the imperial police, who listened in. Zuo unburdened himself of his anxiety. Sun consoled him. Zuo said his guards had told him that "those in power definitely plan to kill Yang Lian," which, if true, meant that he and Wei Dazhong would be killed as well. Sun Qifeng told Zuo that through contacts he had learned that Ke Guangxian, Madame Ke's younger brother, had offered to intercede with his sister in the prisoners' behalf. "How can I seek help from a woman?" huffed Zuo. "I wouldn't be a man if I did."

Wei Dazhong's son Wei Xueyi and Zuo Guangdou's brother Zuo Guangming, traveling under assumed names, needed a place to stay. Sun said his own home was too small and poor, so he arranged for them to stay with Lu Zheng at Jiangcun in Dingxing, a few miles west of Baigouhe.

A day after Zuo Guangdou reached Baigouhe, Wei Dazhong and his guards arrived after their long journey from South China. Zhang Guozhong had gone to Shanhaiguan to confer with Sun Chengzong and Lu Shanji. Sun Qifeng had gone off on an errand as well. Wei Dazhong angrily demanded to wait at Baigouhe for their return, but his guards were in a hurry, and so, unhappily, Wei was forced to depart at once for Beijing.[70]

Wei Dazhong entered Beijing on July 16 and was placed in temporary confinement. Zuo Guangdou may have arrived the day before. On July 18, a Palace rescript ordered the incarceration of both prisoners in the Decree Prison. Their interrogation would wait until Yang Lian arrived.

The other three *junzi* had already been waiting in the Decree Prison since early June. Finally Yang Lian arrived on July 31, and the awful ordeal began.

◀

As the prisoners made their way to Beijing, some of the Beijing officials began to express misgivings about what was soon to take place. Cao Guang, Minister of the Court of Judicial Review, tried to get the prisoners transferred from the Decree Prison to the Ministry of Justice, where they would not be subjected to secret torture. He persuaded Vice Minister of War Zhang Fengxiang to talk to Grand Secretary Zhu Yanxi, whom he thought might be sympathetic. Zhang did so, but he reported back to Cao that Grand Secretary Zhu was unable to help.[71] Several years later, recalling this incident, Zhu Yanxi said he had been "unbearably pained" by the arrest order for Yang Lian, and though he wanted to help, he could not "stop the tigers who had access to the imperial throne."[72] On July 8 and 9, anti-Donglin censors impeached Zhu Yanxi for colluding with Zhang Fengxiang in an effort to make himself look virtuous by alleviating the treatment in store for Yang and Zuo and the others, shifting resentment to the emperor, and placing others in peril. The Palace removed Zhang from civil service, and on July 12, it ordered Zhu Yanxi to retire. Cao Guang was removed from civil service not long after.[73]

Then the remaining two grand secretaries—Gu Bingqian and Wei Guangwei—panicked and entered last-minute pleas in the prisoners' behalf. Minister of Personnel Cui Jingrong wrote an urgent note warning Wei Guangwei of the ugly consequences of what was about to occur. How, he asked, could the grand secretary in good conscience involve himself with an endorsement of a Palace directive to apply lethal torture to Yang Lian and the others? The prisoners had committed serious crimes, but torture was uncalled for, and future generations would surely condemn the grand secretary for assenting to it. Wei Guangwei was taken aback. On August 2, he wrote an endorsement supporting the directive, but he wrote another one protesting it, plus an accompanying note expressing his shock at the Palace's savagery. He begged Gu Bingqian to join him, and Gu followed with a protest of his own on August 3.[74]

Word leaked out that Wei Guangwei's newfound hesitation angered Palace eunuch Wei Zhongxian: "You urged me to take these actions, and now you affect a virtuous pose so as to put the blame on me!" Wei Zhongxian then had the grand secretary shown all the paperwork related to the case that the grand secretary himself had written.[75] The grand secretaries' protests were not well received. Cui Jingrong was dismissed. Wei Guangwei was allowed to resign in September.[76] Gu Bingqian remained for another year as chief grand secretary.

◀

What happened to Yang Lian and the others inside the Decree Prison is known from several eyewitness accounts, including especially that by the pseudonymous "Beijing Guest," who may well have been Gu Dazhang's younger brother, Gu Dawu.[77] The Beijing Guest disguised himself as an orderly and saw more than any other eyewitness what took place in the Decree Prison.

Prison Director Xu Xianchun's first task was to make the prisoners confirm what was in the "confession" of the now dead Wang Wenyan. The ordeal began on July 31.

Interrogations were held outdoors. The prisoners were hauled from their cells and arranged on the ground in front of a building called the Mingxin *tang* ("Hall for Clarifying the Mind"). At a table under the eave of the Mingxin *tang* sat the prison director, and behind him sat a "recorder," actually a Palace agent. Guards and beaters stood along the sides. To some or all of the prisoners, the beaters applied a hundred squeezings of the finger press, fifty applications of the leg crusher, plus forty blows with a stick, with the victims being roped in such a way that they could not move.[78]

Wei Xueyi's informant was not close enough to hear distinctly what was being said.[79] However, an informant for Yang Lian's family heard some bits of Yang Lian's interrogation and reported it partly in the colloquial language. "Why did you take the lead in the Palace Removal [the Palace Case of 1620]?" Yang replied that he was not the only person involved. "Why did you force the emperor into a position where he was made to look unfilial?" To that, Yang Lian replied indirectly: "As the sky and sun are up above, this is the Hall for Clarifying the Mind! Let's not change it into a place for obscuring the mind!" Asked about the capital evaluations of 1623, in which the Donglin people had done well, Yang said he was at home then and had not taken part in it. Finally he was asked about receiving a big bribe from Xiong Tingbi. He denied it: "I impeached

Xiong Tingbi even before his defeat in Liaoyang, so how would I do him favors after the defeat at Guangning? Check Xiong Tingbi's original confession. Or did you alter it?" At this juncture, Xu Xianchun called for torture to be applied to Yang Lian. Cried Yang: "Well, now it's you saying to use torture, you're killing me to curry favor, you'll stand condemned in the eyes of future generations, your flesh won't be fit [even for dogs] to eat!"[80]

After this opening round of interrogation under torture, the prisoners were dragged back to their cells. Word was then relayed from the Palace to the prisoners that if they would agree not to dispute the charges made against them, they would emerge alive from the ordeal. Zuo Guangdou convinced the others to cooperate. "We'll get out of this and some day serve again," he is said to have said. "What benefit is there in just dying here?" None of the other prisoners truly desired to die, and they agreed with Zuo that it made sense to confess even to false charges.[81]

Thus, on August 2 there was a reinterrogation, and this time the prisoners acknowledged guilt in all the charges laid against them in Wang Wenyan's "confession" of early May. Xu Xianchun wrote up a detailed report and sent it to the Palace. The report stated that Yang and Zuo had indeed accepted 20,000 taels of silver each from Xiong Tingbi to plead his case. Yang and Zuo had colluded with Palace eunuch Wang An in forcing Lady Li to evacuate the Qianqing palace in 1620. Yang Lian worked the capital evaluations of 1623 in his own favor. Prisoners Yuan Huazhong and Wei Dazhong "leaned on the ice mountain" and accepted bribes, unashamed of their greed, uncaring of the national right (*guoshi*); Zhou Chaorui and Gu Dazhang had tried to rescue those guilty of military failure and national humiliation.

The Palace rescripted this report on August 3. It now demanded that, since Yang Lian had fully admitted his guilt, he was to be tortured at intervals until the full amount of the bribe he confessed to having taken was repaid, at which time he was to be sent to the Ministry of Justice for final adjudication.[82]

This was a double cross. The Palace rescript amounted to a betrayal of the deal it had struck with the prisoners to obtain their confessions. Apparently Wei Zhongxian had been persuaded that to release "those tigers" would be to invite their future retaliation; that "if we don't kill that fellow [Yang Lian], we will not overawe the realm."[83]

On August 6, the "Six *junzi*" were fetched from their cells—groaning from the effects of the earlier torture, their heads shaved, cotton cloths wrapped around their foreheads—and laid prostrate in front of Xu Xian-chun. Yang and Zuo were in the middle, the others at their sides. What was said is not reported, but no torture was applied to them. Xu Xian-chun clearly wanted the prisoners off his hands. He memorialized a re-quest to transfer them from the Decree Prison to the custody of the *fasi*—the Ministry of Justice, the Court of Judicial Review, and the Cen-sorate. That body should collect the bribe repayments and determine the appropriate punishments. But on August 9 the Palace denied his request. "[Yang Lian's] crimes mount to Heaven," thundered the rescript. "How can Xu Xianchun on his own authority try to send him to the Ministry of Justice? Surely he is doing it for personal reasons. I won't probe into that for now. I order the Prison Office to retrieve all the stipulated amounts of the bribes. Report every five days. Do not be lenient."[84]

On August 11, the prisoners were again laid out in front of the Mingxin *tang*. Having been scolded for his leniency, Xu Xianchun began calling the prisoners by disrespectful pronouns, as though they were servants. Five of the six were beaten ten times with the stick (Yuan Huazhong was ill and was excused).

The procedure was established that the alleged bribes were to be paid in installments. At dawn on collection days, the prisoners' family servants were admitted to the interrogation area outside the Decree Prison with whatever amount of silver they had collected. One at a time, they turned over the silver. As they did this, the servants knelt behind the prisoners and could speak briefly with them, though Xu was obliged to order that they kneel several feet away and speak in a loud voice and not use dia-lect.[85] Identity checks of the servants were loose, however. For example, Wei Dazhong's friend and neighbor Liu Qixian disguised himself as a family servant, and as such he entered the prison and conferred with Wei on collection days.

After each round of silver collection, the Prison Office reported to the Palace the amounts received. The Palace was dissatisfied with the pace of the collections. On August 14 it complained: "Yang Lian and the others are repaying huge bribes in such small installments. When will these ever be repaid in full? For now, I won't investigate Xu Xianchun on the mat-ter. Henceforth apply severity to get the amounts repaid. Don't be lax as you were, or you'll be punished."[86]

On August 15, Xu Xianchun bore down more harshly. He now de-manded that each prisoner pay 400 taels every five days or else they would be beaten heavily with the stick—as they were on this day, perhaps for demonstration effect. Each received thirty blows on the bare upper legs. By this time the prisoners' leg wounds had become infected, Yang's the worst. The wounds were wrapped in cotton cloth. Yang had hoped up to this moment that he might yet survive the ordeal. Now he was sure he would not. He began drinking large quantities of cold water in the belief that it might help him die sooner. He scribbled notes and letters and statements using as ink the blood oozing from his wounds.

The silver payments were still too small. On August 18, the Palace seethed: "Yang Lian and the others aren't making their payments. Obviously the selling of law is going on. Xu Xianchun and Cui Yingyuan are each to be demoted one rank. They are to recover the amounts and report every five days. If they are lax again, they will be heavily punished without mercy."[87]

On August 19, Yang Lian and Zuo Guangdou each received another thirty blows with the stick, and full torture was threatened if their payments continued to fall short. The other four prisoners were excused. Wei Xueyi sent word through Liu Qixian that he wanted to see his father. Wei Dazhong refused, and said: "I'm in extreme pain . . . I can't last, but don't tell my son that." He wanted Wei Xueyi to hasten the silver payments so that he would not have to endure further torture.

On August 21, for reasons unknown, heavy torture was applied to all the prisoners. Yang, Zuo, and Wei suffered a hundred squeezes of the finger press, plus forty blows with the stick. Zhou Chaorui and Gu Dazhang were given half those numbers. Yuan Huazhong received fifty finger squeezings but was spared the stick. Yang Lian was heard to utter scream-like croaks. Zuo Guangdou cried like a child. Wei Dazhong told his people, within the hearing of the "Beijing Guest," that he had no more appetite, that a container of cold water and half an apple was all he could manage to eat in a day, and that it was time to prepare a coffin, because he believed he would not live much longer.[88]

A Palace rescript of August 22 again complained of meager repayments.[89] On the following day, Yang, Zuo, and Wei Dazhong were each beaten thirty times with the stick, which was unusually heavy, because it was raining. Xu Xianchun accused Yang Lian of telling his family servants not to hand in any silver at all. Yang Lian raised his head to argue, but no words came out. The beating session over, Yang and Zuo were dragged away and dropped momentarily at the doorway of the prison, blood seeping from their wounds, and looking as though they had died already.

"Pity!" cried Yang. Zuo Guangdou looked at his family servants, but said nothing.[90]

◄

Meanwhile, the prisoners' servants and relatives and friends were making desperate efforts to collect the silver that the Palace demanded every five days in restitution for the bribes the accused were alleged to have pocketed. Yang Lian's eldest son, Yang Zhiyi, sent his brother-in-law Xu Yingzheng back to Yingshan county in Hubei to sell Yang Lian's property there. A family servant had charge of fulfilling Yang Lian's food requests. Yang Zhiyi himself left Beijing and made hurried visits to several places in north China looking for loans or contributions. The coffin that Yang Lian had had portered up from Hubei was confiscated by the police. Several friends in the capital area took up a collection and bought another one for him.[91]

Wei Dazhong's son Wei Xueyi ran about madly trying to collect silver for his father. The family property in Jiashan county was small, and Jiashan was three thousand *li* away. Silver had somehow to be collected in the Beijing area in a hurry. Sun Qifeng helped to arrange safe houses and escorts. Among those who gave Wei Xueyi a safe place to stay was Xu Xianda of Dingxing county—a kinsman, no less, of Prison Director Xu Xianchun. The Dingxing county magistrate gave Wei Xueyi 100 taels from his own pocket. Lu Zheng traveled all around in the heat and collected some 300 taels altogether, mostly in tiny contributions. "Righteous men have small resources, while the rich are seldom righteous," noted Sun Qifeng.[92]

In Beijing, Wei Xueyi wrote long, urgent, impassioned letters to some of his father's Zhejiang colleagues, in which he defended his father's provocative political behavior and heatedly denied his ever having accepted the 3,300 taels in bribes from Xiong Tingbi with which he was charged. Some of Wei Dazhong's former colleagues, afraid of implicating themselves in the case, refused to help his son. Wei Xueyi later described how in several instances he was treated "like a ghost with the plague." He knocked at someone's gate and found himself eye-to-eye with the man he was looking for. "Come back late tomorrow!" was the answer. "When I showed up again at the appointed time," wrote Wei, "a gateman hissed at me: 'He's sound asleep, and I don't dare disturb him. Come back tomorrow.' I scurried about in terror through the night, fearing death at the hands of the police *(luozu)*, and I never was able to get to see him."[93]

However, some colleagues did help. Cang Zhaoru gave Wei Xueyi a place to stay and some silver.[94] Supervising Secretaries Huang Chenghao and Yu Tingbi, coprovincials of Wei's, contributed funds. Huang contacted other coprovincials and sent a letter to his son back in Zhejiang, directing him to sell 200 *mou* of property there and to forward 1,000 or so taels of proceeds to Beijing. Huang thought Wei's charge of 3,300 taels not too large a sum to raise, and that raising it might deprive Wei's tormentors of an excuse to kill him.[95]

Zuo Guangdou had many friends in north China because of his recent service there as educational intendant and state farms commissioner. Lu Zheng mobilized dozens of government students *(shengyuan)* and other people, and within a few days they collected several hundred taels of silver. Zhang Guozhong and others took turns forwarding the silver to Zuo's servants in Beijing.[96]

One *shengyuan*, Shi Kefa (later a famous Ming loyalist), bribed the prison guards, who let him dress as a night-soil collector and enter the Decree Prison to see Zuo Guangdou. He found Zuo sitting on a mat, leaning against a wall: his face was so disfigured as to be unrecognizable. The bones and tendons below his left knee were mangled. Shi knelt and wept. Zuo could not see, but he recognized the voice, and then he forced open an eyelid with his hand and said in anger: "You idiot, what are you doing in this place? The dynasty is rotting away, and you're doing a stupid thing risking your life to come in here when the realm needs your support! Leave now, or before a traitor gets you, I'll kill you myself!" He groped about for a stick, and made as if to strike. Shi left at once. Later he would tell people about this and saying, "My teacher's lungs and gall were made out of iron and stone."[97]

The silver installments, when paid on time, eased the physical abuse of the prisoners. When their assessments were fully paid, people presumed that the prisoners would be released, although it was not for certain. On August 26, Yang, Zuo, and Wei were put to yet another round of torture. Prison Director Xu Xianchun then ordered the three separated from the others. A guard explained to the "Beijing Guest" that they were going to be killed. That night, a guard by the name of Ye Wenzhong killed them. Their deaths "from illness" were reported to the Palace. A rescript of August 28 acknowledged the deaths of Yang and Zuo "by illness." Another rescript of August 31 acknowledged the death of Wei Dazhong, also "by illness." (Apparently, the split dates avoided the awkwardness of having three "accidental" deaths all occur at the same time.) The *fasi* (judicial officials of the outer court) were ordered to verify the identities of the corpses and release them for burial. Provincial officials were ordered to arrest and imprison the family members of each dead prisoner and force from them the repayment of the "bribery" charges still unpaid.[98] As of August 31, the accounts looked like this:[99]

TABLE I

	Taels Charged	Repaid as of August 30, 1625
Yang Lian	20,000	none?
Zuo Guangdou	20,000	43.6
Wei Dazhong	3,300	550
Yuan Huazhong	6,330	1,224.5
Zhou Chaorui	10,000	1,517.4
Gu Dazhang	40,000	803.3

Tianqi himself, at least in a general way, was aware of all this. On September 13, after a tutorial, he remarked to the grand secretaries that Yang Lian's crimes were many; that although he had died in prison, uncollected bribes remained, and the provincial authorities were going to recover those from his home area.[100]

◀

So three of the "Six *junzi*" were dead, those furthest behind in their repayments. Three were still alive, but not for long. By September 13, former Censor Yuan Huazhong's people paid his account in full, and by September 15, former Supervising Secretary Zhou Chaorui's account was fully paid as well. According to the "Beijing Guest," Zhou's family was rich. Neither prisoner was turned over to the *fasi* for final adjudication, however. On September 20, guard Yan Zi killed Yuan with his own hands. The prison reported that Yuan "died of illness." On September 23, Yuan's corpse was dumped outside the prison for his family to remove for burial.

Prison Director Xu Xianchun reported Zhou Chaorui to be ill, though he was not. The Palace sent in a physician to treat him. Xu sent the physician away. On September 29, guard Guo Er interrupted Zhou while he was at lunch with Gu Dazhang and another prisoner (Meng Shukong, to whom Yang Lian had entrusted his last writings). He marched Zhou off and killed him with his own hands. Again, the death was officially ascribed to "illness."[101]

Former vice director of the Ministry of War, Gu Dazhang, the last remaining prisoner, lingered on for another few weeks. On October 13, he was actually taken before the *fasi* for formal adjudication. He refused to confess. Then he was taken back to the Decree Prison. On October 14, he committed suicide by self-strangulation. The official announcement stated that he had died "of illness." His corpse was ordered removed from the Decree Prison on October 18. Provincial authorities were ordered to press his family back home (in Changshu county in the Yangtze delta region) for the unpaid balance on his account.[102]

◄

So all of the "Six *junzi*" were dead. Four of them still had large arrears outstanding on the bribes they had been charged with having received. The job of retrieving those amounts was shifted from the Decree Prison to the *fuan*—the leading officials in the victims' home provinces. In that connection, former Grand Secretary Ye Xianggao commented that "the cruelty of these punishments is something wholly unprecedented in history."[103]

On August 31, the corpses of Yang Lian, Zuo Guangdou, and Wei Dazhong were wrapped in hemp cloth and reed mats and tied with rope and pushed through a small stone door in the rear of the Decree Prison. The men had been dead several days in hot weather. Their stench filled the street. Maggots fell from their wrappings.

Family servants brought Yang Lian's coffin back from Beijing to Yingshan county.[104] People wept and performed rituals as Yang's coffin passed through the villages. One elder with a load of firewood on his back stuck a note on Yang's coffin. "The master's heart was a heart that was loyal to his ruler, and his mouth a mouth that hated traitors," it read. "He is dead, but he will live a thousand ages!" The old man refused to give his name.[105]

In Yang Lian's home county of Yingshan, the officials confiscated the family property, forcing Yang's widow and stepmother into the streets.

But provincial and local officials did what they could to ease things, arranging, for example, for public contributions to help pay Yang Lian's assessment. It was secretly arranged for a young grandson to be taken away to Lushan in Jiangxi province to live disguised as a Buddhist monk, to continue the Yang line in case none of the family in Yingshan should survive. The local authorities also helped by being dilatory in making the repayments. A Palace edict of January 26, 1626, complained that nothing had yet been sent, and demanded immediate action.[106] Yang's nephew and two of his five sons were imprisoned. One of the sons died in prison, as did several servants. By the time of the death of Tianqi and the collapse of the Wei Zhongxian regime in 1627, nearly all of the 20,000 taels charged to Yang Lian had somehow been collected.[107]

Zuo Guangdou's corpse was picked up by two of his brothers and an in-law as well as his student Shi Kefa. The proceeds from the confiscation of Zuo's property in Tongcheng county came to less than a thousand taels. Zuo's eldest brother died in prison. The county magistrate wept as he punished Zuo's son; it was unjust, he acknowledged, but there was nothing that he as a lowly magistrate could do about it. Some kinsmen fled into hiding. But apparently all 20,000 taels were collected by 1627.[108]

On September 1, guards deposited the decomposing corpse of Wei Dazhong in the street outside the prison. Apparently he had been suffocated to death, because his face was squashed flat. His son Wei Xueyi and some others gathered up his remains, placed them in a coffin, and hurried away with the deceased back to Jiashan county, some eight hundred miles to the south. En route, Wei Xueyi wrote a long, searing letter to an acquaintance detailing in graphic language the excruciating and completely unjustified torment his father had just been put through.[109]

Back in Jiashan, the local elders offered to take up a collection, but Wei Xueyi declined, showing them a note written from prison by his father on August 5 refusing any such charity: "I have been poor all my life, and have never given any charity to my neighbors; my personal disaster is not the public business of the [people of the] county, and I cannot obligate them." But Wei Xueyi did beg the elders to encourage someone to buy their "dilapidated house and a few *mou* of fields" and to "give some food and shelter to my mother."

For his part, Wei Xueyi refused to go to prison and there serve as hostage for the forced repayment of his father's silver arrears. He went into deep mourning for the father whose life he had been unable to save. He rejected food and drink. "Who gave our father anything to drink at

midnight in the Decree Prison?" he said to his younger brother, Wei Xuelian. Wei Xueyi died of slow suicide on December 20, 1625.[110] The provincial authorities put Wei Xuelian in prison. The local elders took up a collection of silver after all. By July 24, 1626, the Palace acknowledged that
the Zhejiang provincial officials had collected 2,360 taels on Wei Dazhong's account, and it directed that the sum be delivered at once to Beijing to help pay for palace reconstruction in the Forbidden City.[111]

◀

The Palace rested its case. Never mind Gu Dazhang—all the principals
had confessed! All of them, starting with Wang Wenyan, had (most re-
grettably) died "of illness" in prison. The public execution of the villain
general Xiong Tingbi was announced in September 1625. Provincial officials were at work recouping all the silver Xiong and others had allegedly handed out as bribes.

At last, on October 21, the *fasi* (legal organs of the outer court) convened and prepared the formal criminal charges *(yuanshu)*. On October 27,
the Palace gave its public response. Now the main charge was no longer
Xiong Tingbi but the Palace Case, wherein Yang Lian, Zuo Guangdou,
Zhou Chaorui, and Wang Wenyan had conspired together and had inhu-
manely driven Lady Li from the Qianqing palace, forcing Tianqi into a
posture of filial impiety. Following that crime, the same four had leagued
with Wei Dazhong, Yuan Huazhong, and Gu Dazhang and pocketed
mountainous bribes from Xiong Tingbi, in return for which they had
sought to win leniency for him. Nothing at all was said of Yang Lian's
"Twenty-four Crimes" memorial.

The Palace ordered that all the documents relating to these two infamous cases be sent to the History Office for eventual publication, so that
the true facts might be made clear to posterity—or, in the words of the
Palace, "to make manifest the justice, enlightenment, benevolence, and
filiality of Our rule, and convince the minds of the future generations of
the realm."[112] No less than the martyrs, the Palace hoped that history
would ratify the extreme measures it had been compelled to take. This
was not yet the end of the story, however. More arrests, tortures, and
secret murders were about to follow.

CHAPTER 4

The Murders Continue: 1626

◀

IT IS ALMOST beyond belief that the shocking arrests, doubtful charges, tortures, and secret murders of six leading Donglin figures in 1625 failed to satisfy the Beijing authorities' desire for retribution. Obviously, however, the authorities felt that they had not yet done enough. The year 1626, therefore, saw a second and equally grim round of arrests and murders, this time targeting seven of the most renowned and articulate scholar-officials of south China. Again, contemporaries recorded for posterity the harrowing stories of this new wave of martyrs, with undiminished relish for intense, day-by-day detail.

By 1625–1626 an elaborate machinery of political repression had developed. There were two principal organs. One was the so-called Eastern Depot, of which palace eunuch Wei Zhongxian was director. It consisted of some one thousand uniformed police and two headquarters complexes, one inside the Forbidden City, and the other outside, at the Forbidden City's eastern wall. The Eastern Depot could not directly arrest or interrogate officials, or anyone who enjoyed official status *(jinshen)*; its jurisdiction was confined to commoners.[1] The available records show that, indeed, Wei Zhongxian was regularly rewarded for his work in prosecuting thieves, counterfeiters, Manchu spies, and other small-time suspects who were not of the official class.

The prosecution of officials (such as the Donglin) was the responsibility of the Embroidered-uniform Guard, whose offices and infamous "Decree Prison" were located south of the Imperial City, in the same government quarter that housed all the other military offices of the outer court. The Guard's Northern Prison Office *(Bei zhenfusi)*, of which Xu Xianchun was director, conducted the interrogations and tortures of officials. The Embroidered-uniform Guard grew in size from 17,760 in 1620 to 36,360 in 1627.[2] Thus Wei Zhongxian's hand in the arrest and torture of the Donglin and other officials was indirect and came by way of his informal control of Tianqi's powers of edict and rescript rather than by his direct management of the Eastern Depot.

With the cooperation of the Palace, anti-Donglin officials proceeded during 1625–1626 with the piecemeal removals of hundreds of perceived enemies from bureaucratic life. Most were reduced from official to commoner status and were ordered to hand back the patents of official rank that had been awarded to their parents. However, for a select few of those purged, much worse was in store.

In the spring of 1626, there was engineered a second round of arrests of seven more leading lights in the Donglin faction. They were made because the Tianqi court was still struggling to recover China's moral high ground, and the seven men, although they had been removed from office, were still seen as threatening the country's moral credentials. These arrests struck at the cultural heart of late Ming China, the wealthy region of Jiangnan, including especially the city of Suzhou.

◀

Censor Zhou Zongjian (who in 1623, in a failed bid for Donglin leadership, had scathingly assaulted Wei Zhongxian and his then collaborator Guo Gong) was home on mourning leave in Wujiang county, not far south of Suzhou, when in April 1625 he was placed second in a list of four Donglin officials accused of partisan activity and removed from civil service. Zhou was also accused of taking bribes. The governors *(fuan)* of Nanzhili province were ordered to determine and recover the full amounts of the alleged bribes.[3]

After nearly a year had elapsed, the Palace had received no report from the Nanzhili governors about their investigation of Zhou Zongjian. It therefore ordered a detachment of the Embroidered-uniform Guard to go to Wujiang, arrest Zhou, and bring him to the Decree Prison for interrogation.[4] Upon receiving this directive, Governor *(xunfu)* Mao Yilu belatedly reported having collected 1,000 taels from Zhou. The Palace was dissatisfied with Mao's report; it said there was much more silver than that to be accounted for, and it directed Mao to "severely press" Zhou Zongjian's family for more.[5]

Also placed under arrest by the same Palace rescript was Miao Changqi of Jiangyin county, about twenty-five miles northwest of Suzhou. In February 1625, Miao had received permission to leave Beijing and go home to recuperate from an illness.[6] Three months later, while he was at home, Miao Changqi was removed from civil service because he was one of those named in Wang Wenyan's "confession" for taking bribes from the imprisoned commander Xiong Tingbi. Miao allegedly took 3,000 taels.[7]

Had Miao then secluded himself, he might have escaped arrest. He was

certainly warned. Li Yingsheng warned him.[8] So did Qian Qianyi, by letter from Beijing dated May 16, 1625 (and thus probably too late to have
any effect). Qian gave Miao Changqi a detailed account of how the anti-
Donglin men were exploiting what he firmly believed was Wang Wenyan's falsely concocted confession to prepare the ground to kill their enemies. "Living at home, you must be exceptionally careful," he cautioned.
"You'll find it hard to keep your tongue quiet, but things have come to
the point where we're not just in an age of decline *(moshi)*, but in a killing
cycle *(shayun)* as well, so you must keep quiet to save your life. . . . When
you left the capital, I warned you, and you agreed, but you didn't restrain
yourself. . . . These things get reported to the eunuch [Wei Zhongxian].
You were lucky not to get arrested. . . . I don't know why you defended
Xiong Tingbi that day, but it has provoked this big case. . . ."[9]

The Palace rescript of March 15, 1626 (which also ordered Zhou Zongjian's arrest) noted that, despite Miao Changqi's removal from civil service, he continued to wear official paraphernalia, to invite guests, and to
act with no restraint, and therefore his arrest was required.[10]

About two weeks later, on March 28, the Palace ordered five more arrests of Donglin principals. This order came by way of a rescript to a memorial of complaint ostensibly sent up by Li Shi, eunuch Textile Commissioner of Suzhou and Hangzhou, but actually drawn up in the Palace
itself by eunuch Li Yongzhen and others acting at the behest of Wei
Zhongxian.

Nominally, the key figure in this roundup was Zhou Qiyuan, a long-
time partisan battler in the Donglin behalf, who, in 1624, as governor
(xunfu) of Nanzhili, had clashed with Li Shi in a dispute over Palace silk
procurement.[11] Early in 1625, Zhou Qiyuan was removed from civil service for that and other offenses.[12] Li Shi's memorial of March 1626, actually composed in the palace, alleged that Zhou Qiyuan had not only defied
imperial orders in the silk procurement matter but had pocketed funds
intended to pay the silk workers. And not only that! He was now using
daoxue—that is, Confucian study and discussion—as an excuse to gather
sympathizers Zhou Zongjian, Miao Changqi, Zhou Shunchang, Gao
Panlong, Li Yingsheng, and Huang Zunsu. And, in addition, Huang
Zunsu recently had a spy or agent serving right in Li Shi's staff. And
Zhou Zongjian had acted disrespectfully when he was arrested, just as
though he had chosen not to recognize his ruler-father! And Zhou
Shunchang! Removed from the official register, he should have retired in
self-reproach; instead, he continued to dress as an official, to act in a

domineering way, and even went so far as to urge the imperial silk weavers to stop work.[13]

As in 1625, so again in 1626, squadrons of imperial police proceeded south from Beijing to the homes of the accused to carry out the arrests. However, both Li Shi's memorial and the imperial rescript to it were confidential, so no one who saw or was aware of the departure of the police knew for certain who they were after. Any of a number of famous personalities living in the greater Jiangnan area had reason to believe he might be the target. Each of them had to consider carefully what to do and how to behave in such circumstances.

Some fled into hiding. Others defiantly stood their ground. Perhaps neither response was correct. Already in 1625, Gao Panlong wrote a letter counseling Liu Zongzhou in the matter. "To close your gate and refuse guests is the right way," he urged. "If they want to kill us, barring the gate won't stop them, but that's to die fulfilling the Way.... Principle (*daoli*) lies at the apex of the ordinary. Even the slightest mind to escape death ruins the Way. Even the slightest mind to seek death wrecks it as well. I'm afraid that in your extreme anguish you haven't thought of that."[14]

Zhou Zongjian

The imperial police (by now commonly referred to as *tiqi*, or "horsemen dressed in colored silk") came down to south China and arrested Zhou Zongjian and Miao Changqi about a month ahead of the other five.

Zhou Zongjian somehow found out ahead of time that the *tiqi* were coming for him, and so he left his home in Wujiang without telling his family where he was going and proceeded on his own to Suzhou, the prefectural capital, where he turned himself in. The order of arrest was read out in a public ceremony. Zhou was then placed in a prisoner transport cart. Crowds of Suzhou people gathered about the cart and wept. It was murmured that the arrest order was a fake concocted by palace eunuch Wei Zhongxian and should not be obeyed. Some onlookers hovered about, looking as though they might try to rough up the guards. Zhou scolded them, and they backed away. (A month later, when Zhou Shunchang was arrested, the Suzhou crowds rioted in earnest.) By May 5, prisoner Zhou had arrived in Beijing and was placed in the Decree Prison for questioning under torture.[15]

Miao Changqi

Meanwhile, on April 1, in Jiangyin county, Miao Changqi went by himself to the magistrate's office, where he was placed in irons and forbidden any further contact with his family.[16] Scholars and common people wept in the streets of Jiangyin as prisoner Miao departed, by boat, to the prefectural capital, Changzhou. En route, a brief meeting was somehow arranged with Gao Panlong. "To humiliate a high official is to humiliate the dynasty, and I will not be humiliated," asserted Gao. Miao replied, "Unless I go to prison, I cannot fulfill my duty, so that is what I am doing."[17]

At Changzhou, "several tens of myriads of country people crowded the roads" to greet Miao on his arrival. "They all put their palms together and chanted the Buddha's name. They said: 'Today we see a bodhisattva appear in the world!' Miao laughed and thanked them, acting as though this was just an ordinary affair."[18]

In Changzhou, where the charges were publicly read out, Miao was fortunate to fall into the hands of prefect Zeng Ying, a Donglin supporter, who eased his circumstances and offered him some financial assistance. Family servants were allowed for the first time to bring Miao food and drink. Miao's sons paid a short visit to their father. Miao had prepared an autobiography, and he gave it to one of his sons. His former colleagues Li Yingsheng and Zhou Shunchang also visited him.

At length, Miao's prison cortège departed Changzhou. Across the Yangtze at Yizhen, the local students (shengyuan) tendered Miao a reception and wept as they escorted him out of town.[19] He arrived in Beijing on May 5, and on May 6 was consigned to the Decree Prison, where Zhou Zongjian had also just arrived.[20] While prisoners Zhou and Miao were still on the road to Beijing, the arrests of the other five former officials got under way.

Zhou Qiyuan

Zhou Qiyuan lived the farthest away, in Haicheng county, Zhangzhou prefecture, Fujian province. The date of the arrival of the two tiqi and their entourage is not known, but, as in every other such instance, the local expenses of the police were paid by contribution or extortion.

Zhou was somehow aware of his coming arrest, and he made his own way from Haicheng some hundred miles northeast to the prefectural capital. As he left, onlookers gathered and sighed as they observed his three little sons clinging to his knees. Zhou patted the boys on the head. "Your father won't get to teach you," he was heard to say. "You let your mother raise you. Don't cry."

Disturbed by the news of his arrest, local citizens received official permission to place collection boxes at Zhangzhou's four city gates to help pay Zhou Qiyuan's expenses. Many donated, anonymously tossing in a few taels. They say old women from the back alleys pawned their hairpins for cash and donated that. Even chair bearers carrying passengers were seen throwing a few coppers into the collection boxes as they rushed by.

Then came the public reading of the charges. A retired official, aged and bedridden, demanded to be taken by sedan chair to the yamen where the reading took place. He had something he wanted to say. "You've offended the government by opposing the eunuch [Li Shi] in the people's behalf," wailed the invalid. "You've repaid the favor the dynasty gave you in nurturing you. You'll die right. I wish I weren't too old to join you in the punishment." Replied Zhou: "When I wrote those memorials, I knew today would come. I have no regret."

It was possible for street mobs to overpower the imperial police. Whenever a mob gave signs that it was about to become violent, it was essential that the prisoner-hero himself intervene to help defuse the situation. So when the angered crowd in Zhangzhou indeed threatened the police, Zhou Qiyuan got on his knees and pleaded with them: "When the subject official serves his ruler, his body is no longer his own. Thunder and rain come by favor of the ruler. If you local people care for me, you won't have me put in legal jeopardy." The crowd calmed down. The police were grateful. At length the prison cortège left Zhangzhou, escorted by thousands of weeping locals.[21] So long was the journey that Zhou Qiyuan did not arrive in Beijing until early August, by which time all the other Donglin victims had undergone their ordeals and were dead.[22]

Li Yingsheng

Li Yingsheng at thirty-two years of age was the youngest of all the Donglin martyrs of 1625–1626. Removed from civil service, he did not want to draw attention to himself and went into seclusion in his native Jiangyin county. Miao Changqi—whose wife was Li's aunt—lived in the same Jiangyin county and had behaved provocatively and been arrested on

April 1. But it did not matter; on April 13, Li received written notice of his own arrest.

Li's wife and mother fell weeping into each other's arms. Li's little son Li Sunzhi grabbed his robe and cried. Li consoled his family and departed by boat to the prefectural capital, Changzhou, which he reached on April 15. There he met his old teacher and others, and jokingly speculated that his arrest must be revenge for some wrong he had committed in a previous incarnation. Li said he would not commit suicide, because his father was still alive.

The reading of the charges was delayed while the imperial police went about extorting compensation from the people in the streets. Angry mobs gathered. Word was passed that Li's arrest was completely unjust. Threats were uttered. There were scufflings and flurries of violence as some of the police were assaulted. Prefect Zeng Ying tried to calm things. Li Yingsheng—described as young, vigorous, refined, and like a "sylph visiting from another world"—rode through the streets on horseback pleading with the crowd, which then relented. The imperial police were removed from the streets and brought inside the yamen for their own safety. Prefect Zeng paid them some silver from his own pocket. The reading then took place on April 19 under tight security because news had just arrived of the full-blown riot in Suzhou, April 11–14.[23]

Li and his escort of guards left Changzhou, crossed the Yangtze to Yizhen, left Yizhen on April 24, and reached Dezhou, in northern Shandong, about 175 miles south of Beijing, on May 10. There Li wrote his father: "Changed from sedan chair to cart, which is uncomfortable, but no matter. Here I guess we wait for Zhou [Shunchang] and Huang [Zunsu] to arrive. . . . As for the silver, there's no way to get it except to sell fields. . . . Elder brother must keep himself well hidden in the capital . . . he'll tell you all the rest. I don't know if I'll be able to write again."[24]

Gao Panlong

Gao Panlong, cofounder and leader of the Donglin academy in Wuxi county (thirty miles northwest of Suzhou, twenty miles south of Jiangyin), was living not altogether quietly at home since his removal from civil service in 1625. He had made it clear to close colleagues what he planned to do in case of arrest, but he did not tell his family.

The Gao home was surrounded by water. By activating a movable bridge, Gao Panlong admitted occasional students and select guests. While he was entertaining some guests on April 12, news came from some friendly source in Suzhou that his arrest was imminent. "If this news is true," smiled Gao, "then I just look on death as a return. There is no life and death, no life and death. How can we make life and death two things? If on the verge of death you begin rethinking your thoughts, you fall into the bitter sea. How can you achieve your fixed fate that way?"

That evening, Gao assured his family that he would submit to arrest. But during the night, while everyone was asleep, he crept out of bed and out of the house to the water's edge, where he plunged in, fully clothed. The next morning they found his body floating upright in the water, his hat on the surface, not far away.[25]

The Palace was informed by governor Mao Yilu of Gao Panlong's suicide and was not pleased. It wanted to know how Gao had learned ahead of time that he was under arrest and ordered the seizure and interrogation of his son, Gao Shiru. However, Prefect Zeng Ying was able to protect Gao Shiru, and the Palace never did find out the source of the leak.[26]

Gao Panlong left a note for the imperial police to take to Tianqi: "I have been removed from civil service and the patents given my parents have been rescinded. But once I was a high official, and when a high official is humiliated, the dynasty is humiliated. I kowtow facing north and follow the example of Qu Yuan [by drowning myself]. I have left unrepaid the ruler's favor; I hope to settle that in a future life. Written by your servant Gao Panlong, on the verge of death. (I ask that a messenger deliver this to the emperor.)"[27]

Zhou Shunchang

The arrest by *tiqi* of Zhou Shunchang ignited the famous Suzhou riot of 1626. Even more than Beijing, Suzhou was the cultural and fashion center of China in the late Ming. Zhou Shunchang lived in Suzhou—in self-imposed poverty, in a small house of three rooms, decorated only with a few potted plants—with his plainly dressed wife and eight children. He had been there since 1622, when as a vice director in the Ministry of Personnel he took leave to see to the burial of his parents. He was active as an advocate for the people of the city (as Yang Lian too had been, in Yingshan). He exchanged letters with colleagues and friends and so kept abreast of political developments in Beijing. He was a Donglin sympathizer of long standing, because, as he put it when asked, it happened that those colleagues with whom he found himself naturally attuned were all Donglin adherents. "There was an attraction of flavor, an unplanned-for union, and they didn't have to recruit me like those who bang the drum to gather outlaws under some banner."[28]

Zhou Shunchang made no secret of his hatred for the Donglin baiters at court. Indeed, he deliberately provoked them. In 1624, he wrote a message for Governor Zhou Qiyuan upon his impeachment, in which he said such things as "never in the two hundred years of the Ming has anyone so qualified and of such good repute been removed from officialdom by the emperor"; that "the emperor's action only enhances your reputation"; that "the stars are fading, the frost descends, and heroes of talent are no longer welcome."[29] Within a month, it is said, copies of this message were circulating in Beijing, where his enemies could of course read them.[30] Then came his well-publicized embrace of Wei Dazhong in 1625, when Wei, under arrest, passed through Suzhou and Zhou betrothed his youngest daughter to Wei's grandson. In August 1625, the Palace removed Zhou along with several others from civil service.[31]

The imperial order to arrest Zhou Shunchang was delivered to the provincial governors Mao Yilu and Xu Ji in Suzhou on April 11, 1626.[32] The governors in turn directed Suzhou prefect Kou Shen to order Chen Wenrui, magistrate of Wu county, to go to Zhou's house that night and inform him that he was under arrest. As it happened, Zhou Shunchang knew Magistrate Chen well; Chen had been an outstanding local student when Zhou was an official in Fujian province some years before. Chen Wenrui leaned on Zhou's bed and wept as he broke the news to him. "I knew all along this order was coming," said Zhou. "I expected it. Don't be upset."

There were several other ousted Donglin officials living in Suzhou, and they soon learned of the arrival of the imperial police. Each man thought the target of the arrest order might be himself. In the afternoon of April 11, someone roused former Hanlin Senior Compiler Wen Zhenmeng from a nap and told him the terrifying news. Wen had been sent home in 1622 for his scathing critique of Tianqi's personal shortcomings and was surely a possible target. However, after some hours, Wen's son-in-law came by to tell him it was Zhou Shunchang they were after. To Wen it seemed like waking from a bad dream. Although it was raining, Wen Zhenmeng and several other friends went over to Zhou's house that night to console him. They found Zhou calm. Two of his sons were standing by. His wife had fainted.

At dawn on April 12, Zhou changed into prison garb and climbed into a sedan chair. News of his arrest had meanwhile spread throughout Suzhou, and the streets were filling with sad, angry, and perplexed people wanting to know why villains far away in Beijing had incriminated a pure, loyal, and blameless official like Zhou. Governor Mao Yilu hoped to avoid a riot, and so, as crowds gathered at one detention site, he would move the prisoner to another. The day appointed for the public reading of the charges was April 14.

On April 13, the streets again filled with sad and angry people, as the imperial police negotiated with Zhou Shunchang's self-appointed personal agent, Zhu Zuwen, a student who worshipped Zhou, about their recompense. The police said they needed 800 taels. They said they knew Zhou Shunchang could not pay such an amount, but surely the Suzhou gentry *(xiangshen)* could donate funds in his behalf. Zhu Zuwen told them that was not possible, because of the fear that informers would denounce those who donated. Nor could Zhou's relatives and in-laws help; they were poor. But the police found resources somewhere and managed to raise some 1,300 taels for themselves.[33]

Rain was falling again in Suzhou as dawn broke on April 14. Zhou Shunchang was placed in a prisoner cart at the county magistrate's yamen, and he and his guards made their way with difficulty through thick crowds of weeping and muttering people to the Western Censorate office, where the imperial police were waiting and the charges were to be read out. At several points, Zhou had to plead for the crowd to make way so that the cart could proceed.

The Western Censorate building stood in its own walled compound. Even before the front gate had opened to admit the prisoner, some men had climbed the wall and stood around. They refused to climb down. Outside and below, the crowd increased in size. Eventually Provincial Inspector Xu Ji arrived, followed a bit later by his superior, Mao Yilu. Mao ordered the gate opened. In swarmed a great crowd of people, including some five hundred students. As they all stood in the mud left by the rain, before them on a platform in front of the building lay the prisoner, while above him stood two imperial police officers. Near at hand lay the fetters that would be placed on Zhou after the reading of the charges.

Several student leaders surrounded Mao Yilu. A long and heated argument began as the students, supported by the mood of the crowd, demanded to know why this unjust arrest could not be postponed and appealed, and why an imperial order forged by palace eunuch Wei

Zhongxian could not be legitimately resisted. Mao's face turned pale and sweaty from the strain. He pleaded with the students. No matter how the arrest order was arrived at, it was still an imperial order, he insisted. How could the students defy their father-ruler and still call themselves disciples of Confucius?

The argument went on and on, and the imperial police grew impatient. The crowd pressed closer and closer in order to hear what the students were saying. Xu Ji seemed to sympathize with the students. Mao Yilu was promising them that he would submit a memorial to the throne that expressed their concerns.

The appointed noon hour for the formal reading of the charges came and went. The patience of the imperial police was wearing thin. They made motions to get on with the ceremony. One of them called the students "rats with no right to stick their mouths in." Several commoners in the crowd (later to win immortality as the "Five Men") shouted back that the arrest order was illegal. Then, all of a sudden, as the students shrank out of the way, the hecklers mounted the platform and assaulted the imperial police. The crowd below began flinging stones and tiles and wooden mud-clogs at them. The police covered their heads and scattered. One climbed a tree and got on the Censorate roof. Another hid in a latrine. Imperial policeman Li Guozhu escaped over the wall of the compound, but the crowd outside seized him and kicked him to death.

While the mêlée was in progress, Mao Yilu and Xu Ji managed to call in a local defense unit for protection. Prefect Kou Shen and Magistrate Chen Wenrui used their good reputations to go out into the crowd and urge everyone to go home, promising that they would do all in their power to protest Zhou's arrest through official channels. But it was dark before the crowds dispersed.

Late on the very same day, April 14, another squadron of imperial police, en route south to Yuyao county in Zhejiang province to arrest Huang Zunsu, had decided to stop for the night in Suzhou. Having no idea of what was taking place inside the walls, they moored their boat outside the Xu gate on the west side of Suzhou, which, unknown to them, was the gate closest to the epicenter of the riot. The guards proceeded to make the usual peremptory demands for food, drink, and accommodations. The street crowd would have none of it. Fights broke out. Word spread and more rioters appeared. They tossed the policemen's baggage overboard and set their boats on fire. The imperial arrest orders were lost. Most of the police escaped the mob by clinging to pieces of lumber and paddling out of harm's way. The two commanders eventually made it to Nanjing, where they informed the court by written memorial of what had happened.

For the next several days, remnants of the crowd camped in the streets and refused to go home. Zhou Shunchang, nearly forgotten in the commotion, was moved from the Western Censorate office to the Wu county yamen, where he expressed his annoyance to his devotee Zhu Zuwen. "Except for the riot, I'd be on the road by now. Why all this turmoil?" Zhou was impatient to get the whole ordeal over with. Finally, in the early morning hours of April 22, eight days after the riot, Zhou was placed on a boat, and the much harried imperial police at last made off with their prisoner for Beijing.[34] Zhou Shunchang arrived in Beijing in late May. A Palace rescript of May 23 ordered him placed in the Decree Prison.[35]

◀

But what was the Palace going to do about the riots? Let them go unpunished? Or conduct mass arrests? Rumors flew about Suzhou that mass arrests and executions were imminent, and many people began fleeing from the city.

In Beijing, some of the anti-Donglin officials in power urged savage reprisals. Palace eunuch Wei Zhongxian was ultimately responsible for delivering imperial edicts and rescripts, so everything depended on how he was persuaded. It is related that Suzhou native Xu Ruke, on duty as chief minister of the Court of Imperial Entertainment, lobbied hard with chief Grand Secretary Gu Bingqian to convince him that harsh retaliation would (1) jeopardize the vital flow of Suzhou tax revenue to Beijing and (2) invite a mob attack on the grand secretary's own family estate in nearby Kunshan county.[36]

It is also related that when the first reports of the Suzhou riot reached Wei Zhongxian, he burst into the Grand Secretariat yelling that "the emperor was angry" and demanding that the grand secretaries draft a rescript calling for harsh retaliation. Gu Bingqian was sick at home. But Grand Secretary Ding Shaoshi convinced Wei that a harsh crackdown might provoke another riot as well as cause serious revenue losses.[37]

Thanks to such representations, the Palace in its rescript of May 5 made the prudent decision "not to deeply probe" the matter.[38] Mao Yilu and Xu Ji were instructed to identify and punish a few ringleaders, no more.

The "Five Men" who incited the riot were executed on August 28. Five student leaders were expelled. A few other rioters were flogged and exiled. The legal case was thereby closed, but the rioters as moral heroes lived on in history and literature, and in dramatic presentations on the popular stage.[39]

Huang Zunsu

There was still Huang Zunsu to be arrested. Imperial police had been sent to fetch him, but their mission was aborted by the riot in Suzhou on April 14. The Palace decided not to send another mission. Instead, it ordered the governors of Zhejiang province to make the arrest. The governors in turn ordered the Yuyao county magistrate to go to Huang Zunsu's house with troops and fetch him.

The magistrate did so. But Huang Zunsu was not there! The magistrate guessed that he had fled into hiding. Actually, after hearing what had happened in Suzhou, Huang had gone on his own to the prefectural capital of Shaoxing to turn himself in. "Even if I covered my head and hid like a rat I would not escape death," wrote Huang to the magistrate. "How can you think so little of us real men of the realm?"[40]

In Shaoxing, there was an opportunity for Huang to have a meal at a Buddhist temple with a philosopher and former colleague Liu Zongzhou. There were tears. Huang and Liu discussed "national right" (guoshi). Liu came away realizing that he had not yet achieved sufficient psychic equilibrium to get through the "barrier between life and death" without his heart racing out of control.[41]

By early June, the Zhejiang provincial authorities delivered prisoner Huang Zunsu to Beijing, and a Palace rescript of June 13 ordered him placed in the Decree Prison for interrogation under torture.[42]

◀

The interrogations of the men who had arrived in Beijing in May were already long under way. According to rumor, which the Palace evidently believed to be true, Miao Changqi was the actual writer of Yang Lian's "Twenty-four Crimes" memorial of 1624, and Prison Director Xu Xianchun applied especially heavy torture to him for that reason. Miao was initially asked why he had associated with Yang and Zuo to do such a thing. Miao's reported reply was: "When Yang Lian was magistrate of

Changshu [in 1608–1614], I visited with him. Zuo was a year-mate of mine. We were friends. Why wouldn't I associate with them? And I don't know what you mean by 'such a thing.' " Miao also denied ever having accepted bribes. "The Hanlin academy is a 'cold' office; it has always prided itself on its purity and honor. How would I engage in bribery?" The Palace was not satisfied with these "vague and unclear" replies and demanded further interrogation under torture.[43]

After ten days of interrogating him under torture, Prison Director Xu Xianchun reported that Miao Changqi had confessed to having taken 1,000 taels in bribes. The Palace was not satisfied with that amount, nor with the 5,200 that fellow prisoner Zhou Zongjian had confessed to, and it demanded that Xu Xianchun press both men harder.[44] On May 20, the Palace finally agreed to the revised figures of 3,000 taels from Miao and 7,000 from Zhou.[45] Meanwhile, prisoner Li Yingsheng arrived in Beijing. On May 18, the Palace ordered him placed in the Decree Prison for interrogation under torture and the restitution of all bribes.[46]

At this juncture, chief Grand Secretary Gu Bingqian unburdened himself of some misgivings about the interrogations going on in the Decree Prison. In a memorial to the emperor, he said that the Grand Secretariat had been routinely endorsing the rescripts relating to Miao and Zhou that were issuing from the Palace, but just now, he said, a eunuch had told them orally that a rescript was en route from the Palace ordering Li Yingsheng to be placed in the Decree Prison, and the Grand Secretariat would surely endorse that; however, he suggested that after their interrogations, Miao, Zhou, and Li should be sent before the judicial authorities of the outer court, so that the officials there could examine and restate their crimes in an open and credible way. Should the prisoners die in their present custody without appearing before the *fasi*, then, predicted Gu, the people of the realm will think they were all unjustly killed in the "black prison," and, instead of vilifying them, will mourn them as martyrs.[47] To this memorial the Palace did not reply.

Having confessed to 3,000 taels, Miao Changqi was subjected to the bribe-restitution procedure. Every five days his family servants had to produce so much silver, while Miao lay ready to be beaten and tortured if they failed. On or about May 24, Miao died "of illness." On May 26, the Palace ordered officials to verify the identity of the corpse and deliver it to his relatives for burial. It demanded that the provincial officials press from his family the balance of the 3,000 taels with which he was charged.[48]

Meanwhile, prisoner Zhou Shunchang at last arrived in Beijing from Suzhou, and on May 23 he was ordered to be placed in the Decree Prison. Zhou's student and admirer, Zhu Zuwen, had already reached Beijing twenty days earlier and had worked frantically during that time to set up a system for the repayment of the bribes, amount yet to be determined, with which Zhou would be charged. Zhou had provided Zhu with letters for Sun Qifeng and Lu Shanji, who had helped Yang and Zuo when they were arrested in 1625.

On the afternoon of May 11, Zhu Zuwen (who recorded everything in his diary) reached the Lu homestead in Dingxing county. Lu Shanji was no longer on duty at Shanhaiguan but was right there, at home. He ordered a servant to take Zhu to see Sun Qifeng in Rongcheng county, some eight or nine miles south. They arrived that night. Sun urged that Zhu contact Wang Qimin, an Embroidered-uniform Guards officer who had helped Wei Dazhong the year before.

Zhu departed from Rongcheng at once and reached Beijing early the next morning. Security in the city was tight. He needed a place to stay. What about the Zong family, whom his father had known in military service? Zhu went to their gate, and spoke with two of the Zong sons. They explained that it was unsafe for them to take him in. There were spies everywhere. They could not let him leave baggage there either. They suggested that Zhu and the two servants of Zhou Shunchang who were with him look for an inn.

Zhu was carrying 500 taels' worth of silver deposit tickets from Suzhou. He desperately needed to find some trustworthy people in Beijing who would agree to redeem them, so that Zhu would have the silver in hand whenever the Decree Prison decided that the repayments should begin. Meanwhile he hunted up Jiang Shiheng, a family friend from Suzhou who was a student in the Imperial College and was living in student lodgings. He asked Jiang to contact Xu Ruke (minister of the Court of Imperial Entertainments) and Gu Zongmeng (a censor), both Suzhou natives, and to ask them to arrange with Wang Qimin for a safe place to redeem the silver tickets. Zhu did not know Wang Qimin personally and could not approach him himself. Zhu stayed overnight in Jiang's dormitory bed.

At dawn on May 15, student Jiang went out to look for Xu and Gu. After a long time, he returned and told Zhu that he had learned that Wang Qimin had been removed from service, but that Xu Ruke and Gu Zongmeng had agreed to help with the silver. They suggested another

Embroidered-uniform Guards officer—Zhu Ruzhong, a Suzhou native—
as a good person to help set up a facility for redeeming the tickets. Zhu
Zuwen at once contacted Zhu Ruzhong, gave him the silver tickets, and
begged him for a place to stay. However, the officer refused, directing
him instead to a Buddhist temple. Over the next several days, Zhu Zuwen
deployed Zhou Shunchang's servants on various errands, endeavoring all
the while to ensure that their activities were inconspicuous to the ever-
present spies and informers. A "climate of fear" *(weihuo jingxiang)* lay
thick over Beijing.

On the night of May 20, Zhou Shunchang and his police escort
reached Beijing. Family servant Qian Zhen had accompanied them, and
somehow he found Zhu Zuwen and told him some other bad news—that
prisoner Zhou Zongjian's son had not come, and that Zhou Zongjian
had only four servants to help him; and that city police had arrested
Huang Zunsu's father, confiscated the 50 taels he had on him, and released him only after receiving a further 500 taels' bribe.[49]

Zhu Zuwen did not dare try to see Zhou Shunchang in person. For
news of him he relied on Zhou's servants, who had taken quarters near
the Decree Prison. They said Zhou had been tortured for the first time
on May 23, and on May 25 was charged with having taken 2,000 taels in
bribes.

Two thousand taels! How could such a huge sum be raised? Zhu Zuwen spent a sleepless night thinking about it. It was a fifty-day round trip
from Beijing to Suzhou and back!

A servant delivered to Zhu a note from Zhou in prison, in which Zhou
urged that Zhu himself should return to Suzhou. Meanwhile Zhu received news that the amount charged to Zhou had been raised to 3,000
taels, and that installments of 100 taels every five days was the repayment
rate demanded by the Decree Prison. Zhu decided not to return to Suzhou himself, but to send servant Tang Yuan there with letters for Zhou's
friends asking them for money. Zhu himself went back to Dingxing county to find Lu Shanji and Sun Qifeng and have them help collect silver
nearer Beijing.

On May 28, three mounted patrolmen stopped Zhu Zuwen and the
two servants accompanying him south from Beijing. Zhu and one servant
distracted the patrolmen with talk, giving servant Tang Yuan the opportunity to destroy the letters he was carrying to Zhou Shunchang's friends
in Suzhou. Finding nothing suspicious, the patrolmen let them all go. After that narrow escape, they proceeded to Zhuozhou, forty miles south-

west of Beijing, where they parted ways, servant Tang Yuan for Suzhou, and Zhu Zuwen and the other servant for Dingxing.

On May 30, Zhu Zuwen appeared at Lu Shanji's gate, and they discussed the situation. Sun Qifeng was summoned. He and Lu agreed to help with funeral arrangements in case Zhou Shunchang died in prison. They also agreed to fan out and ask friends in north China to make loans or contributions of silver in Zhou's behalf.[50]

◀

At exactly this juncture—with Miao Changqi dead and prisoners Zhou Shunchang, Zhou Zongjian, Li Yingsheng, and Huang Zunsu undergoing abuse in the Decree Prison, servant Tang Yuan en route to Suzhou, and Zhu Zuwen in Dingxing arranging silver collections—a series of tremendous explosions occurred in Beijing at around nine o'clock in the morning of May 31. Shock waves caused damage in the Forbidden City. A timber was blown off the Huangji palace, which was then undergoing reconstruction. In the emperor's private apartment in the Qianqing palace, some big screens fell over, injuring two eunuchs. There was damage in Wei Zhongxian's office.[51] According to one story, the emperor was in the palace dining hall when the explosions occurred. He ran out in panic, followed by a eunuch, who was struck in the head by a tile from the Jianji palace, some distance away. Tianqi was fortunate to escape harm.[52]

It took some hours before officials were able to investigate and inform the Palace of what had happened. Censor Wang Yehao ventured on horseback out into the smoke and fire and reported that he saw "women and children and old people weeping in the streets and realized many buildings had been destroyed and many people crushed. I urged my horse ahead and saw crowds fleeing in panic because the elephant house had been destroyed and the elephants were running loose." Censor Wang ascertained that gunpowder stored in big jars in an arsenal known as the Wanggongchang, adjacent to the elephant house, had exploded.[53] The arsenal lay about two miles southeast of the Qianqing palace.

In the days following, the authorities determined the extent of the damage: 537 male and female casualties, and some twenty thousand units of housing leveled. Tianqi contributed 10,000 taels of his own silver for relief purposes.[54]

By edict of June 1, the Palace—perhaps it was even Tianqi himself—expressed deep unease about the portentous implications of this awful

catastrophe. The emperor announced that he would undergo ritual puri-
fication and then conduct a solemn sacrifice at the imperial ancestral temple. All the officials were commanded to don plain costume and "wash
their minds" before doing their duties. Everyone must introspect. Ways
to stop "Heaven's disorders" needed to be found. And the prisoners in
the Decree Prison could rejoice: the Palace ordered the suspension of all
tortures and punishments![55]

◀

Down in Dingxing county, Zhu Zuwen learned of the explosion in Beijing two days after it happened. Later he read the details in the Capital
Gazette and was especially cheered by the imperial edict of expiation and
stay of punishments. He thought it likely that Zhou Shunchang might
survive and continued the job of arranging loans and contributions with
renewed vigor. He did note, however, that "this area is desolate and there
are very few rich families in it." By June 13, he had collected a mere 300
taels from some half-dozen different sources.[56]

On June 15, accompanied by a servant of Lu Shanji's, Zhu returned to
Beijing with the 300 taels and gave it to Zha Xianke, an imperial college
student, who in turn passed it to one of Zhou Shunchang's servants for
delivery to the Decree Prison. Zhu noted that the Beijing gate tax had
doubled since the previous month, and that the atmosphere (*qixiang*) of
the city was even tenser than it had been. On June 19, Zhu received a personal note from Zhou Shunchang. Zhou was worried about the silver
repayments. He urged Zhu to go to Wuqiao county, some 150 miles south
of Beijing, to look into the possibility of raising funds from Fan Jingwen,
an official colleague who lived there.

Zhu did not know Fan Jingwen, but he left Beijing and on June 24
came to Lu Shanji's gate in Dingxing. Lu knew Fan well: "That is one of
the best men in the realm!" he exclaimed. He wrote a letter of introduc-
tion and plea for funds and gave it to Zhu. Zhu then visited Sun Qifeng
at Rongcheng, and over the next several days, June 28 to July 2, he made
his way on horseback in intense heat over the hundred miles from Rongcheng south to Wuqiao.

Fan Jingwen was receptive. Out of friendship for Lu Shanji, he agreed
to help raise a loan of 300 taels. Together with silver forthcoming from
Suzhou, and from Xu Ruke and other friends of Zhou's in Beijing, Zhu

Zuwen calculated that he would have a total of 800 taels, which should suffice to meet the five-day payments for some weeks yet and spare Zhou the abuse for failure to meet payment deadlines.[57]

Fan Jingwen promised to forward as soon as possible the 300 taels to Lu Shanji, so Zhu left Wuqiao on July 7, and after another hot ride reached Sun Qifeng's place in Rongcheng on July 11. Zhu was worried that all his travels might have attracted the notice of informers. Sun agreed to have his younger brother Sun Qiyan make the next silver-delivery trip to Beijing; and while he reassured Zhu that he had "one or two" contacts among the palace eunuchs who could extend some protection, he agreed that Zhu should do as Wei Xueyi had done, and not make himself conspicuous.[58]

Zhu arrived at Lu Shanji's place the next day. On July 14, Fan Jingwen's emissary appeared with 200 taels and an elaborate explanation from Fan as to his failure to gather the full amount of 300 that he had promised. No matter. On July 15, Sun Qifeng's brother, accompanied by a servant of Zhou Shunchang's and a servant of Lu Shanji's, left Dingxing county for Beijing with 380 taels—Fan's 200, plus 180 collected by Lu Shanji—to deliver to those in Beijing who were managing the silver fund in Zhou Shunchang's behalf.[59]

It was all in vain. On July 17, Zhou's servant returned from Beijing with the shattering news that Zhou Shunchang had died in the Decree Prison. Zhu Zuwen was devastated. "I had every hope that the emperor was regulating his conduct because of the adverse portents," he wrote in his diary. "I never expected this, and I am extremely disturbed. I couldn't talk, even to Lu [Shanji], and Lu too was distraught."[60]

◀

Zhu Zuwen later learned the details of what had happened to Zhou Shunchang in the Decree Prison. An unexplained hardening in the Palace's plans for Zhou and the other remaining prisoners had indeed taken place.

For a while, it had appeared as though the torture murders might be called off altogether. Some leading anti-Donglin officials in the bureaucracy were persuaded that the killings must now stop. Zhang Lüduan, a bureau secretary in the Ministry of War, drafted a memorial stating, among other things, that the Decree Prison abuses were ruining the emperor's virtue, and that, in order to ensure justice, the prisoners and their cases should be turned over to the *fasi*. He took the draft to his superior, Minister of War Wang Yongguang, who gave it careful thought, and on or about June 2, revised it and submitted it in his own name to the Palace. In the course of his wide-ranging criticism of the Palace, Minister Wang called attention to a "serious situation" in the Decree Prison, where "people have been killed in the process of recovering bribes. . . . I ask that henceforth all penal cases be given to the legal authorities, that punishments be reduced, and that there be shown concern for the children, grandchildren, and parents of the victims."[61]

On June 15, the unease initiated by the arsenal explosion was further deepened by an unexplained fire that burned down the Chadian palace, some two miles northwest of the Forbidden City, once occupied by the Yongle emperor but now used by the officials to rehearse rituals and store their ceremonial robes.[62] On June 18, Minister of Rites Li Sicheng publicly interpreted that fire as a sign of Heaven's displeasure, insisted that "everyone" agreed with what Wang Yongguang had said in his memorial of early June, and urged the emperor to heed it.[63] On June 19, Wang Yongguang spoke out again in defense of what he had stated earlier.[64] On June 24, Minister of Personnel Wang Shaohui, a notorious hater of the Donglin, sent up an emotional plea in behalf of the prisoners whose "wails of grief and resentment rise, but nowhere can they appeal."[65] On June 28, there were earthquake tremors in Beijing. Early in the morning of June 29, an infant son of Tianqi's died.[66]

Almost inexplicably, in the face of these mounting signs of Heaven's anger and the protests coming in from the top levels of the bureaucracy, the Palace took a defiant stance. A long, rambling Palace edict of July 4 restated the criminal acts and refractory behavior that Zhou Zongjian, Zhou Shunchang, and the others had engaged in; they had brought on their own torments—by taking themselves so lightly, by humiliating the ruler, by placing blame on the Palace for their own misdeeds; the emperor was being forbearing and was actually treating them leniently; those officials who were questioning what was going on in the Decree Prison should calmly ask themselves whether they thought the ruler was really acting on the basis of mere whim and rumor. Surely they knew he had unimpeachable evidence of the crimes charged![67]

Minister of Personnel Wang Shaohui sent up a rejoinder to that edict on July 5. He argued that the "villain clique" had already been extirpated and that the unnecessary prolongation of the repression was creating resentment. The Palace called Minister Wang's rejoinder inappropriate and rejected it.[68] So the Decree Prison tortures resumed.

◀

Prisoner Zhou Shunchang, from the time he was placed in the Decree Prison on May 23, refused to confess to anything. He was aware of the perfidy of the Palace the year before, when it had promised leniency to Zuo Guangdou and the others and then reneged on its promise. According to the report of his personal servant Gu Xuan, Zhou's first day of interrogation featured forty blows with the stick, sixty squeezes with the ankle crusher, and a hundred and twenty applications of the finger press. After the arsenal explosion of May 31, things eased for him. Torture resumed on or about July 4, when he received ten blows with the stick.

On July 9, it appears that Zhou suffered another round of torture, after which he stumbled while wearing a heavy cangue on his neck, struck his head on a stone, and bled profusely. A discussion was witnessed between Wei Zhongxian and Prison Director Xu Xianchun. It is not known what was said. However, the Decree Prison reported to the Palace on July 10 that Zhou Shunchang had "died of illness." According to servant Gu Xuan, Zhou was smothered to death by jailer Yan Zi (the same guard who had killed several Donglin prisoners the year before) sometime during the middle of the night July 9–10. On July 13, the Palace ordered Zhou's corpse verified and released, and it directed that the provincial *fuan* (Mao Yilu and Xu Ji) force his family back in Suzhou to pay the remainder of his silver assessment.[69]

Former Censor Zhou Zongjian also died sometime during the night of July 10. Censor Zhou had been in the Decree Prison since May 5. His initial dose of torture featured finger presses applied to each hand, an ankle press on one leg, eighty blows with a big stick, and forty blows with a light stick. Zhou confessed at first to having taken 5,200 taels in bribes, a figure with which the Palace was not satisfied. On May 20, the Palace agreed to a new confession of 13,500 taels. Collection deadlines were announced, at first every five days, then every three. Then he, like Zhou Shunchang, was taken to the "black room" and killed by jailor Yan Zi, either with a rock on his chest or a sandbag over his face, or perhaps both.[70] On the next day, July 11, the Decree Prison announced Zhou's death "of illness." Zhou's corpse was released five days later. The provincial *fuan*, Mao Yilu and Xu Ji, were ordered to collect from his family all the silver remaining on his account.[71]

Four of the original "Seven *junzi*" in the arrest orders of 1626 were dead: one (Gao Panlong) by suicide, the others by secret murder in the Decree Prison. That left Li Yingsheng and Huang Zunsu still alive in the prison and Zhou Qiyan still in transit from Fujian.

On June 25, Prison Director Xu Xianchun presiding, Huang Zunsu was heavily beaten and abused and charged with having taken 2,800 taels in bribes. It was arranged that repayments be made every three days. Whenever the payments failed, Huang was flogged forty times with the heavy stick.[72] Unfortunately Huang's father was discovered and arrested in Beijing, as was noted above. That left Huang's son, sixteen-year-old Huang Zongxi, in charge of collecting silver in Beijing to meet the installment payments, which meant taking out loans from Zhejiang merchants in the capital and dunning his father's colleagues for whatever they could contribute.[73]

Huang Zongxi was making good progress collecting money when on July 23 a friendly guard warned Huang Zunsu that a "eunuch-transmitted Palace directive" *(neichuan)* ordered him to be killed that night, and that he should write down any final arrangements he wished to make. According to a later statement of his son's, Huang Zunsu then kowtowed facing north, thanked the emperor for his mercy, and wrote a poem of which the last two lines read: "[My] upright *qi* will forever linger sadly over the seas and mountains; resolutely I go off—what more is there for me to seek?"[74] On July 23 (the date was later confirmed by a merchant who was a cell-mate) Huang was taken away and killed. On July 27, the Palace issued what by now had become its routinely false and delayed statement that Huang had died "of illness." Provincial officials back in Zhejiang were ordered to recover the remainder of his assessment from his family.[75]

Li Yingsheng was put in the Decree Prison on May 18. Some time in June he was able to have smuggled out a letter to his father back in Jiangyin county:

I was interrogated as soon as I got here and was injured badly, but there's been no more, and I'm still alive. After a month lying down, the wounds still haven't healed; they need another month....Once the bribes are fully repaid, I'm to be sent to the Ministry of Justice. Now they're doing collections every five days. I'm desperate to get a letter from home. There's no way to appeal here, no way to escape torture. Here in prison I worry about the payments by day and suffer pain at night, but I'm in good spleen and my health is strong and I have more food and drink than before, which should relieve some of your worries.... I've gotten you parents in trouble over [my love of] honor *(mingjie)*....[76]

The assessment charge against Li was 4,000 taels of silver.[77] A second letter to his father was smuggled from prison some time in July. Li still hoped he might survive the ordeal, but things were not looking favorable for him:

> I still have some hope of surviving this, but I worry that the silver might not arrive. Yangsu [Liu Yangsu, a friend] has been rushing here and there, and he's been able to redeem 1,000 taels, thanks to my friends. Recently things had eased because of the ominous disaster [the arsenal explosion], but now they've tightened again. You see cruel wounds [on the prisoners]. Myself and Bo'an [Huang Zunsu] are the only ones [of the original group] still alive. And they've gotten very severe on collection days. Twice I've received thirty blows of the heavy stick. Bo'an has let me use a lot of his silver. I'm really indebted to him. Elder brother [i.e., his elder cousin, Li Yimao, a minor official] has been sick all month, and Yangsu has had a hard time running about, plus he's been looking after each one of the family servants.[78]

A final farewell note dated noon on July 25 was smuggled out to Li's father. Five days later, responding to a Decree Prison report of Li's death "by illness," the Palace issued its usual rescript. Li's corpse, on release, was scarcely recognizable. Neither Li Yimao nor Liu Yangsu was ever able to learn the details of how or when Li Yingsheng died.[79]

The last of the "Seven *junzi*," former governor Zhou Qiyuan, arrived in Beijing early in August. A Palace rescript of August 9 charged him with having embezzled and received in bribes a total of 100,000 taels.[80] Three-day repayment deadlines were imposed, and heavy torture was applied. As in the case of the others, the Palace did not intend to wait long, and on November 1, Zhou's death "by illness" was reported by the prison, and the Fujian provincial officials were ordered to collect the remainder of what he owed from his family.[81]

◀

What did the Tianqi court intend to accomplish by all these arrests? During the years 1625–1626 it purged hundreds of presumed Donglin sympathizers from the government, while singling out thirteen of their leaders for the special treatment just described.

The court could not have made its intentions more plain. The prisoners were not, after all, arrested and spirited away in secret. They were made to stand in broad daylight before the general public while the crimes with which they were charged were read out for everyone to hear. They were then taken away in cages mounted on carts, like zoo animals on exhibit, so everyone could see their humiliation. Obviously, the people were being invited to share in the Tianqi court's moral indignation, rally to the court's side, and, perhaps, rage in anger at the miscreants whose misdeeds their ever-vigilant government had exposed.

Evidently, the court had endorsed at least partway the Donglin's own philosophy. It agreed with the Donglin that the men of this world are divided into the two colors white and black, into "gentlemen" and "small men," into selfless heroes and deceitful and corrupt villains. It differed with the Donglin only on the derivative question of the identity of the men to whom the labels ought to apply.

There is more. That the arrests were made in public shows that the Tianqi court was morally serious, that it believed it was right in what it was doing. Now it was Donglin belief that, in the final analysis, the absolutist moral philosophy expounded by the few derived from the inchoate moral leanings of all the people of China. The name for this was the "national right" (*guoshi*). "National right," once wrote Miao Changqi, "emerges from the unforced collective mentality (*qunxin zhi ziran*) and it expresses itself in a unison of voices. As such, it is determined neither by the ruler nor by the court officials, but by every man and woman in the realm. That which every man and woman in the realm labels as right or wrong, neither the ruler nor the officials may overrule."[82] Elsewhere, he explained: "Because the common men and women have no part in governing the realm, they abide it passively, yet they see it clearly. It penetrates their breasts, rises to their throats, and rushes out their mouths, and this is how right and wrong in the realm gets determined."[83]

As though acting upon this belief, the Tianqi court took its case over and over again to the people of China as they gathered in the streets and yamens, and it asked them, in effect, to serve as the ultimate bar of moral judgment and to validate the purging the court was endeavoring to carry out.

But, judging from the reactions it kept getting in the streets, the court failed in its appeal to the people's sense of what was right and wrong. Those whom the court would label villains, the people considered heroes. Even children got involved. Spectators were amused to watch young street boys making a game of flogging each other to unconsciousness. "We're strengthening our bones and tendons to await the day when we become loyal officials at court!" the boys explained.[84]

Indeed, the Tianqi court was able to sustain its public stance of commanding moral righteousness only to a certain point. In Beijing, the court never went so far as to sentence Yang Lian and the other Donglin prisoners to public execution, because, clearly, it could never develop a sufficiently convincing case against them. Nor could it release the prisoners, in part because that would call into question the justification for the purge of the hundreds of lesser Donglin officials that was then in progress. Thus the Tianqi court groped for the tools of secret murder and overt terror.

But the Tianqi regime intended that the utter extirpation of the Donglin faction should be its opening card, not its final act. It clearly hoped to put the repression behind it, relegate it to past history, and move on to develop an attractive new political ethos for China and give its attention to solving the Manchurian and other crises that had been bedeviling the Ming court for so long.

CHAPTER 5

Repression, Triumph, Joy, Collapse
(1625–1627)

◀

THE TIANQI REGIME openly prided
itself on three main achievements. First, it had worked mightily to cleanse
China of the Donglin and all its lingering influences. Second, it had man-
aged to finish the expensive rebuilding of three decaying palaces in the
Forbidden City. Third, after years of Ming defeat, it had scored two en-
couraging military victories in Manchuria (at Ningyuan and Jinzhou).
These things it somehow accomplished in the short space of three years.
Then, in the fall of 1627, the Tianqi emperor died, and the whole Tianqi
order collapsed forthwith. The triumphs, the new anti-Donglin vision for
China espoused by the regime, and then the precipitous demise of the
whole affair all shed light on the intensely personal nature of political
power in the late Ming era.

The repressiveness of the Tianqi order owed much to the vengeful anger of its principal actors. Key players in the regime shared one experience
in common—one or more stinging personal rebuffs by an exclusive, self-
styled moral elite of superior men *(junzi)*. The Donglin attitude of
absolute self-righteousness seemed to create enemies as a natural by-
product: Fu Kui, Ruan Dacheng, and Wei Guangwei, to name just three,
not to speak of Wei Zhongxian (who at the outset had tried to reach out
to Donglin men), and even Tianqi himself.

Feng Quan and Cui Chengxiu

The brilliant but flawed Feng Quan was one of the prime movers behind
the Donglin repression. He too had been stung by Donglin moral barbs.
A northerner from Zhuozhou, he had won his metropolitan degree in
1613 at the exceptionally young age of eighteen and was placed in the
Hanlin academy. Sometime late in the Wanli era, Feng's father, a military
intendant in Liaoyang, was impeached for deserting his post. In vain did
Feng turn to his colleagues for help in clearing his father. Even his close
friend Miao Changqi (in 1626 a Donglin martyr) for some reason turned

against him and repeatedly humiliated him in front of others.[1] Because of the impeachment of his father, Feng Quan was forced to resign from government and return home. Then, early in 1624, Wei Zhongxian made a ceremonial visit to Zhuozhou (where Fu Kui and Ruan Dacheng also contacted him); and there, according to rumor, Feng Quan knelt before the eunuch and in tears explained how the Donglin had ruined his father, and Wei Zhongxian, always eager to have support in the bureaucracy, helped him recover his Hanlin post. Wei Zhongxian desperately needed that support when Yang Lian submitted his "Twenty-four Crimes" memorial in July 1624. Feng made covert contact with the embattled eunuch's nephew, Wei Liangqing, and through him advised that the "outer court was nothing to be afraid of" and that it could be "cut and controlled" by "big cases" (i.e., the prosecution of political crimes) and the reinstitution of court flogging. And so it turned out.

As did many others who opposed the Donglin, Feng Quan enjoyed the good things of life. The late Ming was an era of urban commercial growth and increasingly sophisticated life-styles and patterns of consumption among the elite. Many Donglin partisans defied this trend. Feng Quan did not. According to the memoirs of eunuch Liu Ruoyu, who knew him, the handsome young Feng Quan always dressed in the finest clothing, constantly checked his appearance in a mirror, and avidly collected valuable antiques, rare books, and lovely concubines. A filial son, Feng saw to it that his mother lived like an empress. He once gave a great party on the occasion of his mother's departing Beijing for Zhuozhou. She was showered with gifts from Wei Zhongxian and others; she was surrounded by an entourage of twenty or thirty beautifully dressed maids and other attendants; and on her procession south to Zhuozhou people cleared the roads for her. To onlookers it appeared as though she were leading a foreign embassy.[2]

Liu Ruoyu has it that Feng Quan created strategy from behind the scenes during the final imprisonment and torture of Donglin power broker Wang Wenyan in the spring of 1625. Feng Quan, Cui Chengxiu, and others conferred at night; Wei Liangqing delivered their plans to palace eunuchs Li Yongzhen and Li Chaoqin, who read them aloud to the illiterate Wei Zhongxian, who then forwarded instructions via Li Chaoqin to the recorder sitting behind Prison Director Xu Xianchun at the interrogation sessions. According to Liu, Xu would not proceed without those instructions.[3]

In April 1625, the Palace approved a big bill impeaching four Donglin men (including Zhou Zongjian, Li Yingsheng, and Huang Zunsu) and recommending ten anti-Donglin men. The memorialist was not one of the expected speaking officials, that is, censors or supervising secretaries, but a bureau secretary in the Ministry of Works, a Jiangxi man by the name of Cao Qincheng.[4] Feng Quan had been his examiner on the classics portion of the metropolitan exams when Cao achieved his degree in 1619, which created a "student–teacher" bond of obligation between them. Feng Quan called in his former examinee Cao and dictated to him what he wanted him to do. Cao protested that he was not a speaking official and had no business impeaching those who were. According to testimony given by Cao in 1629, Feng then grew angry, saying, "I've already agreed to it, so of course you'll do it." Cao left in fright. A few days after that, Feng called him in again and had his ally Li Lusheng show him a draft of what he wanted. "I've shown this draft to my old examiner, [Grand Secretary] Wei Guangwei, and he's agreed to it," said Li. "If you decline, you'll be in trouble. You attached yourself to the gate of [Donglin partisan] Zou Yuanbiao to get [him to recommend] posthumous honors for your father, so you have no choice." Li warned Cao not to say anything of this. Cao yielded to the blackmail. That night a copyist came to Cao's house and put the draft into proper form as a memorial from Cao, and the next morning Cao reluctantly presented it at the Palace, which was expecting it.

Then, continued Cao in his confession, early in 1626 Feng Quan demanded that Cao agree to send up yet another big impeachment, this one charging Zhou Shunchang and the other six of conspiracy to overthrow the regime. This time Cao refused. He did not say why. Feng Quan had him removed from civil service. In March–April 1626, Cao was on his way home when, he said, some thirty agents of Feng Quan descended upon him at an inn in Xuzhou, on the Grand Canal four hundred miles south of Beijing. Cao hid under a horse trough. Innkeeper Wang Er was killed in the fracas. The agents gathered up Cao's books, papers, and baggage and burned them, to destroy any evidence that might incriminate Feng.[5]

On September 13, 1625, Feng Quan was one of four new men appointed to the Grand Secretariat. At thirty, he may have been the youngest grand secretary in Ming history. Within a matter of days, he actively intrigued to help bring about the dismissal of Grand Secretary Wei Guangwei when Wei showed that he could no longer stomach the ongoing torture murders of the Donglin men.[6]

As grand secretary, Feng hastened the destruction of Xiong Tingbi. Since the Ming collapse of 1622 in Manchuria, both Xiong Tingbi and Wang Huazhen had been held in the prison of the Ministry of Justice while arguments raged over their punishment. The Donglin rallied, or were accused of rallying, behind Xiong. On September 22, 1625, the emperor attended a tutorial in the Wenhua palace, and on that occasion Feng, allegedly in agreement with the other grand secretaries, showed the ruler a printed book called "The Liaodong Story" *(Liaodong zhuan)*, which had been purchased in the streets of Beijing. In its forty-eight episodes, it glamorized Xiong Tingbi. Feng told the emperor that Xiong Tingbi was himself the author.[7] Four days later, the Palace issued a thunderous edict denouncing the awful *Liaodong zhuan* as the last of Xiong Tingbi's "terrible and unforgivable crimes" and ordering his immediate execution. Apparently, the execution took place on September 27.[8]

In February 1626, Feng Quan was appointed one of the three main working editors of the *Sanchao yaodian* (Essential canon of three reigns). Surprisingly, within days of the July publication of that anti-Donglin monument, the young grand secretary was impeached for gross corruption and malfeasance. On July 24, the Palace ordered him to retire home pending clarification of "public opinion" *(gonglun)* on his case.[9] Wei Zhongxian from that point tended to ignore the Grand Secretariat and look to Cui Chengxiu in the outer court as his main source of bureaucratic support.

Like Feng, Cui Chengxiu also had a personal score to settle, because he had been devastatingly humiliated by the Donglin in the past. Cui was twenty years older than Feng, though he won his metropolitan degree in 1613, the same year Feng did. Cui was also a northerner, from Jizhou, fifty miles east of Beijing. In 1624, Cui returned to Beijing for reassignment upon completing a three-year tour of duty as regional inspector of Yangzhou and Huaian.[10] Before reassignment, it was necessary that his record be reviewed and cleared. Here Cui fell into serious trouble.

Gao Panlong, head of the Donglin academy, now censor-in-chief, had already heard bad things about Cui Chengxiu from local students when he traveled north upon being recalled to government service in 1621.[11] Meanwhile other regional censors had sent up damaging reports about Cui's accepting a bribe of several thousand taels in return for recommending a promotion for a salt official. Censor Yuan Huazhong (one of the six *junzi* killed in the Decree Prison in 1625) was sent from Beijing out to Huaian and Yangzhou to find out more about Cui's behavior there, and he returned with a long and shocking list of Cui's malfeasances, including his demand of 14,000 taels for personal expenses.

Thus, in November 1624, Censor-in-Chief Gao Panlong decided the time had come to impeach Cui. He delegated the job of writing the formal impeachment memorial to Censor Li Yingsheng. On the night of November 3, 1624, Cui Chengxiu came to Li's house and "knelt, begging to explain." Li coldly rebuffed him. On November 4, Li submitted the impeachment. On November 7, the Palace ordered Cui to stand down pending further review of his case, and it sent the matter to the outer court for discussion and recommendation.[12] Speaking for the outer court, Minister of Personnel Zhao Nanxing proposed that Cui be exiled to a garrison. Cui insisted in his own defense that the corruption charges against him were based on nothing more than idle street rumor.[13] No immediate action was taken.

Luckily for Cui, by late 1624 the tide was turning against the Donglin faction. Yang Lian's July impeachment of Wei Zhongxian had failed. The November impeachment of Grand Secretary Wei Guangwei transformed a harmless "small man" into a "mad dog that will bite anything," just as Huang Zunsu had predicted. Wei Guangwei made a back-channel link with Wei Zhongxian with a view to engineering the removals of Donglin men. And so now, in turn, Cui paid a bribe to a lower-ranking palace eunuch and through him secured the support of Wei Zhongxian. He secretly gave the Palace several new lists of pro- and anti-Donglin officials.[14] At some point, Wei Zhongxian reportedly welcomed Cui into his "family"—Cui called Wei "master" and Wei called Cui "son"—and when Wei's other "sons" gathered to kneel holding goblets and wishing the eunuch a long life, they say Cui outdid them by kneeling and holding on his head a urinal with his name incised upon it! Wei was pleased by the gesture.[15]

On February 6, 1625, a Palace rescript declared that Cui Chengxiu had been slandered, that there would be no further investigation of his case, and that he was hereby restored to his position in the Censorate.[16] As the destruction of the Donglin proceeded, Cui's star gradually rose, and Wei Zhongxian found him so effective and cooperative as a colleague that in effect he dumped Feng Quan and the Grand Secretariat and forged a direct relationship with the outer court, with Cui as censor-in-chief and concurrent minister of works. People commonly referred to this as the "Cui–Wei" regime. It lasted until Tianqi's death in 1627.

The Publication of the Sanchao yaodian

The Palace and the triumphant anti-Donglin officials felt it essential to explain in detail to future generations how both concrete facts and the fundamental principles of Confucian political morality required that the Donglin be eliminated forever as a factor in the future governance of China. It had to be shown that many of China's most admired officials and intellectuals were not the "upright men" of the "good species" they claimed to be. And solid evidentiary grounds had to be laid in order to identify all Donglin sympathizers and so justify their continuing purge.

The vehicle for making this case was the thick book called the *Sanchao yaodian* (Essential canon of the three reigns). An edict of February 10, 1626, ordered its compilation under the token general editorship of Chief Grand Secretary Gu Bingqian. It was finished in a matter of months. An edict of July 13 ordered the work printed for "distribution to the realm."[17]

The *Sanchao yaodian* reproduced, with editorial comment, memorials and other testimonies relating to the controversial Three Cases, in an effort to refute and overturn the Donglin verdict on them. It traced the origin of the Donglin error back to 1601, when Wanli had formally named Zhu Changluo as his heir apparent; and it continued the story of the controversies over the whole quarter-century down to 1626, the year of its publication.

The original crime of the Donglin partisans was to disbelieve Wanli's word on the succession and to insist that, had it not been for their constant agitation on the issue, the emperor would have deposed Zhu Changluo and given the throne to Zhu Changxun, his younger son by his favorite concubine, Lady Zheng. The *Sanchao yaodian* endeavored to prove that the Donglin objection had been unnecessary and self-serving; Wanli had never intended to depose Zhu Changluo. Yet the Donglin made a case of Zhang Chai's 1615 intrusion into the Forbidden City to argue that behind the hapless stick wielder lay an assassination plot contrived by Lady Zheng and members of her family and directed against Zhu Changluo. That was nonsense! The *Sanchao yaodian* sought to show that there had been no plot, and that Zhang Chai was a lone madman. Then the Donglin tried to argue that the death of Zhu Changluo after only one month of rule was caused by acts of deliberately negligent homicide committed as part of yet another plot by Lady Zheng and her family. Nonsense again! The *Sanchao yaodian* provided evidence to show there had been no plot and no homicide. Finally, the Donglin maintained that, except for the vigilance and forceful action undertaken by Yang Lian and Zuo Guangdou and others, Tianqi's guardian, Lady Li, acting in league with Lady Zheng, would have seized supreme power and ruled China from "behind the curtain." Again, the *yaodian* marshaled its evidence to show that Lady Li had had no such intention, and that therefore the action taken by the Donglin to drive her out of the palace in the middle of the night was not only cruel and unnecessary, but had forced Tianqi to disobey his father's heartfelt request and thereby make himself an unfilial son.

It must be said that the *Sanchao yaodian* does an effective job of calling into question the Donglin belief that the Three Cases plus the "root-of-the-state" issue were all tied together as parts of an unrelenting quarter-century of conspiracy against the security of the Ming throne. But the book's editors were not satisfied to stop there. They went on to advance a questionable conspiracy charge of their own: that the Donglin faction had conspired for years and years deliberately to destroy the emotional fiber and the moral constitution of the Ming ruling family. So states the imperial preface (Tianqi agreed that he was "too busy" to write the preface himself, so he accepted chief editor Gu Bingqian's offer to write it for him).

In the preface, Gu has the emperor charge that "villainous bandits" *(jianzei)* have made themselves appear "loyal and good" *(zhongliang)* by raising paranoid *(caicun)* suspicions about imperial family matters and, in so doing, have put under a dark cloud the emperors' true compassion as fathers and their true filial piety as sons; but now, at last, the battle is being won; uprightness is vanquishing deviance, yang is overcoming yin, and now everyone must continue to strive to root out all bandits from their hiding places in government, otherwise the whole purpose of compiling the *yaodian* will have been in vain.[18]

Listed in the *Sanchao yaodian* along with excerpts from their memorials were the names of hundreds of officials on either side of the Three Cases controversies. By Palace directive, the *yaodian* was to supplant all the earlier enemies lists, which were said to contain mistakes, and serve henceforth as the sole authoritative source for identifying good men for promotion and villains to be eliminated.[19]

Printed copies of the *Sanchao yaodian* were distributed by some means not only to the officials, but to some extent to the general public. In 1627, reportedly, a student groaned aloud while reading a copy of it in a bookshop in the Jiangxi provincial capital, whereupon a police spy "rolled up his sleeves and threatened to take him to the provincial authorities"; but a crowd intervened, and the student was fined and let go.[20]

The Suppression of Dissent

As recounted earlier, the Wei Zhongxian regime sent imperial police into the China countryside far from Beijing to bring off a dozen spectacular and terrifying arrests of leading scholar-officials of the Donglin opposition. But the regime was persuaded that more needed to be done to cleanse China of all lingering Donglin influences. Therefore it also targeted the academies that were centers for *jiangxue* ("learning through discussion") and that also served as Donglin recruitment camps.

A handful of China's many academies were known to be noxious hotbeds of *jiangxue* activity. Chief among these was, of course, the Shoushan, founded in Beijing by Feng Congwu and Zou Yuanbiao in 1622. Feng and Zou had resigned under attack late that same year. But the Shoushan, forgotten in the swirl of other excitements, remained in operation until early in 1625. In February of that year, the Palace replied to a memorial about the matter from Supervising Secretary Li Lusheng. "The Way of the Sages is as bright as the stars and sun; men study it in preparation for government careers, so why after becoming officials should they still have to discuss it?" the Palace wanted to know. "Recently some have used *daoxue* to gather factions and do self-interested things. The damage from that is not small." It thereupon ordered the Shoushan academy converted into government office space.[21] In March, in response to another memorial from Li Lusheng, the Palace changed its mind and ordered the academy made over into a shrine honoring loyal officials.[22]

Then, in August, Censor Ni Wenhuan told the Palace that although the Shoushan academy's signboard had been taken down, the stone stela with former Grand Secretary Ye Xianggao's inscription on it was still on view, which was wrong, because it allowed the followers of false *daoxue* to leave behind a "red banner" in the wake of their defeat. So the Palace ordered the Ministry of Rites to destroy the offending stela.[23] The wreckers not only smashed the stela, but allegedly they also removed Confucius' tablet from its shrine and tossed it into the street.[24] Each room in the academy was then locked and sealed and the whole building was guarded by armed guards.[25]

Beyond Beijing there were yet more dissenting academies. In May 1625, Censor Zhou Weichi explained in a memorial how hateful were the four words *qing mian men hu*—literally, "sentiment and face, gate and door," meaning the affective ties binding together those within a political clique or camp. Those four words, he said, ruin people's behavior! Real morally superior men *(junzi)* stay away from such associations altogether. He urged the emperor to put an end to all cliques by ordering the destruction of academies everywhere in China where villains gather. "The deviant clique should be allowed no place to hide," he concluded, "in order that the national right *(guoshi)* may be clarified." The Palace sent this memorial to the ministries for discussion.[26]

In September 1625, Censor Zhang Na singled out four academies elsewhere in China as especially active centers where members of the evil clique lay in wait, hoping to come back to Beijing and "challenge the supreme unifying power of the emperor." He explained that those academies attracted motley crowds of scholar-officials, relatives of the imperial house, military men, lower degree holders, Confucian students, clerks, fortunetellers, hermits, merchants, and even criminals and outlaws. Their purpose was to influence court appointments, interfere in frontier defense, and manipulate local government. By their stance in the Three Cases controversies, they were working fervently to drive out good officials and diminish the filial piety of the emperor. He further charged that those academies were in mutual contact—as indeed they were—through visits and correspondence.

The Palace rescript to Zhang's memorial ordered the four academies confiscated. Proceeds from the sales of their buildings and fields were to be sent to Beijing to help fund the ongoing palace construction projects in the Forbidden City. The leaders of those academies were ordered to be deprived of their official status.[27]

Included on the list was of course the notorious Donglin academy itself, in Wuxi. Local officials proceeded to confiscate it. In 1626, the Wuxi magistrate reported that the sale of the Donglin land and buildings yielded 687 taels of silver.[28] In Shaanxi, Feng Congwu's Guanzhong academy was dismantled, and Confucius' image was reportedly tossed by the wreckers into a corner of the Xi'an city wall, where it lay exposed to the elements. Feng Congwu was left deeply depressed, certain that his arrest was imminent; according to later testimony by his son, he fell ill and refused to eat, and he died early in 1627.[29]

The Ziyang academy in Huizhou was another target.[30] The fourth victim was the Renwen academy in Jishui county, Jiangxi, and it is perhaps fortunate that its leader, Zou Yuanbiao, had already died of natural causes and was not on hand to witness its demise. However, his successor, Li Rixuan, and his followers managed to continue their discussion meetings in secret.[31]

◀

But voices of dissent could be heard outside the academies. Some of that dissent was directed squarely at Tianqi and Wei Zhongxian. For example, just two months after Yang Lian's sensational 1624 impeachment of Wei Zhongxian, nationwide provincial-level examinations were held. Examiners in five provinces worded some of their questions in such a way as covertly to invite criticism of the emperor and his palace eunuch. The Palace was soon apprised of this matter, but Chief Grand Secretary Gu Bingqian argued successfully in March 1625 for limiting the punishments. As a result, six provincial degree winners were disqualified from taking the metropolitan exams, but only for six years; eight examiners were demoted three grades and sent away from Beijing.[32]

Also in March 1625, a strange incident took place at the imperial tutorial. Hanlin Junior Compiler Huang Daozhou (later a famous intellectual and anti-Manchu resistance leader) was supposed to bring forward the text of the day on his knees and place it before Tianqi. Instead, he walked upright. Also he brought the wrong text. Wei Zhongxian glared at him. Tianqi wanted to know who the offender was. Grand Secretary Zhu Yanxi identified him and pleaded for mercy on his behalf. The Palace agreed to "overlook" the incident.[33] Surely, however, it was a daring expression of personal contempt on Huang Daozhou's part.

Something may have stung the emperor, because four days later, at a classics tutorial on March 20, Tianqi spoke directly to the grand secretaries. "Recently some officials have formed a clique for personal purposes and I've identified them and I'm punishing them," he said. "You tell [the others] that if they renovate themselves and rectify their errors I won't probe deeply into the matter. . . . The Ministry of Personnel and the Censorate should tell that to all the large and small offices in the capital and the provinces, so each official will rid himself of old habits, and satisfy my intention to be lenient." Tianqi's words were issued verbatim in the colloquial language as an edict.[34] A few months later, however, the Palace was apprised that dissent still existed and acted forcefully to suppress it.

In November 1625, a house servant named Cheng Yuande brought to the Eastern Depot (Wei Zhongxian's police headquarters) three doc-

uments from the home of his master, a secretariat drafter by the name of
Wu Huaixian. One document was a copy of Yang Lian's "Twenty-four
Crimes" memorial of 1624, with Wu Huaixian's underlinings and supportive marginal comments. Also he turned in a copy of a letter sent in
1623 by Wu to a cousin, Wu Jing, also a secretariat drafter, in which Wu
Huaixian complained about the increasing ability of "small men" with
connections in the Palace to humiliate high officials. There was also a
copy of a letter sent in early 1625 to kinsman Wu Changqi, a bureau secretary in the Ministry of Works, in which Wu Huaixian expressed a hope
that the current regime *(jumian)* might soon collapse.

The Eastern Depot reported all this to the Palace, together with further damaging particulars; and on November 19 a Palace rescript ordered
Wu Huaixian arrested and sent to the Decree Prison for interrogation under torture.[35]

On November 23, Prison Director Xu Xianchun prepared a detailed
statement of the case. Wu Huaixian was a native of Xiuning county in
Huizhou prefecture. He was rich and, in 1596, had bought the status of a
Nanjing imperial college student. Then he murdered several locals, and
in 1623 he fled Huizhou for Beijing. In Beijing, he gave his local compatriot, the infamous Donglin power broker Wang Wenyan, a bribe of 1,600
taels, in return for which Wang Wenyan got Chief Grand Secretary Ye
Xianggao to appoint him a secretariat drafter. In return for a further bribe
of 200 taels, Wang Wenyan put Wu Huaixian in contact with Zuo Guangdou and Wei Dazhong, and so Wu Huaixian entered the Donglin camp
and leaked to them the contents of rescripts being prepared by the Grand
Secretariat.[36]

This was a shocking confession. On November 25, the Palace ordered
Wu Huaixian transferred from the Decree Prison to the Ministry of Justice for their recommendation of punishment. On November 26, the
transfer was made. But on November 28, Wu Huaixian died of the effects
of the torture he had received in the Decree Prison.[37]

Barely a month after the torture and death of Wu Huaixian, a squadron
of imperial police descended upon the prefectural city of Yangzhou, six
hundred miles away in the southeast. They extorted 2,000 taels from the
locals, and then they placed Prefect Liu Duo under arrest. There was a
public reading of the charges against him: "He occupies a regular office,
but in his mind he favors the [Donglin] clique. He has slandered current
government with a reckless poem. We have that in his own handwriting
as proof. The Embroidered-uniform Guard is ordered to arrest him and

bring him to the capital for interrogation alongside the heterodox Buddhist monk Benfu."

Liu Duo was dumfounded. To be sure he was a noted drinker, poet, and calligrapher, and it also appears that he acted on the advice of his friend and coprovincial, Wan Jing (beaten to death in 1624), and visited the Donglin academy in Wuxi, which was still open in 1625, to hear the lectures and mend his ways. But he had never written any such poem.

Eastern Depot agents, searching a Beijing monastery, had turned up a painted fan featuring a winter snow scene, with a poem that included the line "Dark with miasma, national affairs go wrong." It bore Liu Duo's personal seal. The painting had been in the possession of the monk Benfu, a hanger-on of the Donglin men. The regime, including especially Grand Secretary Feng Quan and his supporters, were eager to prosecute the case. An imperial rescript of February 19, 1626, ordered both Liu Duo and Benfu sent to the Decree Prison for interrogation.

In a lengthy affidavit, Liu Duo forcefully denied the charge. And indeed further interrogation revealed that he had been framed. An Embroidered-uniform Guards commander named Ouyang Hui had written the poem and had cut Liu Duo's seal from another fan he had given Benfu and pasted it on the painting after the offending poem. It may or may not have helped Liu that a fervent testimonial of support was presented to the court in the name of the "common people" of Yangzhou. It certainly helped that he was friendly with Wei Liangqing, Wei Zhongxian's twenty-seven-year-old nephew.

And so Liu Duo was exonerated. In May 1626, the Palace endorsed Minister of Justice Xu Zhaokui's recommendation and had Liu Duo flogged forty times for mediating a small bribe while in prison, after which he was to be returned to duty. Monk Benfu and guardsman Ouyang Hui were each flogged a hundred times. Benfu was then sent into exile. Ouyang Hui was dismissed from the Guards.[38]

But that did not end the matter. On August 28, Liu Duo was rearrested and sent back to the Decree Prison for further interrogation about the bribe he had allegedly mediated.[39] Then, on September 21, Liu Duo's servant Liu Fu was stopped and searched at one of the Beijing city gates by Zhao San, an agent of the Eastern Depot. Liu Fu was carrying 250 taels on behalf of his master. A relative of Liu Duo's by the name of Peng Wenbing, hearing of this, laid a complaint with the Censorate that the arrest of Liu Fu and the seizure of the silver he was carrying had been improper. So the Censorate had both Liu Fu and Zhao San sent to the Decree

Prison for questioning. At this juncture, a sixty-year-old police command-er named Zhang Tiqian saw an opportunity to bring himself to the favor-able attention of the Palace. It appears that Liu Duo's concubine had arranged a *jiao* sacrifice to celebrate Liu Duo's earlier release. But Zhang Tiqian tortured the servant Liu Fu into stating that what had really hap-pened was that Liu Duo had hired a wife killer, occultist, and sometime Buddhist priest named Fang Jingyang to carry out, not a *jiao* sacrifice, but a voodoo rite—aimed at harming none other than Wei Zhongxian! And after the emperor had so magnanimously forgiven Liu Duo for the offensive poem!

Liu Duo was beaten mercilessly. They say he screamed at his tormen-tors: "Your fame is for the moment only. You won't escape the verdict (*gonglun*) of history!" There was no secret murder of Liu Duo; by Palace order dated October 16, he was decapitated.[40] The murder of Wu Huai-xian and the execution of Liu Duo notwithstanding, expressions of dis-sent continued. In early December 1626, an anonymous poster was put up at the north gate of the Imperial City enumerating palace eunuch Wei Zhongxian's "crimes" and listing by name seventy of his accomplices.[41] This prompted the Palace to issue a general edict ordering government offices everywhere to be alert for subversive writings concocted by sup-porters of the "deviant Donglin clique." The edict reminded the realm that when Tianqi came to power in the early 1620s the "deviant clique" had dominated government, diminished the emperor's filiality and virtue, and discarded national territory. That clique has been destroyed, stated the edict. It went on to warn: "Those who have escaped the net have been told repeatedly to change their faces and reform their minds and start anew, and yet there are minds that still remain unmoved. There are still evil elements, 'mountain men,' and 'pure guests,' who make furtive connections and concoct rumors and write anonymously in behalf of the deviant clique!" Only the vigilant exposure of such activity will "rectify minds and leave the national right unsullied."[42]

The organs of repression took heed. In early February 1627, police commander Wang Tingjian, on patrol in the Beijing streets, arrested two men for possession of dissident literature. Censor Men Kexin sent up a memorial stating the preliminary charges. One of the men arrested was a military degree holder by the name of Gu Tongyin. The other was an ex-pelled Confucian student (*shengyuan*) named Sun Wenzhi.[43] Both were natives of Taicang subprefecture, east of Suzhou; and both were one-time housemen of the executed commander Xiong Tingbi. The police found on Gu a written critique of Manchurian affairs that favored Xiong Tingbi. On Sun they found two poetic laments for Xiong. A Palace rescript ordered the two men sent to the Eastern Depot for interrogation.[44]

What came out of the interrogation was sensational. Here was no less than a plot to organize a political underground, right under the emperor's nose! And there was more. The husband of Gu Tingyin's mother's niece was none other than Hanlin compiler and imperial tutor Chen Renxi. Chen Renxi's native place was in Suzhou prefecture, not far from Taicang. He was a clandestine follower of the Donglin, who day and night thought about ways to overturn the regime *(fanju)*. In this, Chen Renxi worked in close contact with his 1622 year-mate, the optimus Wen Zhenmeng, who had been sent home in 1622 for his scathing description of Tianqi. Wen Zhenmeng in turn had ties to prisoner Sun Wenchi. They were all secretly plotting revenge and a return to power!

This report was sent in Wei Zhongxian's name from the Eastern Depot to the Palace. The Palace rescript to the report praised Wei Zhongxian and directed that Gu, Sun, and several friends and servants of theirs be sent directly over to the Ministry of Justice.

Minister of Justice Xue Zhen prepared a lengthy summary of the case along with recommendations for punishment. To this the Palace issued, on February 25, 1627, a rescript ordering the decapitation of Gu and Sun and the flogging and canguing of four of their servants and friends. A rescript of March 14 praised Wei Zhongxian and ordered the removals from civil service of Chen Renxi, Wen Zhenmeng, and former Hanlin bachelor Zheng Man.[45]

Chen Renxi returned home from Beijing, and there he "closed his gate" and "awaited death." Wen Zhenmeng, already at home, did the same. It was the general expectation that the arrest and transportation of both to the Decree Prison was only a matter of time. In Wujin county, south of Suzhou, Zheng Man (who was never able to find out how his name got placed in the imperial rescript) observed agents wearing "Beijing caps" posted day and night by the gate of his house. He decided to escape rather than "await death." He fled overland through Jiangxi, then south over the Meiling pass to Guangdong, beyond the effective reach of Beijing, where friends entertained him and showed him the famous sites. He came out of hiding after Tianqi's death in September.[46]

◀

The regime of Tianqi, Wei Zhongxian, and their coadjutors in bureaucracy was by no means devoid of significant achievements. The great political purge, still in progress in 1626–1627, was but one of them. A more lasting achievement was architectural. Several of the more spectacular buildings in the Forbidden City, visible expressions of the might and grandeur of the Ming empire, had been neglected for many years and had fallen into a state of disrepair. Their restoration was a pet project of Tianqi's, and, to please him, the multitalented Wei Zhongxian gladly took on the role of impresario of construction. The centerpieces of the rebuilding program were the so-called Three Palaces—that is, the Huangji, Zhongji, and Jianji palaces, colossal structures that line up one behind the other midway along the half-mile avenue leading from the Meridian gate at the south entrance to the Forbidden City north to the emperor's palace, the Qianqing. Of course the willing assistance of Cui Chengxiu as minister of works was essential in this. The construction work force was increased in size from 752 men to 5,288.[47]

The official purge and the palace reconstruction were ingeniously interlinked. Palace reconstruction—which the regime routinely called the "great work" *(da gong)*—was funded not from taxes but from fines and confiscations imposed upon the families of the Donglin martyrs and their sympathizers, including especially military recruiters and suppliers who were believed to have embezzled huge sums and had sought protection from Donglin officials.

Work began slowly, but from 1625 it was rushed. The Huangji palace was finished first, in November 1626, and its restoration was celebrated with elaborate ritual.[48] The other two palaces were completed in September 1627. The Ministry of Works reported the total cost, from March 31, 1625 to September 10, 1627, as 5,788,135.8 taels of silver.[49] Some officials urged postponing the construction and diverting the funds to military defense in Manchuria, but the Palace insisted (1) that defense was being adequately funded already and (2) that, as of July 1626, the 1.5 million taels so far spent on construction were "not being taken from the people."[50] The Palace's assertion may have been technically correct. A fairly thorough combing of surviving records yields a by no means complete total of seventy-four men assessed 2,137,638 taels altogether (ranging from small amounts like the 300 taels Censor Wan Jing's family was forced to pay, to the 402,727 taels charged to the former military supply official Tao Langxian, to the 605,000 charged to the Huizhou entrepreneur Wu Yangchun—the attempted collection of which in April 1627 provoked a local riot).[51] The Palace's determination to accomplish the rebuilding in a hurry and in the face of all resistance, as though somehow it was in a race against time, helps explain the ferocity with which it forced the families of what it insisted were frauds and cheats and embezzlers to pay the amounts charged.

And there was more: the military victory in Manchuria. After so many years of setback, news finally came of the repulse under cannon fire of Manchu leader Nurhaci and his forces at Ningyuan on February 19, 1626. Nurhaci himself died on September 28 of the same year.[52] There followed in August 1627 a victory over the Manchus at Jinzhou, in the Liaodong peninsula. No wonder the mood of the regime turned self-congratulatory.

A Counter-Model to the Donglin

The successes of one-time street rowdy, illiterate director of the Eastern Depot, and flamboyant palace eunuch Wei Zhongxian were almost beyond belief. He had destroyed all opposition inside the Forbidden City— with the exception of Empress Zhang, but he was continuing to work for her removal. Outside the Forbidden City, he had broken the "deviant clique," and he was continuing to purge its last remnants from government. He had funded and rebuilt the Three Palaces. He was happy to accept full credit for the Ming military victory at Ningyuan. The *haojie*, the heroic strong man at the helm of national affairs that so many of the late Ming elite believed the situation required, had materialized—not in Yang Lian or Xiong Tingbi, but in palace eunuch Wei Zhongxian.

Tianqi expressed his confidence in Wei on every possible public occasion. He now regularly addressed the eunuch as his "depot minister" *(changchen)*. From around late in 1626, memorials from officials were expected to include praise for Wei Zhongxian in their opening remarks. Rescripts from the Palace came to be issued in the name of the emperor and the depot minister *(zhen yu changchen)*. Some fourteen male relatives, children of Wei's brother, sister, and daughter, were variously ennobled or given hereditary military offices.[53] Wei Zhongxian himself received the unusual title "superior duke" *(shang gong)*.

Some in the realm could not act fast enough to express their admiration and gratitude, and this they did by building those notorious shrines dedicated to the living genius and beneficent merit of Wei Zhongxian. Palace authorization for constructing the first of these was issued late in

July 1626. The request came up from Zhejiang Provincial Coordinator Pan Ruzhen. The Palace was pleased to grant it. It gave the shrine the name "Pude" (Universal Virtue). The new shrine was built on the shore of scenic West Lake in Hangzhou, right between two existing temples dedicated to loyalist military heroes.[54]

Pan Ruzhen scorned and detested the moral pretensions of the defeated Donglin clique.[55] And it is clear from Pan's memorial that, although Donglin martyr Zhou Qiyuan had championed the underpaid rural producers in the earlier dispute over Palace silk procurement, the effect of his stance was to make it impossible for the Hangzhou silk weavers to meet their quotas, with the result that many weavers suffered, and some even died in prison. It was Wei Zhongxian who then intervened to alleviate the weavers' plight. Accordingly, "several thousand people" now asked Pan Ruzhen to beg the Palace's permission to build this shrine in Wei's honor.[56]

The Pude temple in Hangzhou was soon followed by some forty more Wei Zhongxian shrines, built by regional officials and local gentry in various parts of China after receiving imperial authorization to do so. No effort or expense was spared, with glass bricks being used here and red gates erected there, and yellow tiles on the roofs. "For a while," noted contemporary commentator Zheng Zhongkui, "the whole realm appeared to go mad."[57] Inside some temples were installed lifelike statues of Wei Zhongxian, carved in aromatic wood, with a hole in the topknot where seasonal flowers might be inserted.[58] Inside the temple built in Jizhou, a gold statue of the eunuch sported a cap normally worn only by emperors.[59] Matching couplets hung in each shrine were lavish with praise; "His sageliness and godliness establish the pivot between Heaven and Earth/ May his beneficence and long life shine as eternally brilliant as the sun and moon" is an example of the genre.[60] The eunuchs in Nanjing built a grand temple with three sections. Worshippers entering the shrine saw in the central section a wooden statue and also a painting of Wei Zhongxian in court costume with eunuch servants at each side holding round fans and ivory tablets. In an alcove on the left was another painting of Wei Zhongxian, this one portraying him seated in gold helmet and armor with generals holding spears and swords standing alongside; and on the right, one could contemplate Wei Zhongxian seated upright in traveling costume surrounded by little eunuchs in poses of reverence and adoration.[61]

At the Beijing imperial college, located northeast of the Forbidden

City, student Lu Wanling and several classmates petitioned the throne in June 1627 for permission to build a temple in Wei Zhongxian's honor on some vacant land they had bought nearby. The students' brief was that Wei had helped the young ruler Tianqi to become a "Yao and Shun"; that he had exterminated the "deviant clique"; and, most important for the students, he had restored the "study of the Sages" to its former glory. The students intended to worship at Wei's shrine whenever they offered seasonal sacrifices at the temple of Confucius.[62] This petition the Palace approved. "I hated it deeply when the Donglin followers wrecked national affairs and encroached upon the inner court," stated the rescript. "I relied on the depot minister [Wei Zhongxian], who upheld correct opinion, and turned away the evil wind, so that the villainy of the partisan camp was wiped clean as a mirror, and the filial piety and paternal compassion of myself and my father shone again as bright as the sun in the sky. His merit in the world is not small. His benevolent embrace has made possible pacification on the home front as well as the defeat of foreign enemies. . . ."[63]

Officials improvised ceremonies imaginatively. Somewhere in the outskirts of Beijing, an official by the name of Huang Yuntai welcomed the installation of Wei Zhongxian's "benign visage" *(xirong)* into a newly built shrine, lined up his subordinates at the red-lacquered steps in front, where he had them perform five bows and three kowtows, then approach the image shouting "a thousand blessings" in unison, whereafter each official in turn stated his name and office and kowtowed, and thanked him who should live "nine thousand years" and kowtowed again, then finally all repeated the five bows and three kowtows en masse.[64] One official went too far, perhaps as a kind of protest. After performing elaborate obeisances at a Wei Zhongxian shrine, he crept on his knees to a nearby Buddhist temple, where he made only one bow. "How can I be greater than the Buddha?" asked a suspicious Wei when he was informed of the incident.[65]

Official paperwork authorizing new Wei Zhongxian shrines was usually careful to indicate who the petitioners were, so one can see that besides regional civil officials, military officials, and eunuchs posted in Nanjing and elsewhere, they included Beijing merchants; gentry and common people in Tongzhou; local elders in Songjiang; the common residents of Beijing; more merchants in Beijing; and so on.[66] Perhaps not all of this popular enthusiasm was genuine.[67] Nonetheless, it appears that one should understand this extraordinary episode—this nationwide building of great shrines in honor of a palace eunuch whom the Donglin had so recently vilified—as Wei Zhongxian's answer to the outpourings of love and grief on behalf of the Donglin heroes exhibited by crowds of people in such places as De'anfu, Tongcheng, Jiangyin, Zhangzhou, and of course Suzhou, scene of the famous riot of April 1626. The Donglin heroes had died for an ideal; they had stirred the emotions of the realm through their willing endurance of blood, pain, humiliation, and death. Wei Zhongxian's appeal to the people of China was founded on precisely the opposite emotional grounds. Far from grief and death, the shrines symbolized radiance, abundance, and joy, and endorsed the acquisitive side of human nature—much in the same way that, perhaps, after 1989, the Communist regime replaced the self-sacrificing Tiananmen spirit with a new propaganda emphasizing materialistic values.

◀

The tiny emperor, too, enjoyed what he could of the good life. His fondness for building and crafts has become legendary. Liu Ruoyu described how Tianqi and several eunuch companions would make lacquerware, and how Tianqi did not like being interrupted at that activity, and if a high-ranking eunuch approached him with an important memorial at such times, Tianqi would wave him off, saying, "I understand; you just go take care of that."[68] Wei Zhongxian also occasionally staged palace theatricals for Tianqi. The emperor enjoyed these, but report has it that his adored Empress Zhang walked out offended when one scene turned lewd and refused ever to attend again.[69]

Along the western edge of the Forbidden City was a park and a lake, the Taiyichi, where the little emperor loved to go boating. Once Tianqi invited Empress Zhang aboard a boat and rowed her up and down the lake himself. It is said that the empress used the occasion to admonish Tianqi that he should be reading memorials, that he should listen to the good scholars who attended his tutorials, and that he should not let the crowd of "small men" take advantage of him. "You are my teacher," said Tianqi. "I'll try hard to be diligent." But he soon forgot his promise, and in less than a month he was enjoying himself again.[70]

Late in the afternoon of June 22, 1625, Tianqi and two young eunuchs were playing on a small boat in a deep part of the lake when a sudden gust of wind tilted the boat and dumped the three of them into the water. Of course none of them could swim. People on shore blanched in fright. Wei

Zhongxian and Madame Ke were drinking on a big boat not far away. Wei tried but failed to reach Tianqi and got himself all wet in the effort. Finally several eunuchs on shore managed to row out to where the emperor was thrashing about and save him, but they did not reach his two young companions in time, and they drowned.[71]

◀

Despite his many consorts, Tianqi had an unbroken sequence of sad experiences in producing offspring. Not one of his three sons and two daughters lived to see its first birthday.[72] Some people thought Tianqi failed to give the babies adequate protection. Supervising Secretary Li Mou stated just that in a memorial of 1624, by which time four imperial infants had died; Li thought the deaths were due to the prenatal and postnatal shocks they had received from the earsplitting reverberations of the cannon the Palace army kept firing inside the Forbidden City.[73] Palace eunuch Liu Ruoyu agreed that the imperial infants had not been well protected, and he noted the irony of the comparison between the emperor's sickly infants and the robust peasant children one might observe running about in the north China countryside.[74]

The emperor's own medical history, what it was that caused his early death at the age of twenty-one, is difficult to construe, but all of his reported symptoms were in some way respiratory. Occasionally he felt ill enough to call in the officials. On April 17, 1624, Tianqi called the grand secretaries to his bedside in the Qianqing palace. "The emperor was sitting wearing imperial regalia," noted Ye Xianggao, "and we kowtowed and asked after his health. 'Yesterday I came down with cold and diarrhea,' replied Tianqi, 'and I feel weak, so I wanted to see all of you, that's all.' I urged the emperor to take care of himself. He nodded. We got up and stood on either side of him. The imperial physician knelt taking his pulse. When he finished, we knelt and said, 'Your face is calm and your speech clear, and you should recuperate all right, but you should rest.' The emperor said he understood. He ordered a eunuch to escort us back to the Grand Secretariat. He gave each of us gifts of silver and cloth. . . ."[75]

On September 11, 1624, Tianqi was sick again, with a nosebleed. This time representatives of the supervising secretaries and the censors joined the grand secretaries at the emperor's bedside.[76] Ye Xianggao had by then resigned.

Liu Ruoyu noted in his memoirs that from mid-June 1627 the emperor began feeling increasingly unwell, and from July he never left his bed. For a time they moved the invalid from the Qianqing palace to the Moujindian, a smaller structure immediately to the southwest. Wei Zhongxian covered the walls of the ruler's sickroom with red silk cloth and fetched a gold character reading *shou* (long life) from storage and hung it by his bedside.

These arrangements failed to improve the emperor's health, and at some point it appears the patient was moved back to the Qianqing palace. It was not clear to his physicians what was wrong with him. Minister of War Huo Weihua sent a prescription for a medicine obtained from the condensation of steamed rice. The Imperial Dispensary and the Imperial Academy of Medicine prepared it. Tianqi liked it, as did the palace eunuchs, who drank the leftovers; but after a while the emperor's condition worsened, and he refused any more of it. His body swelled up. Wei Zhongxian grew angry with Huo Weihua.[77]

On September 19, the grand secretaries and other high officials were suddenly called to the emperor's sickbed in the Qianqing palace while the physicians examined him and gave him medicine. Tang Changshi, a minor official in the Ministry of Works, recalled that day in his memoirs. Eunuchs came rushing to the ministry to fetch Cui Chengxiu. Everyone in the ministry was alarmed, not knowing what was going on. They awaited anxiously for Cui to return from the Forbidden City and tell them; and around noon, he did so. "We were called in to receive [the emperor's] final instructions (*guming*)," reported Cui. "He called in the grand secretaries, the Nine Ministers, and representatives of the censors and supervising secretaries. We bowed and knelt, and he sat up and said to us: 'I've been troubled by eastern affairs [in Manchuria], and I've taken ill, and no remedy works, and it's all over. [My brother] the Prince of Xin is in the capital, and you capital officials must conscientiously guide him.' After he said that, he lay back down. We waited prostrate. Then he sat up again and said: 'Tell the Prince of Xin. You officials go away for a bit. The Prince of Xin will soon be here.' The emperor told us to visit the prince. Then he glanced left at Wei Zhongxian and he said to us: 'This depot minister has served me too.'"[78]

Censor Ni Wenhuan reported back to the Palace his version of that meeting, which he too had attended. There was nothing in his report about the prince of Xin. According to Ni, the emperor had stated that he was troubled that he was too sick to attend to official business; that palace eunuchs Wang Tiqian and Wei Zhongxian were experienced and wholly dedicated, and the grand secretaries should consult with them on all important matters; and that without Wei Zhongxian it would have been impossible for the emperor to rebuild the Three Palaces and bring about victory in Manchuria.[79]

The next day, the Palace issued an edict explaining that the emperor was ill because he had not been physically robust to begin with and had overtaxed himself worrying about national affairs. The edict directed the officials to confer with eunuchs Wang Tiqian and Wei Zhongxian. It also informed them that Tianqi had called in his younger half-brother and had spoken with him.[80] It appeared as though death might be near.

Late in the morning of September 28, eunuch Li Yongzhen left the emperor's bedside and entered one of the offices of the eunuch Directorate of Ceremonial nearby. He had with him a large, bloody clot of some sort wrapped in a piece of tissue, which he said had come from Tianqi's nose. The other eunuchs examined the clot and agreed that it was not good news. They rewrapped the clot, wrote the date on the tissue, and tacked it high on a wall. Later that day, the imperial physicians came by and examined it in order to determine whether the emperor needed a different medication.[81] What conclusion they drew from it is not stated.

Death came to Tianqi late in the afternoon of September 30. He was two months short of his twenty-second birthday.[82]

◄

There was speculation among the lettered classes of China that Wei Zhongxian was surely going to make an attempt to seize the Ming throne. But there was also doubt among some of them that such an attempt, if made, would succeed. In Jiashan county, Zhejiang, Chen Longzheng explained why. If you contemplate the matter carefully, wrote Chen, you will observe that the eunuch has performed no great feat. His only merit is "commonplace service" to his ruler. Therefore there is no groundswell of public support for him to ride. His followers and adherents are people of low quality. The empress does not favor him. His palace army is too small to control the entire country. And he seems to have no better plan than to compel everyone to praise him.[83]

Chen Longzheng was right. Wei Zhongxian's political fate was tied to Tianqi's. He had tried to make his position more secure, of course. But his persistent efforts to maneuver Tianqi into deposing Empress Zhang had not succeeded. Rumor had it that at some point he tried to persuade

the empress to agree to adopt an infant son of his nephew, Wei Liangqing, as heir apparent to the Ming throne, and to let Wei Liangqing himself assume power as a "regent-emperor" *(she huangdi)*. To that proposal, the empress is said to have replied, "You'll kill me if I agree to that,
and you'll kill me if I refuse; but if I die refusing you, I'll be able to hold
up my head before the imperial ancestors." Wei had no reply to that, and
he backed down.[84]

On September 19, when Tianqi called the officials to his bedside to witness his final words *(guming)*, Wei Zhongxian wanted his name placed at
the head of the list as chief witness *(guming shou)*. This the Grand Secretariat, though lately a rubber stamp, refused to endorse.[85]

At some point during Tianqi's last days, Empress Zhang visited with
the emperor's younger half-brother (Zhu Youjian, the soon-to-be Chongzhen emperor) and urged him to agree to the dying ruler's wish that he
succeed him. She also tried to arrange to have Chongzhen's exact where-
abouts hidden; and she warned him not to eat any food prepared in the
palace, because of the chance it might be poisoned.[86]

Official notification of Tianqi's death was issued on the next day, October 1. It came by way of an edict from Empress Zhang to the Ministry of
Rites, which in turn released it to the public. It was short and to the
point:

> The Ministry of Rites makes public this edict of the empress: The health of
> the emperor was never strong. On top of that, he got sick worrying over
> eastern [Manchurian] affairs. Medicines had no effect. He died at the *shen*
> [3–5 P.M.] hour of the 22d day of the 8th lunar month of the 7th year of
> Tianqi [September 30, 1627].
>
> As to the funeral rites to be carried out, I order the Ministry of Rites to
> meet as soon as possible with the Hanlin Academy and report here the ap-
> propriate arrangements they propose.[87]

Having received news of Tianqi's death, the officials rushed to gather
at the Longdao pavilion, just outside the Qianqing palace compound,
near the eunuch Directorate of Ceremonial. The eunuchs sent them all
away to change into mourning costume. When they rushed back wearing
proper costume, they were told to return later, as things were not yet
ready. The officials pleaded, and finally they were let in to perform a ceremonial weeping at Tianqi's bier. Wei Zhongxian was observed standing
by, saying nothing, his eyes swollen. As the officials filed out, Cui Chengxiu (recently made minister of war) was called back to the palace for con-

sultation. The officials looked at each other and someone spoke out in protest. "How can Cui monopolize the realm's affairs?" he wanted to know. If Cui heard the remark, he ignored it and went inside, where he reportedly told Wei Zhongxian that he was not able to help him with a last-minute usurpation of the throne.[88]

It is not clear who wrote Tianqi's final edict, which appears to have been released to the public on October 1. Apparently no complete copy of it survives, which is puzzling. It may have been tampered with. In the longest version, the dead ruler points up his successes (rebuilding the Three Palaces; victory in Manchuria—but nothing about the purge of the Donglin); praises the "imperial fifth younger brother" and transmits the throne to him; and gives instructions limiting expressions of national mourning.[89] There is no mention whatever of Wei Zhongxian. His name may have been edited out.

CHAPTER 6

A Reversal of Fortunes

◀

ON OCTOBER 2, 1627, the Tianqi emperor's younger half-brother, Zhu Youjian, assumed the throne under the reign title Chongzhen. (As things turned out, his was the last reign of an intact Ming China.) He was sixteen years old, but, unlike Tianqi, he played an assertive part in government from the very beginning of his reign. He also seems to have kept his own counsel. He certainly tolerated no decision-making surrogates, as Tianqi had done. During the first several months of his tenure as emperor, he adroitly handled the dismantling of the "Cui–Wei" regime, a task made easier for him by the passivity of Cui Chengxiu and Wei Zhongxian, who, in the absence of Tianqi, failed to find a way to defend their positions.

At its core, the Tianqi regime had been truly warm and familial, a *guojia* in the emotionally literal sense of the word. Madame Ke and Wei Zhongxian daily attended Tianqi as his personal, parent-like guardians. Wei Zhongxian in the inner Palace and Cui Chengxiu atop the outer bureaucracy accepted each other as father and son. But Tianqi was the center of it all, and his premature death destroyed the tissue of pseudofamilial affections out of which power at the highest level in Ming China had been constructed. With Tianqi dead, there was no way to reestablish those same affectionate arrangements around Chongzhen, who did not love Madame Ke and Wei Zhongxian and, indeed, had no reason to do so.

For several weeks, however, Chongzhen gave no hint that things might change. On October 8, he refused to act on Wei Zhongxian's offer to resign. On November 5, he agreed to Wei Zhongxian's request that no new temples be built in his honor, but he allowed construction to proceed on those already authorized. On November 12, Chongzhen agreed to a memorial from the acting chief supervising secretary of the Office of Scrutiny for Personnel, Chen Eryi, that the Eastern Depot, Embroidered-uniform Guard, and censors on city patrol duty must together be made to exercise special vigilance because, according to rumor, "remnant villains of the Donglin" were lurking in Beijing hoping for "a change in the weather," and though the former emperor had already cleansed those elements, there was a danger that, unless continually watched, "dead ashes" might well come to life again.[1]

There were some faint signals of a new dispensation, but they were difficult to interpret. On October 11, Tianqi's wet nurse, Madame Ke, vacated her quarters in the Forbidden City and moved to her private residence outside. Eunuch memoirist Liu Ruoyu reports that in the predawn hours of that day, Madame Ke went in mourning dress to the Renzhi palace where Tianqi's coffin still lay and wept as she burned the contents of a small box that contained her dead charge's baby hair, baby teeth, scabs, and nail cuttings.[2] And on October 31 Chongzhen replied affirmatively to a request to have the legal authorities investigate student Lu Wanling and others for fraud and coercion in their role in arranging and funding the construction of a Wei Zhongxian temple at the Imperial University.[3]

In October and November, certain Beijing officials began probing Chongzhen's intentions by repeatedly calling his attention to Cui Chengxiu's overweening position in the Ming government. On October 22, it was requested that Cui and others be relieved of duty so that they might retire home to observe the prescribed mourning regulations.[4] Cui's mother had died, but Tianqi (or, rather, Wei Zhongxian) had considered Cui so indispensable that his mourning obligation had been waived. Cui now asked to be relieved of duty, but Chongzhen denied his request.

A month later, on November 21, Censor Yang Weiyuan impeached Cui Chengxiu for accruing excessive powers (Cui was concurrently minister of war and censor-in-chief, while his younger brother served as military commander in Zhejiang province), and for corruptly dominating government. Yang charged that while Wei Zhongxian had repaid Tianqi's trust with his hard work and his willingness to accept the world's resentments, Cui had not been faithful to Wei Zhongxian. Chongzhen angrily rejected the impeachment. But Yang Weiyuan thought he was on to something, because five days later he submitted a second impeachment of Cui Chengxiu, this time underscoring Cui's selfishness and greed and emphasizing Wei Zhongxian's impartiality and disdain for material things. Chongzhen now changed his mind; his rescript indicated that he was considering doing something about Cui, and indeed, on November 28, he relieved Cui of his two positions and authorized him to go home to observe mourning.[5]

Some of the censors and supervising secretaries now smelled blood. On December 1, Censor Wu Shangmo memorialized his objections to the mildness of Chongzhen's rescript. On December 3, Censor Jia Jichun (notorious for his defense of Lady Li in the 1620 palace crisis) sent up a harsh impeachment of Cui, listing his illegally gotten wealth, his collection of concubines, his unspeakably lewd behavior, and the excessive honors he acquired for his dead parents. On the same day, Supervising Secretary Xu Kezheng impeached Cui's brother Ningxiu. On December 7, Chief Supervising Secretary Wu Hongye brought it to Chongzhen's attention that Cui's son Cui Duo had been improperly awarded a *juren* degree in the recent Shuntian prefectural exams (Chongzhen ordered that Cui Duo be retested, and he failed a retest given on December 20).[6]

At home in Jizhou, Ming China's most powerful bureaucrat apparently sensed that sooner or later the new emperor would respond to these increasingly violent impeachments and order his arrest and execution. He was also very likely informed of Chongzhen's edict of December 11 ordering the arrest of eunuch Wei Zhongxian. Report has it that on December 12, a party was held in the Cui household that concluded with a smashing of the expensive cups from which everyone had drunk.

Shortly after this party, neighborhood security chief Gu Youde entered the Cui home and discovered the corpse of Cui Chengxiu hanging by a wet towel from the rafters of the library and, on the floor in the same room, the still-breathing body of his lover and favorite concubine, Xiao Lingxi, her throat cut with a knife. Gu Youde at once reported this shocking news to Jizhou subprefectural magistrate Zhao Sanji. Magistrate Zhao informed Jizhou military intendant Sun Zhimian, who in turn notified Shan Mingyi, grand coordinator of Shuntian prefecture. Grand Coordinator Shan ordered Magistrate Zhao plus police, clerks, and coroners to revisit the scene and double-check the original report. This they did, and the results were sent up to Chongzhen by Shan Mingyi on December 14.

How long concubine Xiao survived with her throat cut is not recorded. However, on the same day, December 14, Censor Wang Huitu sent up an impeachment of concubine Xiao's younger brother Xiao Weizhong, who had been improperly appointed to a military position under Cui Chengxiu's auspices. He also included a detailed report of his investigation into the social origins of concubine Xiao and her family. They were street entertainers! The beautiful Xiao Lingxi used to stand by the gate of the military encampment at Miyun (about fifty miles northwest of Beijing) and "present smiles" while her little brother Xiao Weizhong played the *pipa* and performed acrobatics. Censor Wang went on to describe how in later years concubine Xiao would revisit Miyun and behave imperiously. Facts like these, he concluded, showed why the "Cui–Wei" crimes needed to be fully exposed.[7]

Within days, Chongzhen endorsed a request that Cui's property be confiscated, the proceeds to be earmarked for military expenses. On December 26, a preliminary report noted that some 71,245 taels of silver plus other assets had so far been seized from Cui's estate. In March of the following year, Cui's corpse was publicly dismembered at Jizhou. He had not, by his suicide, cheated the executioner.[8]

◄

It was likewise by increments that disaster closed in on the archvillain himself, Wei Zhongxian. On November 30, two days after Cui Chengxiu left Beijing, Lu Chengyuan, a minor official in the Ministry of Works, complained in a long memorial that Wei Zhongxian had been rewarded to excess by Tianqi; that he had not declined to let Tianqi treat him as virtual co-emperor; that he had let himself be honored with the building of temples; that he had been put on a par with the duke of Zhou and Confucius; and that he had sent Palace eunuchs to control the frontiers and other vital points in the realm, supplanting the regular bureaucracy.[9] Chongzhen laid the memorial aside.

On December 2, Qian Yuanke, a newly appointed minor official in the Ministry of War, followed with a long impeachment of Wei Zhongxian, reiterating many of Lu Chengyuan's complaints and demanding to know why Chongzhen continued to protect this offending eunuch who was, after all, no more than a low-born illiterate from the streets![10] Chongzhen "noted" receipt of this statement. On December 3, Shi Gongsheng, a vice-director in the Ministry of Justice, weighed in with another anti-Wei memorial, which Chongzhen also "noted."

Then, on December 4, a "ten crimes" memorial arrived from one Qian Jiazheng, which was copied and recopied by people in Beijing and achieved some considerable fame. Qian Jiazheng was not an official. In 1621 he had failed the Shuntian examination for the *juren* degree and by special imperial act had been appointed an Imperial University student. Donglin stalwarts Zou Yuanbiao and Gao Panlong had liked him. Having lain low in Beijing through the Tianqi years, student Qian decided the time had come to assert himself on the dynasty's behalf and resolutely denounce Wei Zhongxian in a format echoing Yang Lian's failed "Twenty-four Crimes" memorial of 1624. The story has it that Chongzhen, impressed by Qian's memorial, called in Wei Zhongxian and had him listen and then reply as each of Qian's ten allegations was read aloud to him; but Wei had no replies and could only kowtow in silence through the ordeal. On December 6, Chongzhen "noted" this, but he indicated that although his mind was made up he wanted to hear more from officialdom. As a university student, Qian Jiazheng of course had no right to memorialize the throne, but the emperor waived the penalty.[11]

At this juncture, timidity lifted, the floodgates opened, and over the following weeks, "more than a hundred" officials sent up memorials denouncing Wei Zhongxian.[12] Meanwhile, on December 5, Chongzhen granted Wei Zhongxian's plea to retire to his private mansion on the ground of illness. The emperor put him at his ease, however, warmly noting in his rescript how Wei had labored so long and hard for Tianqi, rebuilding the Three Palaces and defending the national frontiers.[13]

The emperor's reassurance was not sincere. Three days after giving it, on December 8, Chongzhen issued a long and thunderous edict listing Wei's monstrous crimes; but, because Tianqi's burial had not yet taken place, he ordered that the eunuch be sent south to Fengyang in exile "for the time being."[14]

And so, on or around December 8, Wei left Beijing accompanied by a large retinue and baggage train. Soon after Wei's departure, an official of the Ministry of Revenue memorialized in alarm that merchants arriving in Beijing from the south reported that they had passed Wei's convoy en route and had counted over a hundred carts and over a thousand horses and mules carrying bags! And what was in the bags? No doubt loot stolen from the Palace, or from the people.[15] Commissioner Yang Shaozhen of the Office of Transmission warned the emperor that Fengyang was full of ruffians and fighters, and that Wei might well recruit them and join Cui Chengxiu's brother Ningxiu and his Zhejiang troops in a rebellion. Therefore, he felt he must urge Chongzhen to arrest Wei immediately.[16] On December 11, in response to these warnings, the emperor rescinded his earlier edict and ordered the Embroidered-uniform Guard to go fetch the eunuch back under arrest, and seize his entire retinue.[17]

Informants rushed from Beijing and overtook Wei to warn him of what was coming. On December 13, Wei and his entourage stopped for the night at the You family inn in Foucheng county, about 150 miles south of Beijing and still a long way from Fengyang, their destination.

In the early hours of December 14, a servant of Wei Zhongxian's secretary, Li Chaoqin, discovered the body of his master hanging by the neck from a rafter of the inn, and next to it, also hanging from a rafter, the body of Wei Zhongxian himself. The two had used their belts as nooses and had committed suicide together. The servant immediately sent word to county magistrate Yang Baohe. Magistrate Yang placed the suicide scene under guard and arrested the servant and the inn owner as well as another eunuch and several muleteers. The rest of Wei's retinue fled before they could be caught. Later that day a commander of the Embroidered-uniform Guard sent to arrest Wei arrived in Foucheng, listened to Magistrate Yang's report, and informed the throne of it. Sometime later, Censor Zhuo Mai, on duty as Zhili regional inspector, examined the corpses and verified their identities. In a rescript responding to these reports, the emperor ordered the authorities to bury the two suicides temporarily in Foucheng, and to haul all the accompanying luggage to Hejian prefecture for inventorying. The arrested eunuch was ordered returned to Beijing for questioning. The other figures arrested were interrogated in Foucheng and then released.[18]

In obedience to an edict of March 1, 1628, the corpse of Wei Zhongxian was exhumed and carted to Hejian prefecture for posthumous execution by slicing *(lingchi);* rumor had it that while Li Chaoqin's remains had already rotted to the bones, Wei's still oozed body fluids, "just as though he had been awaiting Heaven's punishment."[19] (A wild rumor, which persisted into the Qing, had it that Wei had forced a look-alike to hang himself, had escaped into hiding, and was never caught.)[20]

The construction of the great mausoleum that Wei was having built for himself at the Biyunsi in Beijing's Western Hills was never finished, but it is said that eunuchs managed to bury some articles of his clothing there, and for many years they guarded the inscribed stelae prominently on view at the site, carefully erasing hostile graffiti left by visitors. Not until 1701 did the Kangxi emperor, responding to a memorial, order the complete demolition of all remains of the site.[21]

◀

Madame Ke, bearer of the title Fengsheng Furen (Lady Who Supports the Sage), was in the dying Tianqi emperor's thoughts in September 1627. In a public edict, he recalled how he was sickly and weak as a child, and would not have survived without Madame Ke; and how, after first his mother and then his father died, she protected him all the more, in ways that "the outer court cannot imagine." He rewarded her for "twenty-three years of total and unwavering loyalty" by promoting in honors her younger brother and her son.[22]

As noted, Madame Ke vacated her Palace quarters on October 11. Sometime in December, the Chongzhen emperor ordered that her and Wei Zhongxian's private residences be confiscated.[23] Reportedly, Madame Ke, now homeless, proceeded on foot some miles to the Wanyiju (literally, Laundry Office), a secluded retirement facility for eunuchs located northwest of the Imperial City.[24] On December 24, she there confessed under torture that the eight pregnant maidservants whom police had just found living in her private residence had earlier accompanied her on her visits to the Forbidden City. This was unspeakable! Who had fathered the babies they were carrying? In a few more months, one of those babies might have been made Tianqi's successor as emperor of China! Madame Ke's interrogator, a eunuch named Wang Wenzheng (or Zhao Benzheng), beat her to death. Unknown to Chongzhen, her corpse was cremated in a Buddhist hall nearby, and her ashes scattered. (In March 1628, Chongzhen ordered her corpse located so that it could be subjected to posthumous execution.[25] Of course, it was never found.)

◀

During the early months of 1628, the Ministry of Justice presented detailed criminal charges against Wei Zhongxian, Cui Chengxiu, and Madame Ke, all now deceased. The emperor agreed to the further confiscation and execution of Wei's nephew, Wei Liangqing, and Madame Ke's son, Hou Guoxing. He also ordered that all the rest of their many relatives, with the exception of some very young children, be permanently exiled to malarial regions. Decree Prison officials Xu Xianchun and Zhang Tiqian, responsible for the deaths of the Donglin martyrs, were ordered to be executed.[26]

The emperor's strategy, however, was not to conduct a complete purge of all officials tainted by contact with the "Cui–Wei" regime, but to limit prosecutions to those who, on the basis of clear written evidence, could be proved to have been its ardent partisans. Thus there was issued early in 1629 the so-called *Ni an* (Treason Case), which publicly listed 161 names of Cui–Wei partisans and their punishments: 24 people sentenced to execution; 11 exiled to garrisons; 71 reduced to commoner status; 32 demoted and forced to retire; 12 simply demoted; and 11 simply forced to retire.[27]

On December 8, 1627, the many temples recently built in Wei Zhong-xian's honor, or still under construction, were ordered to be dismantled. Proceeds from the sale of the building materials were to be added to the military defense budget. (A year later, the Ministry of Revenue reported the collection of 25,538 taels of silver from those sales.)[28]

In an edict of December 17, 1627, the emperor declared an "era of ren-ovation" *(weixin zhi zhi)* and announced his intention to rehabilitate the Donglin martyrs, end the persecutions of their families, and release all the other political prisoners who were still being held in the Decree Prison.[29] Chongzhen reviewed each case individually and in most instances grant-ed releases and exonerations.

Sons of the martyrs journeyed to Beijing to offer pleas and accusations in their dead fathers' behalf. Zhou Shunchang's young son Zhou Maolan pierced his tongue and wrote in blood a memorial accusing two officials (Ni Wenhuan and Mao Yilu) of having engineered his father's wrongful death.[30] And there came a day early in 1628 when there was held in Beijing a formal judicial interrogation *(huishen duibu)* of eight or so eunuchs and Decree Prison personnel. Several of the martyrs' sons were in the crowd of onlookers. Among them were Zhou Zongjian's son Zhou Yanzuo and Huang Zunsu's son Huang Zongxi. Both brought sharp awls. Zhou Yanzuo got blood all over himself from jabbing the prison guards Yan Zi and Ye Wenzhong, who with their own hands had killed several of the martyrs. (He and Huang Zongxi were later on hand to watch as both guards were flogged to death.) At the same interrogation, Huang Zongxi stuck his awl into his father's tormentors, former Decree Prison director Xu Xianchun and the eunuch Li Shi, and he yanked hairs from the beard of Xu Xianchun's deputy, Cui Yingyuan. Several of the sons also conduct-ed a sacrifice in their fathers' memory at the central gate of the Decree Prison itself.[31]

◀

There was a need to decide what to do about the *Sanchao yaodian,* the definitive official treatise on the Three Cases that the Cui–Wei regime had sponsored, of which a second printing had been made as late as Octo-ber 10, 1627.[32] On December 19, a minor official of the Ministry of Rev-enue suggested revising it.[33] Chongzhen ordered court officials to discuss the matter. On January 8, 1628, Supervising Secretary Chen Weixin com-plained that some officials, hoping to reverse the final verdict on the

Three Cases, failed to understand that the purpose of the *Sanchao yaodian* was to celebrate the paternal compassion and filial piety of the Ming
imperial family. They did not see that the "fixed verdict" *(dinglun)* in the
Three Cases was reached before Wei Zhongxian ever came to power!
Therefore, while the treatise must no longer be used as an enemies' list,
neither must it be tampered with.[34] Chongzhen "noted" receipt of this
memorial.

On May 1, 1628, a minor official sent up a memorial from Nanjing demanding that the *Sanchao yaodian* be revised so as to remove from its text
all the false indictments composed by former Decree Prison director Xu
Xianchun, all the memorials written by Cui Chengxiu and other condemned eunuch-partisans, and all the charges of "villainy and hetero-
doxy" laid against the Donglin adherents.[35] This demand the emperor
rejected.

Hanlin Expositor-in-waiting Ni Yuanlu was probably following the emperor's cryptic clues. In a memorial of June 1, soon to become famous,
he laid before Chongzhen the argument that the Three Cases were unde-
cidable; that there were meritorious intentions on either side of the controversy; and that the *Sanchao yaodian* itself was Wei Zhongxian's "personal compilation," which favored one side for purely political reasons.
Therefore, concluded Ni, it was advisable neither to preserve the text nor
to revise it in such a way as to overturn the verdict; the only acceptable
alternative was to destroy it altogether.[36] Chongzhen was impressed with
this argument, and he ordered the Ministry of Rites to gather historians
from the Hanlin to discuss Ni's proposal.

A heated debate must have ensued. On or around June 11, Hanlin
Expositor-in-waiting Sun Zhixie, beside himself with disappointment and
frustration, stormed weeping into the Grand Secretariat, where allegedly
he howled to Heaven, jumped up and down, spluttered expletives, ripped
up his cap, and vowed to die, all in protest over the threatened destruction of the *Sanchao yaodian*.

The scene shocked everyone. Supervising Secretary Zhang Chengzhao
impeached Sun for his behavior. Censor Wu Huan rebutted Sun's argument that Chongzhen would in effect be ignoring his own brother's imperial command if he should order the book destroyed. Sun Zhixie was
dismissed from office.[37] The imperial rescript went ahead and ordered all
palace copies of the *Sanchao yaodian* destroyed, and it directed local and
educational officials all over China to destroy all printing blocks and all
stocks of printed copies on hand.

The emperor indicated by his action in the *Sanchao yaodian* dispute that he intended to strike a hard blow against partisanship of any kind whenever he had the opportunity. He was resolutely destroying the Wei Zhongxian gang. He had agreed to rehabilitate Wei Zhongxian's victims. His purpose in destroying the *Sanchao yaodian* was to bury the Three Cases altogether as a bone of partisan contention. On at least two occasions he rejected requests to reopen the academies as centers of *jiangxue* (discussion and study).[38] By edict he warned the bureaucracy not to engage in further partisan polemics.[39] But his hopes were in vain, because the Donglin wanted total vindication.

On December 17, 1627, Chongzhen agreed to a palace eunuch's request to rehabilitate Wang An, the pro-Donglin eunuch who had been removed and killed in 1621. But on January 4, 1628, when a surviving brother of Wang An sent up another plea in Wang An's behalf, Chongzhen denied the plea and sent the petitioner away from Beijing for fear he might start some sort of "incident."[40]

"What is the Donglin?" asked Ni Yuanlu in a plea of February 11. "It is the 'talent grove' of the realm. Though sometimes too harsh and aggressive, it represents purity. Though sometimes too opinionated, it stands for lofty enlightenment." Remnants of the "deviant clique" of Cui and Wei were even now suppressing it, said Ni, using the "iron case" labeled by the slogans *daoxue* (dissenting Confucianism) and *fengqiang* (territorial losses in Manchuria) to beat it down.[41] Chongzhen declined Ni's invitation to issue a blanket endorsement of the Donglin faction.

Censor Yang Weiyuan rebutted Ni in a memorial of February 24. How, he asked, can Ni deny the presence of greedy, arrogant, and philosophically deluded people in the Donglin? And why was he making "Cui–Wei" into a "case," namely, a partisan issue?[42]

Ni responded with a long and emotional riposte of March 2. In it, he asserted that making a "case" *(duian)* of Cui–Wei was precisely the right thing for the "loyal and upright" men of the world to do, because the low moral character *(pinjie)* of Cui and Wei was perfectly evident; they had killed good men of talent and reputation because they feared them, and so "using [the names] 'Cui–Wei' to discriminate the deviant from the upright is just like using a mirror to tell the difference between the ugly and the beautiful." Should the Donglin killers be immune from all criticism?[43] Chongzhen replied that opinions should be united, and he chided the writer for arguing.

Censor Yang replied on March 7 that the crux of the matter was not

"Cui–Wei" at all. The real case *(duian)* was "making contact with Palace eunuchs" *(tongnei)*. Ruan Dacheng further argued in a memorial that it was Wang Wenyan who had started the turmoil with his link to Wang An, an arrangement that was simply copied by Cui Chengxiu and others when they made their links to Wei Zhongxian.[44] The emperor "noted" these memorials, but it was clear he agreed with them, because on March 30 he issued an edict reminding the officials of what had happened in the Tianqi era and warning them never again to make contacts with palace eunuchs.[45] (Because Yang Lian and many of the other Donglin heroes had in fact made such contacts, it was impossible for the avengers of the Donglin to achieve a complete partisan victory over those whom they labeled the "Cui–Wei" forces.)

Was Political Partisanship Legitimate?

Late Ming political discourse suggests that, on balance, the answer to that question is no. Partisan mobilization seems only to have been justifiable, not as a good thing in its own right, but as a response to the refusal of the emperor, beginning specifically with the Wanli emperor, to supply moral leadership to the realm. And the Donglin partisans, who stepped into the breach, foundered when, as an association of morally superior "gentlemen," they had for practical reasons to enlist the help of certain "small men" in the struggle for political supremacy in Beijing. Although they tried, it proved impossible for the Donglin spokesmen to gloss over this contradiction.

The Donglin academy in Wuxi, founded in 1604 by Gu Xiancheng and Gao Panlong, for twenty years made a deep impression upon a significant fraction of scholar-officials and students from all over China. Through its study by discussion *(jiangxue)* method, Gu and Gao and other invited lecturers taught how the discovery of one's essential moral self must be achieved by way of outwardly directed moral effort.[46] They warned their listeners that "small men" everywhere were trying to build a world without gentlemen and without fathers and were "drowned in self-seeking freedom, while pretending to be concerned with *tao* [*dao*] and other virtues."[47] Gu and Gao also sought, through patronage and personal influence, and through hard infighting, placement for their degree-holding friends and protégés in available bureaucratic positions in Beijing. It was in political struggle of that sort that the outwardly directed dictum of "loving good and hating evil" proved useful as an energizing imperative.

(However, Gao Panlong was careful to explain in a lecture that loving good and hating evil was a dictum that was intended only for men of the "first caliber" [*yideng*] to act upon; men of the "second or third caliber," he cautioned, lack the moral development requisite to making their own judgments in such matters.)[48]

In a 1613 memorial, Donglin sympathizer Liu Zongzhou conceded that Donglin partisan mobilization was not inherently a good thing but a side effect of the Wanli emperor's refusal to lead and govern the realm. Lacking the hand of a morally right-guided autocrat, the Donglin, he argued, were left to rally behind the doctrine of loving good and hating evil to defend or attack other officials on the basis of their perceived moral worth *(liupin)*—that is, as gentlemen *(junzi)* or as small men *(xiaoren)*. Liu admitted that at times this activity led to an excess of "cruelty and unfeeling" *(canke er buqing)*. He also insisted that it was not appropriate that gentlemen should form factions among themselves that were based upon different "views" *(yijian)* in controversial political issues. They should just agree to differ.[49]

In practice, Liu's approach did not work. The Donglin did take "views," arguing in the Three Cases that persons of high moral character might rally behind a single view, leaving only persons of low moral character to champion the contrary positions. Liu's friend Gao Panlong helped press for this radicalization. In a memorial of 1622, and again in 1623, Gao gave a ringing endorsement of the rectitude of the paranoid reading of the evidence in the Palace Case of 1620.[50] In effect, he associated high moral character with the holding of a certain "view" in an issue of political controversy.

Gao Panlong further argued that partisan groups or factions or cliques *(dang)* form inevitably, but they comprise all gentlemen on one side and all small men on the other. In the case of small men, the factions they form are inherently "biased" (they are a *piandang*). Gentlemen, by contrast, naturally group together as members of a single species *(lei):* they constitute a *danglei zhi dang,* that is, a clique or fellowship that forms on the basis of common characteristics that each member recognizes or senses in the other—and that nonmembers also recognize, and condemn. In a long October 1622 message addressed to his Beijing colleagues, Gao argued that strictly speaking there was no "Donglin *dang*," as Supervising Secretary Zhu Tongmeng had charged when he attacked the Shoushan academy as a center for partisan organization. Gao stated that anytime anyone says or does anything that is correct, anytime any excellent person is appointed to a vacant position, the small men raise a clamor and accuse such people of being Donglin men. "No matter that they are men from every different part of China, who have no connection with each other—if they act with uprightness, they are regarded as members of this single *dang!*"[51]

In his controversial essay on factions, however, Gao argued that it was a mistake for gentlemen in the heat of battle to deny that they constitute a *dang*. But no *dang* was capable of achieving anything all by itself. Autocratic support was absolutely essential. According to Gao, there was only one way to bring an end to the disastrous partisan strife of the 1620s: the emperor had to identify and appoint to the highest positions the handful of outstanding personalities among the *dang* of gentlemen and reject the handful of outstanding leaders among the small men. The rest of officialdom, being of middling quality, would follow as a matter of course the lead of the outstanding gentlemen.[52]

Early in the Tianqi reign, Liu Zongzhou had made an argument of just this kind in a personal letter he wrote to Grand Secretary Zhu Guozhen, urging him neither to sit by and "observe from a distance" (*guanwang*) nor to follow chief Grand Secretary Ye Xianggao and "work out compromises" (*tiaoting*). He implored Zhu to strive to make the young ruler a moral autocrat—a Yao or Shun. Liu accurately foresaw that Tianqi would try to withdraw from government as his grandfather Wanli had done, placing actual rule in the hands of some effective practitioner of harsh methods, as early in his reign Wanli had done with Grand Secretary Zhang Juzheng.[53] Of course Tianqi's surrogate was not a grand secretary but palace eunuch Wei Zhongxian.

After the deaths of Tianqi and Wei Zhongxian, arguments over the legitimacy of factions were resumed at court. In 1628–1629, as the time for the sexennial evaluations of Beijing officials approached, some speaking officials at court tried to eliminate all talk of factions. Officials, they said, were either upright or deviant; history had shown that to assume or to charge that those making such judgments did so on partisan grounds was to invite dynastic collapse.[54]

Censor Ren Zanhua patiently explained that when one talked about "gentlemen" and "small men" one was talking about species or categories (*lei*), not factions. It was like the colors red, white, blue, and so on, which are easily distinguishable from each other. It was like dogs and horses, which from birth (from the time they receive *qi*) are of a different species from human beings. How puzzled we would be if dogs or horses should point at us and call us all members of a human faction! Unless we avoided the word "faction," we could not even say that the categories of human being, dog, or horse even exist! So the emperor just needed to separate officials by moral quality *(liupin)*, and on that basis determine the right or wrong of what they said.[55]

Supervising Secretary Liu Mou said there was no need to consider parties or cliques as real entities. Government was a matter of partiality or impartiality in individuals. It was not eloquence or talent that characterized upright gentlemen, but impartial thinking. Gentlemen kept not their own interests but the interests of the ruler, the dynasty, and the people in mind. In the Tianqi era, it was the self-concerned thinking of people like Grand Secretary Wei Guangwei that led them to identify their critics as members of a Donglin camp *(menhu)*, which in turn occasioned the fateful transfer of power to Wei Zhongxian in the inner Palace and the near collapse of the Ming.[56]

The Chongzhen emperor emphatically agreed with these arguments. He insisted that all talk of factions and camps destroyed government and therefore must cease. On February 18, 1629, he met with a large gathering of officials in the Wenhua palace in conjunction with a fierce dispute in which each side was accusing the other of partisanship—of old links to the Donglin and Cui-Wei factions. "Well, just consider this," said Chongzhen after a long day of listening to both sides. "When have [the speaking officials] ever had the dynasty *(guojia)* in mind? I can tell when they're really focusing on the *guo*, the *jia*, the national territory, the well-being of the people. But they don't send up anything unless it suits their selfish purposes. What kind of time is this? We have alarms east and west, we have war north and south, yet they have no anxiety for the dynasty, all they do is divide into camps, all they talk about is some clique *(dang)*, some Donglin, and of what benefit is that to national affairs?"[57]

The case for or against factions could, in the end, never be definitively resolved, couched as it was in Confucian moral theory, and vividly colored as it was by recent memory of the events of the disastrous Tianqi reign. Even if not asserted by members, faction could always be inferred and imputed by others.

If one followed Gao Panlong's argument, "factions" were natural sociomoral formations, and in order for China to be ruled well, the emperor needed only to coopt into his administration the leaders among that self-selected faction which was made up of individuals of recognizably superior moral type.

If, further, one followed the argument made later by Hou Fangyu (1618–1655), then only gentlemen formed factions. And it was right that they should do so. The argument that factionlessness should prevail (which Chongzhen preferred) was nothing but a clever ploy advanced by small men. Small men clung to the specious slogan "stand independent and minimize collegial ties" *(duli guayu)*, which in fact just licensed opportunism, allowing them to feint and shift, straight today and crooked tomorrow.[58] Even from youth a good gentleman must have his close friends! If he is friendless, it means worthies have rejected him and he must be evil, or else humble to excess. "How," asked Hou, "can a gentleman with a will to serve the world stand independent and minimize collegial ties?" Partisan circles *(dang, menhu)*, he pointed out, were to be found everywhere in China. Sometimes an entire province was made up of small men. Sometimes there were gentleman and small-man cliques in the various prefectures and counties. And it happened that even inside families, fathers, sons, and brothers divided into gentleman and small-man cliques![59]

Liu Zongzhou (back in office, as prefect of Beijing's Shuntian prefecture) protested in a long memorial of November 1629 that while the label *"menhu"* was the reason for the killing of "countless upright men [embodying] primal *qi*" in recent years, the emperor was keeping the *menhu* struggle alive by the very balancing act (between the upright Yang–Zuo and the deviant Cui–Wei factions) that he hoped would suppress it.[60] The emperor was not pleased by this argument.

The Donglin in Retrospect

Later on, as time passed and the Tianqi era could be viewed in longer perspective, most commentators took the position that the Donglin's politicization of virtue had been a grave mistake. According to Feng Ban (1602–1671), gentlemen should associate with each other not on the basis of party but on the basis of impartiality and righteousness. The Donglin experience showed that when gentlemen form a party, harm results. The Donglin men were upright gentlemen, but it was unfortunately self-interest *(siyi)* that led them to create a camp *(menhu)*.[61]

Lin Shidui (1615–1705) thought that some in the Donglin suffered from an excess of heat and ardor. The Donglin founders were gentlemen, but they created a camp, and they attracted evil opportunists into that camp.

Real men *(hanzi)*, he said, stand without fear above the storm, and do not seek shelter in the camps of other people.[62]

A dynasty afflicted with *dang*, concluded Zhu Haoling (1606–1683), was like a tree riddled with termites. All *dang* were bad. The Donglin *dang* was organized around opinion; in the struggle over the Three Cases, the Donglin leaders' heroics "eclipsed the sun and moon and drove the wind and storm," but they had to accept help from small men, and the whole "partisan disaster" *(danghuo)* that ensued was responsible for the fall of the Ming. It was always a mistake to identify small men and engage them in battle, as the Donglin had. Gentlemen should remember that they cannot vanquish small men through partisanship. They vanquish small men when they act with impartiality and perfect calm; they must never yield to emotionalism and rancor.[63]

Back in the Tianqi era, noted Chen Tingjing (1639–1712), the scholar-officials prided themselves on being Donglin stalwarts. They so eagerly sought respect and fame that they frivolously provoked the anger of small men. It did not matter to them that their pursuit of personal reputation came at the dynasty's expense, and, indeed, had those gentlemen not perished, the Ming dynasty might not have collapsed as soon as it did.[64]

The distinction between gentlemen and small men was and had to remain total and absolute, according to Huang Zongxi (1610–1695; son of Donglin martyr Huang Zunsu). Even so, he agreed that the Donglin ("our party") had been too radical. Huang Zongxi's father had, after all, tried to stop Wei Dazhong from impeaching Grand Secretary Wei Guangwei, but Wei Dazhong cared more for his own reputation *(mingjie)* than he did for the fate of the dynasty. "If the small men were driven to the extremity of using the eunuch [Wei Zhongxian] to wreak vengeance, the fault for that lay with the gentlemen of the Tianqi era," he concluded.[65]

There was wide agreement in the Qing that the fate of the Ming was sealed by what had happened in the Tianqi era. There were differences, however, about who or what bore the main responsibility. Was it the Tianqi emperor? Anthologist Chen Ding (b. 1651) thought so. So childish and stupid *(tonghun)* a ruler was Tianqi that, wrote Chen, not even the duke of Zhou could have controlled the crowd of "tigers and wolves" that came to dominate his court. Tianqi was scarcely aware that Wei Zhongxian was stealing his power. "Heaven sent disaster to the dynasty by giving birth to that characterless *(bucai)* ruler," he concluded. After

the damage Tianqi had done, there was nothing his successor, the Chongzhen emperor, could do to save the realm.[66]

However, historian Tan Qian (1594–1658) did not think that Tianqi personally was all that much to blame. He noted that in the fifteenth century the Yongle emperor had trained his grandson, the Xuande emperor, so
that upon his succession Xuande would be able to cope with the demands
of the job. The Wanli emperor, by contrast, did not attend court, and the
child Tianqi grew up in the Cining palace where he knew nothing of outside affairs and had no one but eunuchs and palace women to educate
him. For all the evils of his reign, noted Tan Qian, Tianqi must be given
credit for having refused to revive Wanli's policy of having eunuchs run
the nation's mines, and especially for his vouchsafing the succession of the
throne to his younger brother, the Chongzhen emperor.[67]

Or was no one specifically to blame? The Ming dynastic history, published in 1739, comments (after its biographies of the Donglin martyrs):
"When a dynasty is about to perish, it first destroys its own good species
(shanlei). After that, there come flood, drought, and banditry. So at the
beginning point of [a time of] disaster and chaos, it is the gentlemen
among the scholar-officials who, remarkably, suffer the poison first. In the
case of the Ming, all the court officials argued endlessly the so-called
Three Cases, and the great villains used that as a means to extirpate the
good species, which is how Yang [Lian] and Zuo [Guangdou] and the
others ended up as corpses in the [Decree] prison. It was like the late
years of the Eastern Han all over again. Nothing could have saved the
Ming."[68]

There never was a final, single verdict in the Donglin matter. What the
Donglin had stood for and what it had suffered called for everlasting
commemoration. And yet, at the very same time, what hindsight suggested the Donglin had done was to set in motion the collapse of the very
dynasty they had thought they were rescuing, and for this it appeared
they deserved resolute condemnation.

In his preface to his biographical anthology of leading Donglin personalities (the *Donglin liezhuan,* published in 1711), Chen Ding reflected upon the unhappy terminal years of the Ming and considered what the
Donglin had done to shape them. The great legacy of the Donglin, he asserted, was its creation through the technique of *jiangxue* (discussion and
study) of a historically unprecedented spiritual revolution; the Donglin
had raised the moral level of China's long civilization to such a degree
that nothing in the past could compare with it. The Donglin changed the

whole moral atmosphere *(fengqi)* of China. They taught the "study of the sages"; they elucidated "righteous principles"; they encouraged "honesty and sense of shame"; they made people look on the dynasty *(guo)* as a family *(jia)*, on the ruler as a father; they encouraged people to pursue right like water flowing downhill, and to look on death as a return home. And just observe how many people of all classes—from the Chongzhen emperor and high officials, the gentry, even down to commoners and their wives and daughters—"willingly committed suicide as proof of their moral resolve, or suffered slaughter to bring to a completion their benevolence." Chen Ding said that he was able to uncover the stories of some forty-six hundred martyrs, not counting women. Martyrs came forth in solid ranks, heel to heel and shoulder to shoulder, and all thanks to Donglin teaching. "No dynasty," he said in a ringing phrase, "ever fell in more brilliant glory than did the Ming."[69]

It was probably hard for the editors of the Qianlong emperor's "Four Treasuries" project to decide what to do with Chen Ding's work. In the end they decided to accept and recopy it for the imperial library.[70] But the Manchu emperor attached a preface of his own, dated 1778, to Chen's preface; in it, he heavily berated Chen Ding for his false notions. "The Donglin discussion and study began in uprightness," he thundered, "but it ended in chaos, and it brought the Ming down with it.... The gentlemen should have carried on the [Ming] founders' legacy and brought peace to the people. Given that they failed to keep that legacy, it is hardly reasonable to consider their martyrdom in a lost cause as glorious.... When the Donglin let small men into their ranks, that was just like opening the door to invite in the thieves, and that is where the partisan imprisonments began. The Donglin brought this on themselves, and they kept it up until the Ming fell. Chen Ding wrongs the ruler, the bureaucracy, and [the ideal of the] upright man and the gentleman. [Above all], any gentleman should want his dynasty to survive, and the people to prosper!"[71]

There was, and is, no certain way to reconcile these conflicting views of the Donglin legacy. However, though the Qianlong emperor condemned the Donglin men for their political shortsightedness, he did not go so far as to impugn the martyrs' sincerity, or, indeed, to order the destruction of Chen Ding's work, as he could have done. In effect, the emperor left open the possibility that the self-sacrifices of the Donglin heroes might look altogether better if they were not judged in the light of practical questions of governance at all. There was another way to

commemorate those who gave their lives for moral principles and in protest of evil. This way transcended practical issues. It was cosmic.

In 1848, publisher Pan Xi'en wrote a preface to a collectaneum he put
together consisting of the prose writings of 101 moral heroes and martyrs,
ranging in date from the fourth century B.C. to the end of the Ming and
including the Donglin heroes. (Seventy-two of his 101 heroes lived in the
Ming.) He called the collectaneum *Qiankun zhengqi ji,* or "rectified *qi*
(moral climate, ethical energy) between Heaven and Earth." He noted
that *qi* is a cosmic substance that should be "upright" *(zheng),* but in the
course of time and events it turns "deviant" *(xie).* In times of crisis, when
yin and yang struggle with each other, deviant *qi* overspreads the world,
and "if no one steps forth then, and uses all his strength to support and
revive [upright *qi*], then surely Heaven and Earth come to destruction.
By 'upright *qi*' is meant commonality without partiality; making plans for
the entire state, not single families; acting for the whole realm, not the
single individual. And there is no greater instance of *qi* in a rectified condition than when men go so far as to sacrifice themselves and their families for the sake of the state and the realm."[72]

This sort of cosmic thinking is by no means dead in China today.[73] It is
thus on a cosmic battlefield, in the partly pure, partly contaminated fields
of *qi* that fill the space between Heaven and Earth, that human beings
must from time to time take this side or that in an all-out war. To fight
to restore upright *qi* is to love good and hate evil, to uphold the whole
and not the part, and to sacrifice absolutely everything to the cause.
Student leader Chai Ling's startling statements of 1989, linking the unity
of China to love and hate and blood and sacrificial slaughter, seem to
have had, not so much "science" and "democracy," as these deeper philosophical and historical resonances implicitly behind them. Likewise, in
1624, Yang Lian and Wei Dazhong and Li Yingsheng were not thinking
about practical matters of governance at all when they flung their missiles
at personified evil, knowingly placing their lives at risk when they did so.
It is at this rarefied cosmic level that blood and history in China achieve
their full and indeed intended effect.

When the pseudonymous "Beijing Guest" described in awful detail
what happened inside the Decree Prison in 1625, he called his account
"Proof of the Conjunction of Heaven and Man: A True Record" *(Tianren hezheng jishi),* thus evoking the cosmic context for the gruesome facts
he reported. He noted in the spring of 1625 an unusual juncture of the
moon with a certain constellation, which to him meant that "innocent

high officials were about to come to grief." Specifically, the heavenly bodies foretold poisonous disaster for officials of the Censorate—which would be Yang Lian and Zuo Guangdou; and, sure enough, their arrests were ordered a month later. Next the Beijing Guest sighted a noctilucent cloud positioned in a certain way, which prefigured the torture and deaths of Yang, Zuo, and Wei Dazhong on eunuch orders; and, after that, the sun and the planet Venus were visible in the same sky together, normally indicating an inferior competing with the ruler for power *(quan)*, but the eunuch's power was already complete, so the Beijing Guest interpreted the phenomenon to mean the imminent deaths of the remaining Donglin prisoners.

And so it turned out. But the Beijing Guest was not primarily interested in showing the world the accuracy of his astrological predictions. He kept a daily log of what happened in the Decree Prison at the risk of his own life for a different purpose: so that "a hundred generations from now, the air *(feng)* of the [Six Gentlemen] will still be current, and people will continue to mourn them."[74] The narrative itself leaves no doubt of the writer's emotional involvement in the fate of the men who came to know him as a *youxin ren*—"a man with a heart."

Someday, perhaps, the legacy of the demonstrations of 1989 will be reinterpreted by whatever government is then ruling in Beijing in a way somewhat resembling the Qing interpretation of the Donglin legacy of 1620–1627: as a grievous mistake in practical politics but a glorious exercise in collective sincerity, which demonstrated the moral capacity of the people of China, led by the best and brightest among them, to rise to a level high above their mundane and selfish concerns and to write with their blood yet another chapter of a very special history that has a place all its own in defining what China is all about.

Notes

◀

Introduction

1. Heinrich Busch, "The Tung-lin Shu-yuan and Its Political and Philosophical Significance," *Monumenta Serica* 14 (1949–1955): 48.

2. Notably, Xie Guozhen, *Ming Qing zhi ji dangshe yundong kao* (Taipei, 1967), and Ono Kazuko, *Minki tōsha kō—Tōrintō to Fukusha* (Kyoto, 1996), commence the story of partisan conflict with the controversies occasioned by the grand secretaryship of Zhang Juzheng (1567–1582) and bring it down to the years of the Ming collapse and Manchu conquest of the mid-seventeenth century.

3. Charles O. Hucker, "The Tung-lin Movement of the Late Ming Period," in John K. Fairbank, ed., *Chinese Thought and Institutions* (Chicago, 1957), pp. 132–162.

4. Lee Feigon, *China Rising: The Meaning of Tiananmen* (Chicago, 1990), p. 242. However, a few informants told Perry Link that their individual and joint petitions of January and February 1989, in which they urged the leadership to release political prisoners and permit democracy, uneasily reminded them of the Donglin effort of the 1620s, which ended disastrously. See Perry Link, *Evening Chats in Beijing* (New York, 1992), p. 166.

5. Joseph W. Esherick and Jeffrey N. Wasserstrom, "Acting Out Democracy: Political Theater in Modern China," in Wasserstrom and Perry, eds., *Popular Protest and Political Culture in Modern China: Learning from 1989* (Boulder, Colo., 1991), pp. 26–66.

6. John Israel, "Reflections on 'Reflections on the Modern Chinese Student Movement,'" in ibid., p. 85ff.

7. Han Minzhu (pseud.), ed., *Cries for Democracy: Writings and Speeches from the 1989 Chinese Democracy Movement* (Princeton, N.J., 1990), p. 95.

8. Ibid., p. 126.

9. Ibid., p. 284.

10. Ibid., p. 198.

11. Ibid., p. 45.

12. Ibid., p. 123.

13. Ibid., p. 327.

14. Ibid., p. 363.

15. Richard Baum, "The Road to Tiananmen: Chinese Politics in the 1980s," in Roderick MacFarquhar, ed., *The Politics of China* (Cambridge, 1993), pp. 458–463.

16. See, for example, Wai-yee Li, *Enchantment and Disenchantment: Love and Illusion in Chinese Literature* (Princeton, N.J., 1993), p. 62; Katherine Carlitz, "Style and Suffering in Two Stories by 'Langxian,'" in Theodore Huters et al., eds., *Culture and State in Chinese History* (Stanford, Calif., 1997), p. 233.

17. For descriptions of what happened, see Ray Huang, "The Lung-ch'ing and

Wan-li Reigns, 1567–1620," in Frederick W. Mote and Denis Twitchett, eds., *The Cambridge History of China*, vol. 7, pt. 1 (Cambridge, 1988), pp. 577–584; and William Atwell, "The T'ai-ch'ang, T'ien-ch'i, and Ch'ung-chen Reigns, 1620–1644," in ibid., pp. 599–605).

18. Described in detail in Frederic Wakeman, Jr., *The Great Enterprise: The Manchu Reconstruction of Order in Seventeenth-Century China*, 2 vols. (Berkeley, 1985).

19. Tang Tsou, "The Tiananmen Tragedy: The State–Society Relationship, Choices, and Mechanisms in Historical Perspective," in Brantly Womack, ed., *Contemporary Chinese Politics in Historical Perspective* (Cambridge, 1991), pp. 265–327. Tsou does not mention the Donglin episode.

20. A possibility entertained, for instance, in Benjamin Elman, "Imperial Politics and Confucian Societies in Late Imperial China," *Modern China* 15.4 (October 1989): 389.

21. Indeed, it is questionable how "democratic" the thought expressed in the protest of 1989 was. Yan Jiaqi's idea of the role of the common people of China in government, as an ultimate source of correct views and feelings on fundamental issues, is close to what Donglin martyr Miao Changqi wrote. See Yan Jiaqi, *Toward a Democratic China: The Intellectual Biography of Yan Jiaqi* (Honolulu, 1989), pp. 63, 91, 135–136, 212.

22. The classic work on this institution is Charles O. Hucker, *The Censorial System of Ming China* (Stanford, Calif., 1966), especially chapter 5, on the Tianqi reign.

Chapter 1. The Ming Throne Imperiled

1. The Wanli emperor and the succession issue have been discussed in interesting detail by Ray Huang, *1587: A Year of No Significance* (New Haven, Conn., 1981), especially chapters 1, 3, and 4.

2. *Wanli dichao* (1969), 3.2203–2204; Yao Zongdian, *Cunshi lu*, 28b–29a.

3. Gu Yingtai, *Mingshi jishi benmo* 4.37; Sheng Feng, *Jiahe zhengxian lu*, 7.13ab, 28.7b–8a, 31.8ab.

4. Yao Zongdian, *Cunshi lu*, 29b–31a.

5. *Ming shi*, 21.6343–6348 (biography of Wang Zhicai); Xu Qianxue, *Xuben Mingshi liezhuan*, 94.665–669 (biography of Lu Menglong).

6. Tan Qian, *Guo que*, 5.5082.

7. *Sanchao yaodian*, 1.137–139.

8. Ibid., 1.134–136.

9. *Wanli dichao*, 3.2212–2213.

10. Ibid., 3.2215–2220.

11. Charles O. Hucker, biography of Chu I-chün, in Goodrich and Fang, eds., *Dictionary of Ming Biography*, 1.327.

12. *Sanchao yaodian*, 1.168–179; Yao Zongdian, *Cunshi lu*, 36a–37b.

13. *Sanchao yaodian*, 1.186–188.

14. *Wanli dichao*, 3.2240; *Sanchao yaodian*, 1.195–197.

15. In 1623, Chief Grand Secretary Ye Xianggao concluded after hearing both sides of the case that, crazy or not, Zhang Chai had somehow singled out among the "thousands of gates" in the Forbidden City the very one that led to the heir apparent's res-

idence and would have killed the heir apparent had the eunuchs not stopped him, and for those and other reasons the existence of an assassination plot was likely. *Ju bian,* pp. 446–447.

16. Yang Lian, 1.193–200 (memorial).

17. Ibid. The *Sanchao yaodian* wrongly gives the date September 20 for Yang's impeachment.

18. *Sanchao yaodian,* 2.844–857. Explanations of the medical terms and the ingredients of the pill, all commonplaces in traditional Chinese medicine, may be found in Joseph Needham, *Science and Civilisation in China,* vol. 5, pt. 5, p. 26.

19. *Ming shilu,* 126.1161–1165.

20. Ibid., 1062–1064.

21. Ibid., 1153–1155.

22. Zhang Po, 5b.

23. Yang Lian, 1.289 (statement to colleagues detailing the two enthronements). Lady Zheng, of course, was Zheng Guifei, Wanli's favorite concubine and mother of the exiled Zhu Changxun.

24. Zhang Po, under date *jimao.* Wang Tianrui was Taichang's maternal grandfather. Guo Jiazhen was related to a consort of Taichang's.

25. The paragraphs that follow are based principally on Yang Lian's account, which he submitted to the court on December 29, 1620 (*Ming shilu,* 124.174ff.). In addition, later accounts were submitted as official memorials by Donglin figures Han Kuang (in *Ming shilu,* 126.1161–1165), and Zhang Wenda (in *Ming shilu,* 126.1165–1167). There is also Zhang Po's account, in his *Gengshen jishi.*

26. Zhang Po, 4a.

27. Luo Ruoyu, p. 205.

28. Zuo Guangdou, 304(1).19b–20a.

29. Gu Yingtai; 4.53; Xia Xie, 5.2967.

30. *Ming shilu,* 124.66–67.

31. Ibid., 68–69. On November 17, a fire of unknown origin burned the Huiluan palace to the ground. No one was injured. In 1623, Lady Li was declared to be living in the Ciqing palace. *Ming shilu,* 124.103; 128.1742–1743.

32. *Sanchao yaodian,* 3.983–987.

33. Ibid., 994–1005.

34. Yang Lian, 1.209–219; *Ming shilu,* 124.174–178.

35. *Ming shilu,* 124.181–185.

36. Li Changchun, 2.57–59, 73–74.

37. Ibid., 6–10.

38. Yang Lian, 1.229–240.

39. Neither Lady Zheng nor Lady Li was ever asked to give, nor did either provide, their own testimony about the Three Cases. Lady Zheng lived on in the Palace until her death on July 5, 1630, and Lady Li likewise until her death on June 21, 1674. For the latter date, see Wang Shizhen, *Chibei outan,* 2.1b.

40. Huang Zunsu, *Shuo lue,* 12a, reports: "In 1622, I came to the capital for evaluation and selection. At the time, the partisan camps were fighting for adherents. The three cases were being used to test people's attitudes. An influential person asked me how I stood on the three cases. I said: 'It's been a while since Guangzong [Taichang]

died, and the present emperor has been some time on the throne. The three cases are past history now. They are not really the critical issue before the court.' The fellow had no riposte to that, and left."

Chapter 2. Beijing, 1620–1624

1. Liu Ruoyu, pp. 143–148.

2. Including Gu Dazhang and Yang Lian, when the latter was magistrate of Changshu county, 1608–1613.

3. Huang Zunsu, 327(3).5a–6b (biography of Wang Wenyan); Gong Liben, pp. 60–61; Ye Xianggao, *Jubian*, p. 486; *Sanchao yaodian*, 3.1295–1299, 1325–1331.

4. Liu Ruoyu, pp. 156–157.

5. Qian Qianyi, *Muzhai youxue ji*, 28.1a–10b (epitaph for Liu Yijing).

6. Liu Ruoyu, pp. 148–154.

7. *Jubian*, p. 331.

8. Tan Qian, *Guo que*, 5.5191. (The memorial is not reported in the *Ming shilu*.)

9. Liu Ruoyu, p. 155. Nanhaizi was 20 *li* south of Beijing, according to Sun Chengze, *Chunming mengyu lu*, p. 957.

10. Song Qifeng, *Bai shuo*, p. 59. Madame Ke had a son of her own, Hou Guoxing, born ca. 1610, according to later official report (Zhu Changzuo, pp. 143–152). She came from Dingxing county, 60 miles southwest of Beijing, also the home of Donglin supporter Lu Shanji.

11. Liu Ruoyu, p. 225. The official criminal indictment, issued probably sometime in the early months of 1628, states that Madame Ke was 48 *sui*. If she was 48 *sui* at the time of her death in December 1627, then she was probably born in 1580. Tan Qian, *Guo que*, 6.5382 states that she became a palace wet nurse at 18 *sui*, i.e., 1598, and became a widow two years later. But her son Hou Guoxing, was, according to a criminal indictment dated January 26, 1628 (still in the twelfth month of the seventh year of Tianqi), 18 *sui*. That would put his birthdate in roughly 1610. By that time, his father, Hou Er, was already ten years dead. Perhaps 18 is a copyist's error for 28.

12. Liu Ruoyu, p. 210; *Ming shilu*, 124.58.

13. Liu Ruoyu, pp. 201–202, 216; Zhu Changzuo, pp. 131–141, 143–152 (criminal indictments and official testimony dating to 1628).

14. Zhu Changzuo, pp. 2–4.

15. *Cheqian yeyu*, 8b–9b. Interestingly, Liu Ruoyu, who knew Wei Zhongxian and has a great deal to say about him, gives no reason at all why Wei had himself castrated.

16. Liu Ruoyu, pp. 202–204.

17. Zhu Changzuo, p. 4.

18. Liu Ruoyu, pp. 205–209.

19. Sun Qifeng, *Xiafeng xiansheng ji*, 7.22a–25b (epitaph for Gao Shiming). Restated without source attribution in Sun Chengze, *Chunming mengyu lu*, pp. 98–99.

20. Sun Chengzong, 3(572).14ab *Ming shilu*, 124.90.

21. Liu Ruoyu, pp. 77, 538.

22. *Ming shilu*, 124.261.

23. Zhu Yizun, *Pushuting ji*, 53.4ab.

24. *Jubian*, p. 331.

25. *Ming shilu*, 126.1242; 127.1505. The *Dijian tushuo* was already proposed in July 1622 (*Ming shilu*, 126.1145).

26. *Ming shilu*, 127.1384–1388.

27. Li Sunzhi, *Sanchao yeji*, pp. 227–228.

28. Jin Risheng, 4.1503–1510.

29. *Ming shilu*, 127.1384–1390, 1397–1398; Ye Xianggao, *Lunfei zoucao*, 6.3125–3133; *Jubian*, pp. 395–396; Zheng Man, *Zheng Man shiji*, pp. 1509–1510.

30. Ji Yun, *Ming Yian huanghou waizhuan;* Zhu Haoling, 2.698–699 (a note about Zhou Daodeng); *Ming shilu*, 125.436, 482. (Zhou Daodeng had acting charge of the Ministry of Rites and participated in the vetting of candidates. He removed a girl who was related to Zheng Guifei, the notorious concubine of Wanli.)

31. *Ming shilu*, 125.551–552, 712. Ji Yun has it that after the Sun Er affair failed, Wei Zhongxian hired an assassin who tried but failed to kill her in her palace, the Kunning, located some 50 meters to the rear of the Qianqing. Then Wei began attacking the empress's father's family. In June 1622, several Zhang family servants were arrested and placed under the heavy cangue for three months, a punishment sure to end in death. Minister of Justice Wang Ji and chief Grand Secretary Ye Xianggao protested the cruelty of those sentences, but to no avail (*Ming shilu*, 126.1109–1110; Ye Xianggao, *Jubian*, p. 372). Palace rumor had it that when the empress's only pregnancy ended in a still-birth in 1623, it was because a palace maid acting at the behest of Ke and Wei had given her a massage designed to kill her fetus (Liu Ruoyu, p. 140).

32. *Ming shilu*, 125.576–578.

33. Ibid., 730.

34. Zhou Zongjian, 311(2).9a–11a (memorial impeaching Madame Ke).

35. *Yuxuan mingchen zouyi*, 4.2065–2073; *Ming shilu*, 125.735–736, under date November 13.

36. *Ming shilu*, 125.736–737. Censor Wang Xinyi protested that punishment; he too was demoted (Ibid., 125.738; Li Changchun, 2.233–235). Censor Ma Mingqi sent up another attack on Madame Ke and was fined a year's salary (*Ming shilu*, 125.744; Huang Daozhou, 26.3a–4a, epitaph for Ma).

37. *Ming shilu*, 126.834; *Suian xianzhi* (1930), 3.741–742. The Palace took no action against Jiang for this memorial.

38. *Ming shilu*, 125.758–759.

39. *Jubian*, p. 325. Liu Zongzhou, 2.890–896; 6.3524–3525; Ye Xianggao, *Lunfei zoucao*, 6.2787–2788; *Ming shilu*, 125.776–778.

40. Liu Ruoyu, p. 89.

41. *Jingong yilu*, p. 33.

42. Liu Ruoyu, pp. 211–213.

43. Ibid., pp. 445–446.

44. Liu Ruoyu, p. 162. Wei Zhongxian purged Liu Zhao in 1622 and may then have taken over direction of the Palace army himself, or had one of his own eunuchs do it.

45. Ibid., 124.36–37.

46. Ibid., 124.87–88.

47. Ibid., 124.90–91.

48. Ibid., 124.128.

49. Ibid., 124.133–136, 145–146.
50. Ibid., 124.158.
51. Ibid., 124.167–171, 173–174.
52. Ibid., 124.235–236.
53. Ibid., 124.101.
54. Ibid., 124.136.
55. Ibid., 124.171.
56. Ibid., 124.220–222.
57. Li Changchun, 2.10–12.
58. *Ming shilu,* 124.237.
59. Ibid., 124.283–284.
60. Ibid., 124.290–293.

61. Chief Grand Secretary Fang Congzhe, long a target of Donglin attack, was allowed to retire on January 10, 1621 (*Ming shilu,* 124.199). In July 1621 two new grand secretaries, appointed earlier, arrived; they were He Zongren and Zhu Guozuo, both pro-Donglin. Neither was a strong political figure. They joined Liu Yijing (now chief grand secretary) and Han Kuang, both Donglin sympathizers but mediocre politicians. On August 15, the arrival of Shen Que sparked an explosion. A Wanli appointee, he was a strong figure but not a Donglin sympathizer. In summer 1622, his enemies forced him to resign, in circumstances to be related later. Another Wanli appointee, Shi Jijie, arrived in Beijing in November 1621. Supervising Secretary Yang Lian had challenged his original appointment in July 1620, and fierce attacks on him by Censors Ruan Dacheng and Liu Fang followed immediately upon his arrival. In August 1623, the Palace finally gave in and accepted Shi's resignation (*Ming shilu,* 123.11421–11422; 125.546, 549, 583, 591, 717, 746; 127.1614–1616, 1634–1635; 128.1800.

62. But not by pro-Donglin Grand Secretary Liu Yijing, who was allowed to retire in April 1622 (*Ming shilu,* 126.996).

63. Ye Xianggao, *Lunfei zoucao,* 6.2930–2932; *Jubian,* p. 355.

64. Zhou Zongjian, 311(2).1a–4a. Wei Zhongxian is called here by his earlier name, Wei Jinzhong. The rescript to this memorial was issued three days later, on June 10; it acknowledged receipt of the memorial, indicated that Zhou was out to enhance his own reputation, and sent the document down to the ministries.

65. Ye Xianggao, *Jubian,* pp. 362–364.

66. *Ming shih, juan* 259 (biographies of Wang and Xiong); Xiong Kaiyuan, *juan* 8B (biography of Xiong); Ye Xianggao, *Jubian,* pp. 345–348.

67. *Ming shilu,* 126.971.

68. Zhou Hongmo, 19.408–410; Huang Zunsu, *Shuo lue,* 14ab; Ye Xianggao, *Jubian,* p. 348.

69. *Ming shilu,* 126.1066–1068.

70. Ibid., 126.998–1000, 1003, 1065–1066.

71. Ye Xianggao, *Jubian,* pp. 381–382; *Ming shilu,* 126.1095–1096, 1155. The traditional meaning of *guoti* stems from the ancient Guliang commentary to the Spring and Autumn Annals, and bears a strong corporeal metaphor, with leading officials understood as body parts acting in behalf of the head, i.e., the ruler. The modern meaning is a bit more abstract (cf. the Japanese *kokutai*) and refers to a nation's legitimate political system or structural order.

72. *Ming shilu,* 126.1182–1183.

73. Ibid., 126.1195–1197, 1207–1208, 1212–1213, 1218, 1234; Ye Xianggao, *Jubian,* pp. 381–382, 384.

74. *Ming shilu,* 127.1381–1382; Chen Ding, 3.17a–22b (biography of Gu). In June 1623, Minister of Justice Sun Wei memorialized that there was no evidence at all that Gu had taken a 40,000-tael bribe. He had, however, acted too willfully. A Palace rescript fined Gu two months' salary. (*Ming shilu,* 128.1774–1775).

75. Feng Congwu, p. 621.

76. Ibid., p. 673.

77. Ibid., pp. 697, 754; Liu Tong, *Dijing jingwu lue,* 4.1a–5b; Sun Chengze, *Tianfu guangji,* pp. 30–31; Zhou Zongjian, 312(3).1a–2a; Ye Xianggao, *Jubian,* p. 389.

78. Chen Hong, *Lu Zhongjie gong nianpu,* A22a.

79. Feng Congwu, p. 697.

80. Ibid., p. 719.

81. Ibid., p. 717.

82. Liu Tong, 4.1a–5b. In his official capacity as vice censor-in-chief, Feng supported the death penalty for both Wang Huazhen and Xiong Tingbi, to deter those who in future might imitate their behavior (Feng, p. 806). Besides Feng, Zou Yuanbiao also led discussions at the Shoushan academy. Zou talked about the importance of material self-denial. "Unless you're poor, you've not fulfilled the Way; and I would add, unless you've been slandered, you've not fulfilled the Way either." Zou asked his listeners to imagine themselves as pines in winter, not plum trees that bloom for a moment and then fade (Liu Tong, 4.1a–5b). Zou challenged his audience, many of them junior officials and students, with this exhortation to extreme effort: "To know that something is impossible, and yet do it—that is the heart-and-guts (*xinchang*) of the Sages and Heaven and Earth, and that is the true mind of the loyal official and filial son" (Feng, p. 702).

There were many other discussion leaders. Zhang Chun, for example, was a northerner and provincial degree holder who was assistant commissioner of the military defense circuit at Yongping, 125 miles east of Beijing. He came to the favorable attention of Gao Panlong (leader of the Donglin academy in Wuxi) and Zuo Guangdou, both of whom sent notes recommending him to Feng Congwu, who then invited Zhang to come to the Shoushan academy and discuss passages from the *Great Learning* and the *Mencius.* "We who eat the ruler's salary must find real solutions to national affairs," lectured Zhang. "We have no learning if all we do is 'pure discussion' in the Jin style. We simply let the dynasty go to ruin that way" (Zhang Chun, *Zhang Taipu Buerge ji,* 3.1793).

83. Feng Congwu, pp. 806–809 (Yao Ximeng's epitaph for Feng).

84. *Ming shilu,* 127.1302–1303.

85. Ibid., 127.1306–1308. Feng's memorial is dated October 10, the Palace rescript October 13 (Feng, pp. 745–746).

86. Feng Congwu, p. 744. A capital evaluation was scheduled for 1623, and many non-Donglin officials were afraid of Zou Yuanbiao's likely role in that. Zou had rejected Guo Tingxun's recommendation of Pan Ruzhen as grossly overblown and refused to endorse it. Both Guo and Pan were anti-Donglin.

87. *Ming shilu,* 127.1344–1345.

88. Ibid., 127.1345–1349; Ye Xianggao, *Lunfei zoucao*, 6.3093–3100; *Jubian*, pp. 389–390.

89. *Ming shilu*, 127.1357–1358.

90. Ibid., 127.1357–1359; Li Changchun, 3.430–433.

91. Ibid., 127.1363.

92. Feng Congwu, pp. 749–750; *Ming shilu*, 127.1380–1381, 1395.

93. Ye Xianggao, *Jubian*, pp. 392–393.

94. *Ming shilu*, 127.1509–1512, 1526–1527, 1556.

95. Ibid., 127.1524–1525; Ye Xianggao, *Jubian*, pp. 407–409.

96. *Ming shilu*, 125.528, 568; Xiong Kaiyuan, 22b–24b.

97. Ye Xianggao stated that Guo Gong and Zhou Zongjian were both protégés of his (he had been their examiner in the metropolitan examinations), but the two had since become mutual enemies over the matter of Xiong Tingbi. "I constantly advised Guo to put aside past affairs and not keep them entangled in his breast," wrote Ye, "but he wouldn't listen" (*Jubian*, pp. 413–414). Lu Shanji, an official in the Ministry of War, also tried to persuade Guo Gong in a personal letter that his attack on the Liao commander was ill-advised (Lu Shanji, 354(18).13a–14a).

98. Guo Gong's memorials are no longer extant. All that survive are short gists in the *Ming shilu* or indirect references in the responses of other memorialists. Ye Xianggao characterized Guo's language as "crude and full of insinuations."

99. Zhou Zongjian, 312(3).7a–9b; *Ming shilu*, 127.1576–1578.

100. Zhou Zongjian, 311(2).4a–7a.

101. Ibid., 311(2).7a–9a. Ni Yuanlu, 3.863–865 (biography of Zhou) states that Ye Xianggao saved Zhou on this occasion, but Ye's memoirs do not confirm this.

102. In 1621, Zhou Zongjian was engaged in a vituperative dispute with Donglin partisan Wei Dazhong over an appointments case; cf. Zhou Zongjian, 312(3).20b–24a.

103. Ni Yuanlu, p. 865.

104. *Ming shilu*, 127.1605–1606.

105. Ibid., 127.1623–1624.

106. Zhou Zongjian, 311(2).16a–17b.

107. *Ming shilu*, 127.1654–1656; Li Changchun, 3.530–533.

108. Ibid., 127.1653–1654.

109. Ibid., 128.1687–1688.

110. Ibid., 128.1738–1739.

111. Ibid., 128.1998.

112. Huang Zunsu, *Shuo lue*, 16b.

113. Chaoying Fang and L. Carrington Goodrich, eds., *Ming Biographical Dictionary*, 1.130.

114. *Ming shih*, juan 243 (biography of Zhan Nanxing).

115. *Ming shih*, juan 306 (biography of Wei Guangwei); Sun Qifeng, *Jifu renwu kao*, 143.395–399 (biography of Zhao).

116. Ye Xianggao, *Jubian*, p. 421.

117. Chen Ding, 19.4b–9a (biography of Zou Weilian); *Xinchang xianzhi*, in *Xijian Zhongguo difangzhi huikan* 27.677–681 (biography of same); Li Yan, pp. 45–47 (biography of Zhang Yunru); Zhao Nanxing, 277(14).20a–22a, 25b–27b, 29b–31b (memorials).

118. Li Yingsheng, 7.20b–21a (letter to Ruan).

119. Huang Zunsu, *Huang Zhongduan gong ji*, 327(3).6b–7b. As sources for the Ruan episode, I have also used Wei Dazhong, autobiography, in Huang Yu, ed., Bixue lu, in Wu Yingji, ed., *Donglin shimo*, p.103ff.; Li Xunzhi, *Sanchao yeji*, pp. 249–253; and Qian Bingdeng, *Suozhi lu*, appendix, 1aff. The reference to painting the dragon's eyes seems to mean that the anti-Donglin group needed only to recruit Ruan in order to make their position solid.

120. Shen Guoyuan, *Liangchao congxin lu*, 5.2271–2272.

121. Ibid., 5.2270–2273.

122. Ye Xianggao, *Lunfei zoucao*, 7.3549–3552; *Jubian*, pp. 489–490.

123. Ye Xianggao, *Jubian*, pp. 486–488.

124. Zuo Guangdou, 305(2).26a–27b.

125. Wei Dazhong, 331(4).1a–2a.

126. Ibid., 331(4).2a–3a; Wei's autobiography in Huang Yu, ed., *Bixue lu*, pp. 104–105.

127. Shen Guoyuan, 5.2296–2300. No Palace response to this memorial is given.

128. Li Changchun, 4.858–860.

129. Ye Xianggao, *Jubian*, pp. 491–492.

130. Huang Zunsu, *Shuo lue*, 17b–18a.

131. Huang Zongxi, 5.272–276 (biography of Madame Yang, Huang Zunsu's wife); Huang Zongxi, *Nanlei wending*, pp. 173–174 (critique of an unofficial history).

132. Huang Zunsu, *Huang Zhongduan gong ji*, 327(3).5a–6b (biography of Wang Wenyan).

133. Tan Qian, *Guo que*, 6.5278.

134. Zhao Nanxing, 277(14).33a–34b; Shen Guoyuan, 5.2363.

Chapter 3. Political Murders, 1625

1. Qian Qianyi, *Muzhai chuxue ji*, 50.6ab (epitaph for Yang Lian).

2. Yang Lian, 3.1251.

3. *Ming shilu*, 126.1046.

4. Miao Changqi (a friend) remarked in an undated personal letter to Liu Ying-guo, a coprovincial of Yang Lian's, that Yang's loyalty was pure, that his "actions engaged the very gods," and that at the time of Taichang's death and the Palace Case, Yang had "grasped the sun and washed Heaven clean," but that the case was now being reopened, thanks to the evil talk of villains. Miao Changqi, 6B.3ab.

5. Yang, 3.1251.

6. Tan Qian, *Guo que*, 6.5260.

7. Yang Lian, 3.1252–1253.

8. Huang Zunsu, *Shuo lue*, 28b–29a.

9. Huang Zongxi, *Huang Zongxi quanji*, 1.412.

10. Miao Changqi, 8.5b–11b (autobiography).

11. Ni Yuanlu, 2.539–545 (epitaph for Zuo's father).

12. Wu Weiye, 41.1a–3a (epitaph); Li Changxiang, 2.47a–49b (epitaph).

13. Yang Lian, 2.1252 (an anonymous *nianpu*, taken from the Yang lineage book (*zongpu*).

14. Yang Lian states in his letter to colleague Wang Xia that the emperor's appearance had been scheduled for the 29th of the 5th lunar month, i.e., July 14, in connection with public prayers for rain, and it was that appearance that was canceled, because rumors of what Yang planned to do had leaked. Other sources date the occasion to the 1st of the 6th lunar month, i.e., July 15. The "Twenty-four Crimes" memorial is usually dated July 15. I follow the date given by Yang Lian.

15. Charles O. Hucker, *The Censorial System of Ming China,* pp. 200–205. Here Hucker has translated long sections of the opening and closing remarks of Yang's memorial, with summaries of each of the twenty-four specific counts in the indictment.

16. Yang Lian, 2.717–720 (letter to Wang Xia).

17. Xia Xie, 5.3047–3048; Wen Bing, p. 117; *Mingchao shilue,* B.8b–9a; Tan Qian, *Guo que,* 6.5286, 5288.

18. Yang Lian, 2.717–720 (letter to Wang Xia).

19. Ye Xianggao, *Lunfei zoucao,* 7.3589–3591; Jin Risheng, 4.1717–1722 (a violently worded protest of July 18 from Supervising Secretary Chen Liangxun).

20. Ye Xianggao, *Jubian,* pp. 499–502; Jin Risheng, 2.633–634.

21. Ye Xianggao, *Lunfei zoucao,* 7.3611.

22. Ye Xianggao, *Jubian,* p. 502.

23. Miao Changqi, 8.5b–11b (autobiography).

24. Ye Xianggao, *Lunfei zoucao,* 7.3621–3626.

25. Ye Xianggao, *Jubian,* p. 504.

26. Jin Risheng, 3.1183–1197.

27. Ibid., 3.1197. This source errs by ten days in dating the rescript to Wan Jing's memorial. Tianqi's infant son died on July 28. According to Miao Jingchi, 6.549–550, Wan Jing's memorial is dated July 29. Therefore the rescript must be July 30 (Jin dates it Tianqi 4, 6th month, 7th day; it must be in error for 4/6/17).

28. Ye Xianggao, *Lunfei zoucao,* 7.3641–3643.

29. Ibid., 7.3645–3649.

30. Ye Xianggao, *Jubian,* p. 509.

31. Peng Sunyi, 23.8b–9a (account of conduct for Peng Qisheng); Shi Runzhang, 16.1a–7b (biography of Li Banghua); Li Mingjun, biography of Wan Jing, in Wei Yuankuang, ed., *Nanchang wenzheng,* 3.866–868; Huang Zunsu, *Shuo lue,* 29ab; Miao Jingchi, 6.549–550. The exact date of Wan Jing's death is unclear (Xia Xie, 5.3052–3053).

32. Ye Xianggao, *Lunfei zoucao,* 7.3655–3657. In the confrontation about the local crime, Censor Lin had seized and flogged two of the offending eunuchs. Huang Zunsu, for one, thought Lin had overdone it, and that his flogging the eunuchs helped bring on the "humiliation of the *shenshi,*" i.e., the purge of the Donglin (*Shuo lue,* 23b).

33. Huang Zunsu, *Shuo lue,* 30a.

34. Ye Xianggao, *Jubian,* pp. 510–511.

35. *Ming shih,* 23.7108 (biography of Lin Ruzhu).

36. Ye Xianggao, *Jubian,* pp. 512–513.

37. Yang Lian, 1.335–339.

38. Huang Zunsu, *Shuo lue,* 29b.

39. Huang Zunsu, *Huang Zhongduan gong ji,* 327(3).8a–9a.

40. Ibid., 327(3).7b–8a.

41. Li Yingsheng, 2.5a–6a.

42. Liu Ruoyu, pp. 172–173.

43. Xu Zhaotai, p. 258.

44. Chen Zhenhui, *Shushi qize,* 1a–2a.

45. Xu Zhaotai, p. 262; Hu Jixian, 7.34.

46. Miao Changqi, 8.5b–11b (autobiography).

47. Qian Qianyi, *Muzhai chuxue ji,* 47A.50a (account of conduct for Sun). Sun had requested a personal meeting a year earlier, in January 1624, but a Palace rescript politely declined his request (*Ming shilu,* 129.2172–2173).

48. Cai Ding, p. 2158.

49. Qian Qianyi, *Muzhai chuxue ji,* 47A.48a–50a; Mao Yuanyi, pp. 481–488; Xu Zhaotai, p. 264; Wu Yingji, Baofu lu, p.603; Sun Qifeng, *Jifu renwu kao,* 143.313–324; Li Sunzhi, *Sanchao yeji,* pp. 299–303.

50. *Sanchao yaodian,* 3.1318–1319.

51. *Sanchao yaodian,* 3.1318–1319, 1324–1325; Xu Zhaotai, p. 276.

52. Liu Qiao was a southerner and had gotten his position as prison director through the *yin* privilege, as his grandfather had been a high official (*Hubei tongzhi,* 3.3173). Xu Xianchun was a northerner and a relative of Wanli's mother, concubine Li (d. 1614). Reportedly, he hated scholar-officials. See *Yangzhou fuzhi,* 10.3490–3492 (biography of Li Sicheng); Jiang Fan, biography of Huang Zongxi, in *Lizhou yizhu huikan* (Ming Qing shiliao huibian, 6th ser.), 5.28–36; Dai Mingshi, pp. 176–184 (biography of Zuo Guangdou).

53. For Wu Mengming, see Sun Chengze, *Tianfu guangji,* pp. 437–438; *Shaoxing fuzhi,* 5.1196; Mao Qiling, *Xihe ji,* 75.8ab (biography).

54. *Sanchao yaodian,* 3.1325–1331.

55. Xu Zhaotai, pp. 277, 279; Jin Risheng, 7.3421–3430. Wu Mengming was a southerner who gained his position through the *yin* privilege. Former street thug Cui was a northerner.

56. *Sanchao yaodian,* 3.1332–1334; Xu Zhaotai, p. 277. It is not clear why Yang Lian's *nianpu* has the arrest order dated April 25 (Yang Lian, 2.1256–1257).

57. Xu Zhaotai, p. 280.

58. Many of the Donglin men, including those who had used his service, believed he died a hero. But others among the Donglin had scrupulously avoided him and believed he had indeed made the accusations against Yang Lian and the others that Xu Xianchun reported. "When worthies get too close to bad people they suffer for it in the end," concluded Zhou Shunchang. "Once he came to visit me, and it was for good reasons that I coldly turned him away" (Zhou Shunchang, 4.14a [Yin Xianchen's *nianpu* for Zhou Shunchang]). Even in his home county of Xiuning, people were of two minds about Wang Wenyan. Some thought that because he was not a scholar-official, but a former clerk, he could not have been a *zhengren*—an "upright person." Cf. Zhao Jishi, *Jiyuan jisuo ji,* 2.280.

59. Hu Jixian, 7.47.

60. Ibid., pp. 48–54; Yang Lian, 2.1257 *(nianpu).*

61. Yang Lian, 2.1005–1010 (Li Zhichun, inscription for the Zhongxia tang).

62. Xu Zhaotai, p. 295.

63. Jin Risheng, 2.767–770 (notice for the four gates of Tongcheng).

64. Ibid. (statement by Zuo's son Zuo Guozhu).

65. Ibid., 2.771–777.

66. Sun Shenxing, pp. 81–84.

67. Zhou Shunchang, 4.14b (*nianpu* by Yin Xianchen).

68. Sun Qifeng later wrote that this letter prompted the ill-fated attempt by Sun Chengzong to intercede personally with Tianqi. Actually, that event took place the preceding December. Huang Zongxi takes Sun Qifeng to task for this mistake. Cf. Huang Zongxi, *Nanlei wending,* pp. 173–174 (critique of an unofficial history).

69. Qian Yiji, ed., *Beizhuan ji,* 127.20ab (biography of Zhang); Xu Shichang, ed., *Da Qing Jifu xianzhe zhuan,* 2.704–707 (biography of same); Sun Qifeng, *Xiafeng xiansheng ji,* 8.32a (remarks about Zhang); *Xincheng xianzhi,* 1.355.

70. Sun Qifeng, *Yibing jishi,* 1a–4a.

71. Cao Huang, p. 565. Cao Huang is also known as Cao Zhen.

72. *Chongzhen changbian,* 8.1123–1127.

73. *Ming shilu,* 130.2795, 2801–2, 2811; Li Changchun, 4.1088–1090.

74. *Ming shilu,* 130.2861–2862, 2685; Wu Yingji, *Baofu lu,* pp. 617–618.

75. Ye Xianggao, *Jubian,* pp. 535–536.

76. *Ming shilu,* 130.2936. Wei Guangwei died in retirement in September 1627 (Xu Zhaotai, p. 397).

77. Xie Guozhen, *Zengding wan Ming shiji kao,* p. 196.

78. Yan Ke (pseud.), *Tianren hezheng jishi,* in Huang Yu, ed., *Bixue lu,* in Wu Yingji, ed., *Donglin shimo,* p.133ff.

79. Wei Xueyi, *nianpu,* in *Bixue lu,* pp. 107–108.

80. Hu Jixian, pp. 54–55.

81. *Chongzhen changbian,* 7.547–552 (a memorial of 1628 by Qu Shisi).

82. *Sanchao yaodian,* 3.1362–1364; Xu Zhaotai, p. 295.

83. Wu Yingji, *Baofu lu,* p.606; Song Qifeng, *Baishuo,* pp. 59–62.

84. *Sanchao yaodian,* 3.1365–1366; Xu Zhaotai, p. 296.

85. Yan Ke (pseud.), pp. 142–143.

86. Xu Zhaotai, p. 297.

87. Ibid.

88. There is also a long, detailed letter from Wei concerning a coffin, perhaps dictated to Liu Qixian, in *Jiashan xianzhi,* 2.640–642.

89. Xu Zhaotai, p. 298.

90. Yan Ke (pseud.), p. 136.

91. Hu Jixian, pp. 58–59.

92. Sun Qifeng, *Yibing jishi,* 4a–5a.

93. Wei Xueyi, 8.11b–14a (letter to Fan Maoguang).

94. Liu Zongzhou, 3.1750–1756 (epitaph for Cang Zhaoru).

95. Jin Risheng, 5.2173–2176, 2193–2200; Wue Xueyi, 8.10b–11b (letter to Huang and Yu).

96. Sun Qifeng, *Yibing jishi,* 5ab.

97. Cited in Xie Guozhen, *Ming Qing zhi ji dangshe yundong kao,* p. 68. The original story comes from Fang Pao's grandfather; cf. Fang Pao, *Fang Pao ji,* 1.237–238. Dai Mingshi has the story a little differently; cf. *Dai Mingshi ji,* pp. 176–184.

98. *Ming shilu,* 130.2890–2892, 2896–2897; Xu Zhaotai, p. 299; Yan Ke (pseud.), p. 136.

99. Xu Zhaotai, p. 299. The amount charged to Yuan Huazhong is from Miao Jingchi, *Donglin tongnan lu,* pp. 545–546.

100. *Ming shilu,* 130.2919.

101. Xu Zhaotai, p. 302, 304–305; Yan Ke (pseud.), pp. 137–138.

102. Yan Ke (pseud.), p. 139. At the meeting at the *fasi,* Gu had reportedly said: "I've been ordered sent here by the emperor, and I've been convicted, and how dare I dispute that? If I dispute, I defy the imperial directive. Yet if I concur in it, then I lie to myself, lie to the *fasi,* and lie to the future generations of the realm, tantamount to lying to the emperor. So I can neither confess to the charges, nor not confess to them...."

103. Ye Xianggao, *Jubian,* p. 532.

104. A coprovincial, Shen Weiyao of Xiaogan county, was a government military teacher in Beijing who secretly helped with Yang Lian's funeral, a dangerous act because of informers. Cf. Tan Yuanchun, 2.467–469; *Xiaogan xianzhi,* 3.1041.

105. Hu Jixian, p. 74.

106. Xu Zhaotai, p. 326.

107. Hu Jixian, pp. 74–75; Jin Risheng, 6.2783–2801 (memorial by Liu Yingyu, dated December 20, 1627).

108. *Tongcheng xuxiu xianzhi,* 1.281, 295, 318–319; Miao Jingchi, pp. 537–539; Ni Yuanlu, 2.763–776 (account of conduct for Zuo Guangdou), 2.539–545 (epitaph for Zuo's father); Dai Mingshi, pp. 176–184 (biography of Zuo Guangdou).

109. Wei Xueyi, 8.11b–14a (letter to Pan Maoxian); also *nianpu,* pp. 108–109.

110. The date is from Miao Jingchi, pp. 541–542. But Wei Xuelian said his brother died "less than a month" after the death of their father.

111. Wei Xuelian, memorial, in *Jiashan xianzhi,* 2.619–620; Xu Zhaotai, pp. 354–355.

112. *Ming shilu,* 130.2981–2983; *Sanchao yaodian,* 3.1384–1397; Xu Zhaotai, pp. 309–310.

Chapter 4. The Murders Continue: 1626

1. Yu Minzhong, 4.1202–1204; Chen Xi, 1.595–598; Liu Ruoyu, pp. 297–303.

2. *Chongzhen changbian,* 6.145–146.

3. *Ming shilu,* 130.2601–2603; Xu Zhaotai, p. 275; *Chongzhen changbian,* 8.1029–1035.

4. Xu Zhaotai, pp. 333–334.

5. Ibid., p. 336.

6. Ibid., p. 270.

7. *Sanchao yaodian,* 3.1332–1334; *nianpu,* 10b.

8. Li Yingsheng, 8.20a (letter).

9. Miao Changqi, *fulu,* 16b–17a. By "not restraining himself" when leaving the capital, Qian is apparently referring to Miao's willingness to be seen partying in public with accused Donglin officials.

10. Xu Zhaotai, pp. 333–334.

11. Li Changchun, 3.740–743.

12. Tan Qian, *Guo que*, 6.5296.

13. *Ming shilu*, 131.3268–3269. Eunuch Li Shi testified in 1628 that he had had nothing to do with this impeachment but had been forced by Wei Zhongxian to make it appear that way. Cf. *Chongzhen changbian*, 6.339–340.

14. Liu Zongzhou, *nianpu*, 6.3537. The original letter is more colloquial in language than the *nianpu* version; cf. Zhou Lianggong, *Laigutang chidu xinchao*, 1.25.

15. Ni Yuanlu, 3.859–869 (biography of Zhou); Zhang Pu, 1.435–448 (epitaph); Xu Zhaotai, p. 346.

16. Qian Qianyi, *Muzhai chuxue ji*, 48.8b–17a (account of conduct for Miao).

17. Miao Changqi, *nianpu*, 11a.

18. Sun Shenxing, pp. 59–62.

19. Miao Changqi, *nianpu*, 11b.

20. Xu Zhaotai, pp. 346–347.

21. Jin Risheng, 3.1137–1140; *Zhangzhou fuzhi*, 29.26b–28b; Miao Jingchi, pp. 563–565.

22. Xu Zhaotai, p. 356.

23. Sun Shenxing, pp. 62–64 (notes on Li Yingsheng); Li Sunzhi, pp. 373–375; Li Yingsheng, 9.15a–16a (notes by Li Sunzhi); Cai Shishun, *Li Zhongda beidai jilue*; Li Changxiang, 2.47a–49b (epitaph).

24. Li Yingsheng, 9.12b–13a (letter).

25. *Donglin shuyuan zhi*, 7.266–272 (account of conduct by Ye Maocai).

26. Xu Zhaotai, p. 346; Chen Ding, 12.29a–30a; *Ming shih*, 21.6311–6314 (biography of Gao Panlong); Li Changchun, 5.1355 (Mao Yilu's memorial and rescript). Also cf. Zhao Chengzhong, "Zhou Shunchang shoudiqian chuanshu Gao Panlong kao," *Zhongguoshi yanjiu*, no. 4 (1983), 136.

27. Jin Risheng, 3.1108–1109.

28. Zhou Shunchang, 4.12b (*nianpu* by Yin Xianchen). There was a time earlier in his career when Zhou's friends in Beijing gave him a banquet and brought in actors to stage a drama featuring the "evil" Southern Song prime minister Qin Gui's plot to kill the loyalist hero Yue Fei. Zhou Shunchang forgot it was just a play and grew so agitated that he assaulted the actor portraying Qin Gui and then he walked out, as his friends watched in shock. See *Suzou fuzhi* (1883), rpt. Taipei 1970, 6.3480.

29. Zhou Shunchang, 3.1a–2b (message for Zhou Mianzhen, i.e., Qiyuan).

30. Ibid., 4.14b (*nianpu*).

31. Xu Zhaotai, pp. 297–298.

32. To be exact, the governors, or *fuan*, were the Grand Coordinator Mao Yilu and, at a lower rank, Provincial Inspector Xu Ji.

33. Zhu Zuwen, 3a–4a.

34. There are many contemporary accounts of the famous Suzhou riot of 1626. In addition to those used by Charles O. Hucker, "Su-chou and the Agents of Wei Chung-hsien," in his *Two Studies on Ming History* (Ann Arbor, Mich., 1971), pp. 41–83, and Kishimoto Mio, "'Gojin' jō no seiritsu," in Ono Kazuko, ed., *Minmatsu Shincho no shakai to bunka* (Kyoto, 1996), pp. 503–534 (also available as a chapter in her *Min Shin kōtai to Kōnan shakai* [Tokyo, 1999]), I also used Gu Yanwu, 1.12a–16b (epitaph for Kou Shen); Wang Jie, "Kaidu jishi," in Shen Guoyuan, *Liangchao congxin lu,*

6.2777–2782; Wang Wan, 36.1a–2a (reminiscences of Zhou); and *Chongzhen Wuxian zhi,* 4.161–162 (biography of Chen Wenrui).

35. Xu Zhaotai, p. 348.

36. Yang Tingshu, pp. 2137–2140; Qian Qianyi, *Muzhai youxue ji,* 28.26b–34a (epitaph for Xu).

37. Wen Bing, pp. 187–189. The two accounts, which do not necessarily contradict each other, are discussed in *Kun Xin liang xian xuxiu hezhi,* 3.944–945.

38. Xu Zhaotai, pp. 345–346.

39. As described in Kishimoto Mio, *Min Shin kyōdai to Kōnan shakai* (Tokyo, 1999), chap. 4.

40. Huang Zongxi, 1.413–414.

41. Ibid., 1.213–214 (account of conduct for Liu Zongzhou); Liu Zongzhou, *nianpu,* 6.3538–3541.

42. Xu Zhaotai, p. 351.

43. Miao Changqi, *nianpu,* 12a. Actually Miao and Zuo were not year-mates; Miao achieved his *jinshi* in 1607, Miao in 1613.

44. Xu Zhaotai, pp. 347–348.

45. Ibid., p. 348; Miao Jingchi, pp. 555–557, 559–560.

46. Xu Zhaotai, p. 348.

47. *Ming shilu,* 131.3386.

48. Xu Zhaotai, p. 349.

49. The arrest of Huang Zunsu's father is also related in Huang Zongxi, 1.408–409, and in *Yuyao xianzhi,* 2.629. However, neither of those sources mentions the 500-tael bribe. Both state that the police tortured his father to obtain the names of all his associates.

50. Zhu Zuwen, 9a–19b.

51. Liu Ruoyu, pp. 77–78.

52. *Tianbian dichao,* appended to *Bixue lu* (Zhibuzu zhai congshu ed.), 1a.

53. Li Changchun, 5.1367–1369.

54. Ibid., 5.1392–1394 (Censor Li Canran's report); *Ming shilu,* 132.3420, 3425. The number of units *(jian)* of housing destroyed is variously given as 10,930 or 19,031. Which is the correct figure and which the copying error is not clear. There is also a good description of the explosion in Wu Changyuan, *Zhenyuan shilue,* p. 127. Everyone had a strange story to relate about the disaster.

55. *Ming shilu,* 132.3422; Li Changchun, 5.1369–1370.

56. Zhu Zuwen, 19b–20b.

57. Ibid., 24a–27b.

58. Ibid., 28a–29a.

59. Ibid., 29a–30a; Sun Qifeng, *Yibing jishi,* 6b–7a.

60. Zhu Zuwen, 30ab.

61. Huang Zongxi, *Lizhou yizhu huibian,* 5.497–500 (biography of Zhang Lüduan); *Ming shilu,* 132.3450.

62. *Ming shilu,* 132.1450.

63. *Ming shilu,* 132.3456–3458. Peng Runan, supervising secretary of the Office of Scrutiny for Rites, added a long statement of his own in support of Li Sicheng.

64. *Ming shilu,* 132.3462–3463.

65. Ibid., 132.3467–3468.

66. Ibid., 132.3477–3478.

67. Ibid., 132.3484–3487; Xu Zhaotai, pp. 352–353.

68. *Ming shilu*, 132.3489–3491.

69. Zhu Zuwen, 41b–42a; Xu Zhaotai, p. 354; *Chongzhen changbian*, 7.547–552 (memorial of July 1628 by Qu Shisi).

70. Ni Yuanlu, 3.859–869 (biography of Zhou Zongjian); Zhang Pu, *Qiluzhai shi-wen heji*, 1.435–438 (epitaph); Miao Jingchi, pp. 559–560.

71. Xu Zhaotai, p. 354.

72. Miao Jingchi, pp. 571–573.

73. Coprovincial Yu Tingbi, a supervising secretary, helped with silver payments and managed to sneak into the Decree Prison for a visit. Xu Shiqi, a bureau secretary in the Ministry of Works, helped with silver and food. See Jin Risheng, 5.2173–2176; Huang Zongxi, *Nanlei wending*, pp. 71–77 (epitaph for Xu).

74. *Chongzhen changbian*, 7.532–535.

75. Xu Zhaotai, p. 355; *Ming shilu*, 132.3521. Huang Zongxi states in his biography of his father that the official date of Huang Zunsu's death was wrongly stated as July 24. However, both the *Ming shilu* and Xu Zhaotai's collection of Palace rescripts give July 23. Cf. Huang Zongxi, 1.414.

76. Li Yingsheng, 9.14a.

77. Miao Jingchi, pp. 575–576.

78. Li Yingsheng, 9.14b.

79. Ibid., 9.15a–16a (note by his son, Li Sunzhi).

80. Xu Zhaotai, p. 356.

81. Ibid., p. 365; Miao Jingchi, pp. 563–565.

82. Miao Changqi, 2.19a (an essay).

83. Ibid., 2.5b (essay, that public opinion is the *yuanqi* of the state).

84. Wang Yingkui, *Liunan suibi*, B3.2ab.

Chapter 5. Repression Triumph, Joy, Collapse (1625–1627)

1. Wen Bing, pp. 122–123.

2. Liu Ruoyu, p. 608.

3. Ibid., p. 602.

4. *Ming shilu*, 130.2601–2603.

5. *Chongzhen changbian*, 8.1029–1035. Imprisoned in 1628, Cao Qincheng survived until at least 1644. He worked as a prison guard. *Ming shih*, 26.7856–7857 (biography of Cao Qincheng); Li Qing, pp. 155–156; Yang Shicong, p. 197.

6. *Ming shilu*, 130.2920, 2936; Liu Ruoyu, p. 603.

7. No copy of the *Liaodong zhuan* seems to have survived. However, Lin Shidui (1615–1705) saw a copy and remarked that it was much too crude a work to have been written by Xiong. Cf. Lin Shidui, pp. 150–154.

8. Xu Zhaotai, pp. 303–304, 333; *Ming shilu*, 130.2941; Xia Xie, 5.3071; Liu Ruoyu, p. 605. The accounts differ about Xiong's execution, and what happened to his severed head. Cf. Quan Zuwang, A26.19a–20a; Xiong Kaiyuan, 8B.31ab.

9. Xu Zhaotai, p. 355; *Ming shilu,* 132.3519–3520, 3522–3523; Li Changchun, 5.1421–1423. It appears that Feng's high-handedness angered others in the anti-Donglin group. Another key anti-Donglin player, Wang Shaohui, was linked to Feng and impeached as well (*Ming shilu,* 132.3560, 3571; Li Changchun, 5.1413–1415, 1428–1430). Feng lived on to become grand secretary again—after 1644, in the new Qing dynasty.

10. *Ming shi,* 26.7848–7850 (biography of Cui); *Lantai,* pp. 545, 549, 555.

11. *Yangzhou fuzhi* (1810; rpt. Taipei 1974), 10.3534–3535 (biography of Liu Yongqin).

12. Li Sunzhi, p. 277; Li Yingsheng, 2.12a–13a; Gao Panlong, 7.25b–27b.

13. Li Changchun, 4.1001–1003.

14. The eunuch memoirist Liu Ruoyu wrote: "When officials were purged, people were generally puzzled how the emperor knew that so-and-so belonged to the 'deviant clique,' that he was a member of such-and-such a person's camp *(menhu),* that he was related by marriage to Xiong Tingbi, or was a son of Cheng Zhu, or a kinsman of Liu Duo. They thought all this came by way of secret reports from the Eastern Depot, but as time went on, Wei Zhongxian and the others weren't so careful of sources, and they let it leak out that the names were drawn from these lists" (Liu Ruoyu, p. 178).

15. Song Qifeng, pp. 59–62.

16. Xu Zhaotai, p. 271.

17. *Ming shilu,* 132.3506.

18. *Sanchao yaodian,* 1.1–21.

19. *Ming shilu,* 131.3381–3382. The latest such list, the *Donglin dangren bang* (placard of Donglin partisans) of December 29, 1625, had listed 309 men, by no means all of them Donglin men (*Donglin shuyuan zhi,* 467–468). See also Wang Tianyou, *Wan Ming Donglin dangyi* (Shanghai, 1991), pp. 114–115. For a composite roster of all Donglin adherents and suspects, see Ono Kazuko, *Minki tōsha kō* (Kyoto, 1996), pp. 27–43.

20. Zheng Zhongkui, *Er xin,* pp. 44–45.

21. Xu Zhaotai, pp. 270–271.

22. Ibid., p. 272.

23. Li Changchun, 4.1114–1118; *Ming shilu,* 130.2877.

24. Sun Chengze, *Tianfu guangji,* pp. 30–31.

25. Li Changchun, 4.1136–1143 (memorial by Zhang Na).

26. Ibid., 4.1044–1047; *Ming shilu,* 130.2705.

27. Xu Zhaotai, p. 300; Li Changchun, 4.1136–1143.

28. *Donglin shuyuan zhi,* 7.386. Academy destruction was not limited to the originally listed four. In July 1626, Yingtian Governor Mao Yilu reported the further confiscation of academies in Changshu, Yixing, and Jiaxing counties, yielding altogether 2,420 taels in sales of assets. The Palace ordered the sum sent to Beijing to aid in Forbidden City construction (Li Changchun, 5.1404–1406).

29. Feng Congwu, pp. 781–782 (plea of Feng Jianian, 1629).

30. There seems to be no surviving record of the proceeds from the sale of the Ziyang. *Wuyuan xianzhi,* 3.872–874 (biography of Yu Mouheng).

31. *Jishui xianzhi,* 65.233. As in Jiangnan, more than this one Jiangxi academy

was confiscated. In December 1626, Jiangxi Provincial Inspector Cao Gu reported collecting 3,017 taels from the sale of academy assets in Nanchang "and other places." This sum too went to palace construction (*Ming shilu*, 132.3728).

32. *Ming shilu*, 130.2542, 2546–2548, 2567–2568; Xu Zhaotai, p. 273. The exams themselves are reproduced in Jin Risheng, *juan* 23.

33. *Ming shilu*, 130.2567; Hou Zhenping, *Huang Daozhou jinian zhushu shuhua kao*, 1.93.

34. *Ming shilu*, 130.2569–2570; *Sanchao yaodian*, 3.1323–1324.

35. Xu Zhaotai, p. 314, for the rescript.

36. Jin Risheng, 3.1389–1396.

37. Ibid., p. 1396. Wu Huaixian's correspondent, Wu Changqi, was removed from civil service (Xu Zhaotai, pp.321–322). After Tianqi's death in 1727, Wu Huaixian was rehabilitated. It was asserted in his behalf that in the Decree Prison he had said that if he could achieve equal fame with Yang Lian and Zuo Guangdou, he would die without regret. It was also asserted that his downfall was engineered as an act of revenge by Fu Yingxing, a nephew of Wei Zhongxian's, also a secretariat drafter, whose offer of friendship he had earlier spurned. Fu Yingxing's hatred was shared by another Wei Zhongxian nephew, Wei Liangqing. Wei Liangqing's washerwoman had a daughter whom Wu Huaixian had purchased as a bondservant. Wei Liangqing wanted that daughter as a concubine, but Wu refused to let him have her, so Wei Liangqing then bribed Wu's manservant, Cheng Yuande, into submitting those incriminating documents to the Eastern Depot, just out of personal spite. See Jin Risheng, 3.1383–1387, and Li Sunzhi, pp. 344–346.

38. *Ming shilu*, 131.3378–3379; 132.3593–3594; Xu Zhaotai, pp. 328, 343, 344, 348; Jin Risheng, 3.1209–1225; Xia Xie, 5.3087–3088; Liu Ruoyu, p. 607; Chen Ding, 4.15a–16b (biography of Liu Duo).

39. Xu Zhaotai, p. 358; *Ming shilu*, 132.3573–3574, 3593.

40. Xu Zhaotai, pp. 360–363; *Ming shilu*, 132.3593–3594; Zhu Changzuo, pp. 152–158; Wu Yingji, *Qizhen liangchao baofu lu*, pp. 638–639; Li Changchun, 5.1449–1454 (a detailed memorial by Minister of Justice Xue Zhen). Executed with Liu were his kinsman Peng Wenbing, his servant Liu Fu, and the priest Fang Jingyang.

41. Li Sunzhi, pp. 390–391; Wu Yingji, *Qizhen liangchao baofu lu*, p. 640. The Palace made an unsuccessful attempt to link the empress's father (or stepfather) Zhang Guoji to this affair.

42. *Ming shilu*, 132.3711.

43. Fang Chaoying and L. C. Goodrich, eds., *Ming Biographical Dictionary*, 2.1468, gives the pronunciation Sun Wen-chai (Sun Wenzhai).

44. *Ming shilu*, 132.3835.

45. Xu Zhaotai, pp. 377–378; *Ming shilu*, 132.3835; 133.3896–3897; Li Changchun, 5.1518–1522 (memorial from Xue Zhen).

46. Wang Wan, 10.3b–5a (stela for Chen Renxi); Liu Zongzhou, 4.1878–1887 (biography of Chen Renxi); Zheng Man, 3.1513–1514.

47. *Chongzhen changbian*, 6.145–146.

48. *Ming shilu*, 132.3687, 3700–3702.

49. Ibid., 133.4205, 4236. Sun Chengze, *Chunming mengyu lu* (Siku quanshu ed., rpt. Shanghai, 1993), 1.44 gives the total as 5,957,519+ taels.

50. *Ming shilu,* 132.3426–3428, 3484–3487; Xu Zhaotai, pp. 352–353; Li Changchun, 5.1394–1398.

51. Documents relating to the gruesome ordeal suffered by Tao Langxian have been gathered in Tao Langxian, *Tao Zhongcheng yiji;* those relating to the Huizhou riot, in Cheng Minzheng, *Tianqi Huangshan dayu ji.*

52. Meng Sen, *Ming Qing lunzhu jikan xubian* (Beijing, 1987), pp. 81–86.

53. Mammitsch, p. 104.

54. Li Changchun, 5.1401–1402; Li Sunzhi, pp. 395–415; Zhu Yizun, 53.10b–12b; Xu Zhaotai, p. 354.

55. See Pan's preface to Jiang Dongwei, *Furongjing yuyan,* p. 1.

56. *Ming shilu,* 132.3520–3521. It was reported not long after that a retired official by the name of Huang Ruheng was heard to utter some inappropriate remarks as he passed by the new shrine. The eunuch custodian unleashed a gang of thugs upon him, and they beat him to death (Li Sunzhi, p. 395). A brief biographical entry for Huang in *Hangzhou fuzhi,* 7.2107, does not mention this incident, but it is confirmed in a memorial of late 1627; cf. *Chongzhen changbian,* 6.97–98.

57. Zheng Zhongkui, *Er xin,* p. 45.

58. Zhao Jishi, *Jiyuan jisuo ji,* 1.252; Zhu Yizun, 53.10b–12b (notes on poems by my father).

59. Li Sunzhi, pp. 396–398; *Chongzhen changbian,* 6.303–305.

60. *Chongzhen changbian,* 6.303–305.

61. Zhao Jishi, 1.247 (quotation from his grandfather's diary).

62. *Ming shilu,* 133.4064–4065.

63. Xu Zhaotai, p. 388.

64. Wu Yingji, *Qizhen liangchao baofu lu,* p. 643; Li Sunzhi, pp. 399–400.

65. Wu Yingji, *Qizhen liangchao baofu lu,* p. 644.

66. *Ming shilu,* 133.3989, 3990, 4025, 4070, 4088.

67. In Songjiang, for example, Xia Yunyi wrote that the petitioner was a "villain" whose petition falsely purported to represent the desires of the "gentry and people" *(shi min).* An evil government student involved himself in the construction of the shrine and tried to force Xia to yield land for it. Xia resisted. The death of Tianqi and the accession of Chongzhen ended the matter. Cf. Xia Yunyi, *Xingcun lu,* 2.4b.

68. Liu Ruoyu, pp. 214–215.

69. Ji Yun, *Ming Yian huanghou waizhuan,* p. 512.

70. Ibid.

71. Liu Ruoyu, pp. 163–164.

72. Daughter no. 1 was born November 19, 1622, and died July 30, 1623 (*Ming shilu,* 127.1368; 128.1843). Son no. 1, by Empress Zhang, was stillborn on November 4, 1623 (*Ming shilu,* 128.2009; Tan Qian, *Guo que,* 6.5234, gives his name as Zhu Ciran). Son no. 2, Zhu Ciyu, by concubine Fan, was born November 14, 1623, and died July 28, 1624 (*Ming shilu,* 128.2028; Tan Qian, *Guo que,* 6.5288). Daughter no. 2, by concubine Li, was born April 17, 1624, and was dead by early autumn of the same year (Liu Ruoyu, pp. 141–142). Son no. 3, Zhu Cigui, by concubine Ren, was born October 31, 1625, and died June 29, 1626 (*Ming shilu,* 131.2995, 3171). Thus not one of Tianqi's children lived as long as a year.

73. *Ming shilu,* 129.2420–2423.

74. Liu Ruoyu, p. 233.

75. Ye Xianggao, *Ju bian,* pp. 479–481.

76. Tan Qian, *Guo que,* 6.5292.

77. Liu Ruoyu, pp. 79–81.

78. Tang Changshi, pp. 1351–1353.

79. Li Changchun, 5.1622–1624.

80. *Ming shilu,* 133.4215–4216.

81. Liu Ruoyu, pp. 260–261.

82. Some sources date Tianqi's death to September 29 and state that Wei Zhongxian kept his death secret for a day. See Lin Jinshu, *Tianqi huangdi dazhuan,* p. 391.

83. Chen Longzheng, 52.85–87. Also cf. Xia Yunyi, 1.18b.

84. Li Sunzhi, pp. 425–426; Ji Yun, p. 514. There may have been some substance to this rumor, as in August 1627 Wei Liangqing had been sent to substitute for the ailing Tianqi as chief officiant in sacrifices at the imperial ancestral temple and elsewhere (*Ming shilu,* 133.4145).

85. *Chongzhen changbian,* 6.132–138; *Jifu tongzhi,* 5.6282–6284 (epitaphs for Grand Secretary Li Guopu).

86. Ji Yun, p. 514.

87. Xu Zhaotai, pp. 397–398.

88. Li Sunzhi, pp. 425–426; Zhu Changzuo, p. 103.

89. Tan Qian, *Guo que,* 6.5384. The *Ming shilu* text is both abridged and damaged (133.4245–4246). Curiously, neither Li Changchun nor Xu Zhaotai provides a copy of the document.

Chapter 6. A Reversal of Fortunes

1. *Chongzhen changbian,* 6.11, 42, 49–50; Tan Qian, *Guo que,* 6.5389. Chen Eryi was impeached and degraded on December 17 (*Chongzhen changbian,* 6.113).

2. Liu Ruoyu, p. 225.

3. *Chongzhen changbian,* 6.38. Tan Qian, *Guo que,* 6.5389 dates this November 1.

4. *Chongzhen changbian,* 6.28–29.

5. Ibid., 6.28–29, 60–62, 66–68.

6. Ibid., 6.76–77, 80–81, 91; *Ming x-zong x-huangdi shilu,* 1.31.

7. *Chongzhen changbian,* 6.102; Zhu Changzuo, *Yujing xintan,* pp. 126–129 (memorials of Shan Mingyi and Wang Huitu).

8. *Congzhen changbian,* 6.115, 126, 241–242, 292.

9. Ibid., 6.72–76.

10. Ibid., 6.78–80.

11. Ibid., 6.86–89. The *changbian* is careless with dates in this section, and I have instead followed the dating in Tan Qian, *Guo que,* for these memorials, and Xu Zhaotai for the rescripts. For the wide circulation of Qian's memorial, cf. the remarks of Zheng Zhongkui, p. 10. A biography of Qian Jiazheng is to be found in the gazetteer of his native county, Haiyan; cf. *Haiyan xianzhi* (1877), reprinted in *Zhongguo difangzhi jicheng: Zhejiang fuxian zhiji* (Shanghai, 1993), 21.849–851.

NOTES TO PAGES 154–160

12. Zhu Changzuo, p. 108.
13. Xu Zhaotai, p. 406.
14. *Chongzhen changbian*, 6.93–95; Tan Qian, *Guo que*, 6.5397–5398.
15. Chen Changzuo, pp. 121–123. The official was Liu Yingyu.
16. Zhu Changzuo, pp. 124–125.
17. *Chongzhen changbian*, 6.98–99; Tan Qian, *Guo que*, 6.5399.
18. Zhu Changzuo, pp. 123–124, 126, 143ff.
19. Zheng Zhongkui, *Erh xin*, p. 46.
20. Ji Yun, who reports this rumor, discounts it on the argument that Wei was too widely recognized and had no sympathizers in China or contacts outside China. See Ji Yun, pp. 40–41.
21. Xu Ke, 4.10a–13a; Zhu Yizun, 67.7b–8b (inscription on the Biyunsi); Chen Dengyuan, 3.292–294.
22. *Ming shilu*, 133.4207–4209.
23. Zhu Changzuo, p. 123.
24. For this facility and its location, cf. Shih-shan Henry Tsai, *The Eunuchs in the Ming Dynasty*, p. 49.
25. Tan Qian, *Guo que*, 6.5402; *Ming x-zong x-huangdi shilu*, 1.40; Liu Ruoyu, pp. 140–141, 225.
26. Zhu Changzuo, pp. 131–158; *Chongzhen changbian*, 6.243; 7.567.
27. *Chongzhen changbian*, 8.982–986.
28. Ibid., 6.95; 8.829.
29. Ibid., 6.103–104, 114.
30. *Zhou Duanxiao xiansheng xueshu tiehuang ce* (Zhibuzu zhai congshu ed.). The many colophons written to celebrate this memorial attest to its status as a kind of sacred relic.
31. Huang Zongxi, *Huang Zongxi quanji*, 1.346 (memoir of Zhou Yanzuo); Huang *Lizhou yizhu huikan*, 5.28–36 (biography of Huang Zongxi by Jiang Fan).
32. *Chongzhen changbian*, 6.11.
33. Ibid., 6.122.
34. Ibid., 6.156.
35. Ibid., 6.386–388.
36. Ibid., 7.447–452.
37. Ibid., 7.485–486, 492; Sun Chengze, *Shan shu*, p. 18.
38. On February 11, 1628, Ni Yuanlu asked that the academies be reopened. On August 8, 1629, a newly minted *jinshi* by the name of Qian Qizhong made a similar request. Both requests were denied. Cf. *Chongzhen changbian*, 6.205–209; 9.1414.
39. Ibid., 6.299–300.
40. Ibid., 6.149–150.
41. Ibid., 6.205–209.
42. Ibid., 6.223.
43. Ibid., 6.245–252.
44. Ibid., 6.260–262.
45. Ibid., 6.299–300.
46. A good recent discussion of Donglin thought by Willard Peterson may be found in *The Cambridge History of China*, vol. 8, pt. 2, pp. 754–766.

47. Howard L. Goodman and Anthony Grafton, "Ricci, the Chinese, and the Toolkits of Textualists," *Asia Major*, 3d. ser., 3/2 (1990), 129n.106.

48. Gao Panlong, 3.39a–40a, original in colloquial language.

49. Liu Zongzhou, 2.884–890.

50. *Sanchao yaodian*, 3.1231–1245.

51. Gao Panlong, 7.43b–46a. Sun Shenxing later agreed that the "Donglin clique" had been a misnomer because few of Wei Zhongxian's victims actually had ties to the Donglin academy in Wuxi. Rather, Wei's victims were an unlinked community of the good, who, "because they are of similar species, seek each other out" (Sun Shenxing, pp. 81–84, 95–99).

52. Gao Panlong, "Discussion of Cliques," in Xu Bin, ed., *Lidai dangjian* (in Shiliao liubian, rpt. Taipei, 1974), pp. 181–184. Gao Panlong's student and literary executor, Chen Longzheng, disagreed with this essay and removed it from his master's collected works. In 1631, Chen argued that the Confucian classics did not admit of positive implications in the word *dang*. The word *qun* (flock) was more appropriate: a flock was a temporary gathering that was easily divisible, unlike a *dang*. "If I flock with others on the basis of mutual affection, then we'll divide on the basis of that same affection, because I'm closer to some than to others. In no grouping of one hundred are the members equal in quality, or in degree of affection." See Chen Longzheng, vol. 52, p. 87 (explication of "flock" and "faction").

53. Liu Zongzhou, 3.1542–1555.

54. *Chongzhen changbian*, 8.864–867 (memorial by Censor Mao Yujian); 8.879–880 (memorial by Supervising Secretary Shen Weibing); 8.900–903 (memorial by Censor Wang Xiangshuo).

55. Ibid., 8.903–904. That a viewpoint or argument cannot stand on its own merits, but must be accepted or rejected depending upon whether it was advanced by a gentleman or a small man, was a point vehemently made by Huang Zongxi in his critique of Xia Yunyi's history of late Ming factionalism. See Huang Zongxi, *Huang Zongxi quanji*, 1.327–337.

56. *Chongzhen changbian*, 8.933–937. Censor Yuan Jianlie argued that *dang* were real and appropriate—they were regional in nature and consisted of a mix of *junzi* and *xiaoren*. But *xiaoren* everywhere misused the term and wielded it as a weapon in the intrabureaucratic struggle. "No matter how pure, upright, and capable a man is, [our] opponents will claim that it is some *dang* that recommends him," he stated. "No matter how greedy, cruel, or useless a man is, opponents will claim that he is the victim of some *dang*." The ruler must therefore avoid the use of such terms as *dang* or *menhu*. Cf. ibid., 8.994–998.

57. Ibid., 8.1008–1009.

58. Huang Zongxi reports that after Cui–Wei partisan and former Censor Ni Wenhuan returned home to Nanjing, someone asked him how he could ever have attacked such *junzi* as Yang Lian and Zuo Guangdou. "Every moment has its *junzi* and its *xiaoren*," replied Ni. "When I was in the Censorate, everyone reviled Yang and Zuo as *xiaoren*, so I was just attacking *xiaoren*. Now the situation has been reversed, and everyone acclaims Yang and Zuo as *junzi*, and so now I would agree with that." Huang remarked that Ni's remarks were typically those of unprincipled opportunists. Cf. Huang Zongxi, *Huang Zongxi quanji*, 5.366–367.

59. Hou Fangyu, 7.1a–4b ("on cliques").

60. *Chongzhen changbian,* 9.1504–1513.

61. Feng Ban, 8.10a.

62. Lin Shidui, pp. 173–184.

63. Zhu Haoling, 2.651–652.

64. Chen Tingjing, 48.13a–14a.

65. Huang Zongxi, *Huang Zongxi quanji,* 1.411–413.

66. Chen Ding, 17.6b; *juanmo, xia,* 34ab.

67. Tan Qian, *Guo que,* 6.5385.

68. *Ming shi,* 21.6348.

69. Chen Ding, preface, 1a–2b. Chen states that his manuscript containing all these stories was stolen while he was staying at an inn in Beijing. The *Donglin liezhuan* he compiled in Wuxi later; in it he covered some 175 Donglin or Donglin-associated people, not all of them martyrs. Chen also states that until he undertook this project, most people of his acquaintance considered the Donglin a "pit of disaster" and were fearful even of discussing it.

70. The Qianlong emperor's book project has been well described and analyzed in R. Kent Guy, *The Emperor's Four Treasuries: Scholars and the State in the Late Ch'ien-lung Era* (Cambridge, Mass., 1987).

71. Chen Ding, imperial preface, 1ab.

72. Pan Xi'en, ed., *Qiankun zhengqi ji,* vol. 1, preface pp. 3–4.

73. One sees it, for instance, in Ding Yilan's 1979 preface to Deng Tuo's *Yanshan yehua* (Night talks from Yanshan). Deng Tuo (1912–1966) was a martyr in the cause of intellectual resistance to Jiang Qing, Mao Zedong's villainous consort. In 1979 his essays were reprinted "to console the author underground, and to extend rectified *qi* to all those made victims in the unjust case of the 'Three Family Village.' " All of Deng's writings "show a heart of sincere red toward party and revolution, and a fulfilling, loyal love for our great ancestral country and the Chinese nation; and they also show the deepest hatred for the enemy, and an uncompromising fighting spirit and undying abhorrence of erroneous thought and *waifeng xieqi* (crooked winds and deviant *qi*)." See Ma Nantun [Deng Tuo], *Yanshan yehua* (Beijing, 1981), pp. 1–4.

74. The account is contained in Huang Yu, ed., *Bixue lu,* itself contained in Wu Yingji, ed., *Donglin benmo,* pp. 133–144.

Bibliography

◂

Sources

Cai Ding 蔡鼎. 17th century. *Sun Gaoyang qianhou dushi lue* 孫高陽前後督師略. Reprint, *Ming Qing shiliao huibian* 明清史料彙編. 3d ser., vol. 4. Taipei, 1968.

Cai Shishun 蔡士順. 17th century. *Li Zhongda beidai jilue* 李仲達被逮紀略. *Suxiangshi congshu* ed.

Cao Guang 曹珖. 17th century. *Xiansi wangshi* 閒思往事. Reprint, *Beijing tushuguan guji zhenben congkan* 北京圖書館古籍珍本從刊, vol. 13. Beijing, 1987.

Chen Dengyuan 陳登原. (b. 1899). *Guoshi jiuwen* 國史舊聞. New ed., 3 vols. Taipei, 1981.

Chen Ding 陳鼎. (b. 1651). *Donglin liezhuan* 東林列傳. Reprint, *Siku quanshu zhenben* 四庫全書珍本, 5th ser., vols. 88–90. Taipei, 1974.

Chen Hong 陳鋐. *Lu Zhongjie gong nianpu* 鹿忠節公年譜. *Jifu congshu* 畿輔從書 ed.

Chen Longzheng 陳龍正. 1585–1645. *Chen Jiting xiansheng quanshu* 陳幾亭先生全書. Reprint, *Congshu jicheng* 從書集成, 3d ser., vols. 2, 51, 52. Taipei, 1996.

Chen Tingjing 陳廷敬. 1634–1712. *Wuting wenbian* 午亭文編. Reprint, *Siku quanshu zhenben*, 4th ser., vols. 378–383. Taipei, 1973.

Chen Xi 陳僖. 17th century. *Kechuang outan* 客牕偶談. *Zhaodai congshu* 昭代從書, Reprint, vol. 1. Shanghai, 1991.

Chen Zhenhui 陳貞慧. 1604–1656. *Shushi qize* 書事七則. *Changzhou xianzhe yishu* 常州先哲遺書. Reprint, vol. 2. Taipei, 1971.

Cheng Yansheng 程演生. *Tianqi Huangshan dayu ji* 天啓黃山大獄記. Reprint, *Ming Qing shiliao huibian*, 7th ser., vol. 2. Taipei, 1980. Originally published in 1936.

Chongzhen changbian 崇禎長編, Ed. Wan Yan 萬言. 1637–1705. Reprint, *Ming shilu fulu* 明實錄附錄, vols. 6–14. Taiwan: Academia Sinica, 1967.

Chongzhen Wuxian zhi 崇禎吳縣志. 1642. Reprint, *Tianyi ge cang Mingdai fangzhi xuankan* 天一閣藏明代方志選刊續編, 2d ser., vols. 15–18. Shanghai, 1990.

Dai Mingshi 戴名世. 1653–1713. *Dai Mingshi ji* 戴名世集. New ed., Beijing, 1986.

Donglin shuyuan zhi 東林書院志. 1881. Reprint, *Zhongguo lidai shuyuan zhi* 中國歷代書院志, vol. 7. Nanjing, 1995.

Fang Pao 方苞. 1668–1749. *Fang Pao ji* 方苞集. New ed., 2 vols. Shanghai, 1983.

195

Feng Ban 馮班. 1602–1671. *Dunyin zalu* 鈍吟雜錄. Reprint, *Siku quanshu zhen-ben*, 10th ser., vol. 191. Taipei, 1980.

Feng Congwu 馮從吾. 1557–1627. *Feng Shaoxu ji* 馮少墟集. Reprint, *Congshu jicheng*, 3d. ser., vol. 14. Taipei, 1996.

———. *Feng Gongding quan shu: xuji* 馮恭定全書：續集. Reprinted in *Congshu jicheng*, 3d. ser., vol. 14. Taipei, 1996.

Gao Panlong 高攀龍. 1562–1626. *Gaozi yishu* 高子遺書. Reprint, *Siku Mingren wenji congkan* 四庫明人文集從刊. Shanghai, 1993.

Gong Liben 龔立本. 1572–1644. *Yanting yonghuai* 煙艇永懷. Reprint, *Mingdai zhuanji congkan* 明代傳記從刊, vol. 128. Taipei, 1991.

Gu Yanwu 顧炎武. 1613–1682. *Tinglin yuji* 亭林餘集. Reprint, *Sibu congkan*, 四部 从刊. Shanghai, 1919–1936.

Gu Yingtai 谷應泰. 17th century. *Mingshi jishi benmo* 明史紀事本末. New ed., 4 vols. Taipei, 1956.

Haiyan xianzhi 海鹽縣志. 1877. Reprint, *Zhongguo difangzhi jicheng: Zhejiang fuxian zhiji* 中國地方志集成：浙江府縣志輯, vol. 21. Shanghai, 1993.

Hangzhou fuzhi 杭州府志. 1922. Reprint, 10 vols. Taipei, 1970.

Hou Fangyu 侯方域. 1618–1655. *Zhuanghui tang ji* 壯悔堂集. Reprint, Taipei, 1970.

Hu Jixian 胡繼先. 17th century. *Yang Dahong xiansheng zhonglie shilu* 楊大洪先生 忠烈實錄. Reprint, *Ming Qing shiliao huibian*, 6th ser., vol. 7. Taipei, 1969.

Huang Daozhou 黃道周. 1585–1646. *Ming Zhangpu Huang zhongduan gong quanji* 明漳浦黃忠端公全集. Printed ed., 1829.

Huang Yu 黃煜. 17th century. *Bixue lu* 碧血錄. In Wu Yingji 吳應箕, ed., *Donglin shimo* 東林始末. New ed., Taipei, 1964.

Huang Zongxi 黃宗羲. 1610–1695. *Huang Zongxi quanji* 黃宗羲全集. New ed., 6 vols. Hangzhou, 1985.

———. *Lizhou yizhu huikan* 梨洲遺著彙刊. Reprint, *Ming Qing shiliao huibian*, 6th ser., vols. 5–6. Taipei, 1969.

———. *Nanlei wending* 南雷文定. New ed., Taipei, 1964.

Huang Zunsu 黃尊素. 1584–1626. *Shuo lue* 說略. Reprint, *Hanfenlou miji* 涵芬樓 秘笈, vol. 8. Taipei, 1967.

———. *Huang Zhongduan gong ji* 黃忠端公集. Reprint, *Qiankun zhengqi ji* 乾坤 正氣集, vol. 24. Taipei, ca. 1960.

Hubei tongzhi 湖北通志. 1921. Reprint, 8 vols. Taipei, 1967.

Ji Yun 紀昀. 1724–1805. *Yuewei caotang biji* 閱微草堂筆記. New ed., Taipei, 1960.

———. *Ming Yian huanghou waizhuan* 明懿安皇后外傳. Reprint, *Congshu ji-cheng* 3d. ser., vol. 86. Taipei, 1996.

Jiang Dongwei 江東偉. 17th century. *Furongjing yuyan* 芙蓉鏡寓言. New ed., Hangzhou, 1986.

Jiashan xianzhi 嘉善縣志. 1892. Reprint, 2 vols. Taipei, 1970.

Jiaxing fuzhi 嘉興府志. 1879. Reprint, 5 vols. Taipei, 1970.

Jifu tongzhi 畿輔通志. 1884. Reprint, 6 vols. Shanghai, 1934.

Jin'gong yilu 燼宮遺錄. Reprint, *Ming Qing shiliao huibian,* 7th ser., vol. 2. Taipei, 1980.

Jin Risheng 金日升. ed. *Songtian lubi* 頌天臚筆. Reprint, 7 vols. Taipei, 1986.

Jishui xianzhi 吉水縣志. 1875. Reprint, *Zhongguo difangzhi jizheng: Jiangxi fuxian zhiji* 中國地方志集成：江西府縣志輯, vol. 65. Nanjing, 1996.

Kun Xin liangxian xuxiu hezhi 昆新兩縣續修合志. 1880. Reprint, 3 vols. Taipei, 1970.

Li Changchun 李長春, ed. 17th century. *Ming Xizong qinian duchayuan shilu* 明喜宗七年都察院實錄. Reprint, *Ming shilu fulu,* vols. 2–5. Taiwan: Academia Sinica, 1967.

Li Changxiang 李長祥. 17th century. *Tianwenge wenji* 天文閣文集. Reprint, *Qiushuzhai congshu,* 求恕齋從書. Beijing, 1984.

Li Qing 李清. 1591–1673. *Sanyuan biji* 三垣筆記. Reprint, *Jiayetang congshu* 嘉業堂從書. Beijing, 1982.

Li Sunzhi 李遜之. 1618–1672+. *Sanchao yeji* 三朝野記. Reprint, *Ming Qing shiliao huibian,* 3d ser. Taipei, 1968.

Li Yingsheng 李應昇. 1593–1626. *Luoluo zhai ji* 落落齋集. *Changzhou xianzhe yishu* 常州先哲遺書, vol. 19. Reprint, Taipei, 1971.

Lin Shidui 林時對. 1615–1705. *Hezha congtan* 荷牐從談. Reprint, *Ming Qing shiliao huibian,* 6th ser., vol. 7. Taipei, 1969.

Liu Ruoyu 劉若愚. 1584–ca. 1642. *Zhuozhong zhi* 酌中志. Reprint, Taipei, 1976.

Liu Tong 劉侗. 17th century. *Dijing jingwu lue* 帝京景物略. Reprint, *Biji congbian* 筆記從編, 3 vols. Taipei, 1969.

Liu Zongzhou 劉宗周. 1578–1645. *Liuzi quanshu* 劉子全書. Reprint, 6 vols. Taipei, 1968.

Mao Qiling 毛奇齡. 1623–1716. *Xihe ji* 西河集. Reprint, *Siku quanshu zhenben,* 11th ser., vols. 178–185. Taipei, 1981.

———. *Shengchao yongshi shiyi* 勝朝彤史拾集. Reprint, *Mingdai zhuanji congkan,* vol. 50. Taipei, 1991.

Mao Yuanyi 茅元儀. 1594–1640. *Dushi jilue* 督師紀略. Reprint, *Beijing tushuguan guji zhenben huikan,* vol. 9. Beijing, 1987.

Miao Changqi 繆昌期. 1562–1626. *Congye tang cungao* 從野堂存稿. *Changzhou xianzhe yishu,* vols. 17–18. Reprint, Taipei, 1971.

Miao Jingchi 繆敬持, ed. *Donglin tongnan lu* 東林同難錄. Reprint, *Mingdai zhuanji congkan,* vol. 6. Taipei, 1991.

Ming shi 明史. New ed., 28 vols. Beijing, 1974.

Mingshi chaolue 明史鈔略. Reprint, *Sibu congkan,* Shanghai, 1919–1936.

Ming shilu 明實錄. Reprint, 133 vols. Taiwan: Academia Sinica, 1965.

Ming x-zong x-huangdi shilu 明宗皇帝實錄. Reprint, *Ming shilu fulu,* vol. 1. Taiwan: Academia Sinica, 1967.

Ni Yuanlu 倪元璐. 1593–1644. *Hongbao yingben* 鴻寶應本. Reprint, 3 vols. Taipei, 1970.

Pan Xi'en 潘錫恩, ed. *Qiankun zhengqi ji* (1848). Reprint, 40 vols. Taipei, ca. 1960.

Peng Sunyi 彭孫貽. 1615–1673. *Mingzhai ji* 茗齋集. Reprint, *Sibu congkan*, Shanghai, 1919–1936.

Qian Bingdeng 錢秉鐙. 1612–1693. *Suozhi lu* 所知錄. Reprint, Taipei, 1972.

Qian Qianyi 錢謙益. 1582–1664. *Muzhai chuxue ji* 牧齋初學集. Reprint, *Sibu congkan*. Shanghai, 1919–1936.

————. *Muzhai youxue ji* 牧齋有學集. Reprint, *Sibu congkan*. Shanghai, 1919–1936.

————. *Muzhai waiji* 牧齋外集. Reprint, *Ming Qing zhi ji congshu* 明清之際從書, vol. 6. Taipei, 1974.

Qian Yiji 錢儀吉, ed. 1783–1850. *Beizhuan ji* 碑傳集. Reprint, 60 vols. Taipei, 1962.

Qianche yeyu 前車野語. Reprint, Beijing, ca. 1987.

Quan Zuwang 全祖望. 1705–1755. *Jiqi ting ji* 鮚埼亭集. Reprint, *Sibu congkan*. Shanghai, 1919–1936.

Sanchao yaodian 三朝要典. 1625. Ed. Gu Bingqian 顧秉謙. Reprint, 3 vols. Taipei, 1976.

Shaoxing fuzhi 紹興府志. 1792. Reprint, 7 vols. Taipei, 1970.

Shen Guoyuan 沈國元. 17th century. *Liangchao congxin lu* 兩朝從信錄. Reprint, 6 vols. Taipei, 1968.

Sheng Feng 盛楓, ed. *Jiahe zhengxian lu* 嘉禾徵獻錄. Reprint, Yangzhou, 1989.

Shi Runzhang 施閏章. 1619–1683. *Xueyu tang wenji* 學餘堂文集. Reprint, *Siku quanshu zhenben,* 3d. ser., vols. 354–359. Taipei, 1972.

Song Qifeng 宋起鳳. 17th century. *Bai shuo* 稗説. New ed., *Mingshi ziliao congkan* 明史資料從刊. 2d ser. Yangzhou, 1982.

Suian xianzhi 遂安縣志. 1930. Reprint, 3 vols. Taipei, 1970.

Sun Chengze 孫承澤. 1593–1675. *Chunming mengyu lu* 春明夢餘錄. Reprint, *Siku quanshu,* 2 vols. Shanghai, 1993.

————. *Tianfu guangji* 天府廣記. New ed., Beijing, 1962.

————. *Shanshu* 山書. New ed., Hangzhou, 1989.

Sun Chengzong 孫承宗. 1563–1638. *Gaoyang wenji* 高陽文集. Reprint, *Qiankun zhengqi ji*, vol. 40. Taipei, ca. 1960.

Sun Qifeng 孫奇逢. 1585–1675. *Yibing jishi* 乙丙紀事. Reprint, *Shiliao congkan* 史料從刊, vol. 6. Taipei, 1968.

————. *Jifu renwu kao* 畿輔人物考. Reprint, *Mingdai zhuanji congkan*, vol. 143. Taipei, 1991.

————. *Xiafeng xiansheng ji* 夏峰先生集. *Jifu congshu* 畿輔從書 ed.

Sun Shenxing 孫慎行. 1565–1636. *Enxu zhugong zhilue* 恩卹諸公志略. Reprint, *Mingdai zhuanji congkan*, vol. 68. Taipei, 1991.

Tan Qian 談遷. 1594–1658. *Guo que* 國榷. New ed., 6 vols. Beijing, 1958.

Tan Yuanchun 譚元春 (d. 1638). *Tan Youxia heji* 譚友夏合集. Reprint, 3 vols. Taipei, 1976.

Tang Changshi 唐昌世. 1596–1684. *Suibi manji* 隨筆漫記. Reprint, *Ming Qing shiliao huibian,* 1st ser., vol. 3. Taipei, 1967.

Tao Langxian 陶朗先. 1584–1625. *Tao Yuanhui zhongcheng yiji* 陶元暉中丞遺集. Reprint, *Congshu jicheng,* 3d ser., vol. 51. Taipei, 1996.

Tianbian dichao 天變邸抄. Appended to Huang Yu, ed., *Bixue lu. Zhibuzu zhai congshu* ed. 知不足齋從書.

Tongcheng xuxiu xianzhi 桐城續修縣志. 1827. Reprint, 3 vols. Taipei, 1975.

Wang Shizhen 王士禎. 1634–1711. *Chibei outan* 池北偶談. Reprint, Taipei, 1960.

Wang Wan 汪琬. 1624–1691. *Yaofeng wenchao* 堯峰文鈔. Reprint, *Sibu congkan.* Shanghai, 1919–1936.

Wang Yingkui 王應奎. 1684–1757. *Liunan suibi* 柳南隨筆. *Jieyue shanfang huichao* ed. 借月山房彙鈔.

Wanli dichao 萬歷邸抄. Reprint, 3 vols. Taipei, 1969.

Wei Dazhong 魏大中. 1575–1625. *Cangzhai wenji* 藏齋文集. Reprint, *Qiankun zhengqi ji,* vol. 25. Taipei, ca. 1960.

Wei Xueyi 魏學洢. 1596–1625. *Maoyan ji* 茅簷集. Reprint, *Siku quanshu zhenben,* 4th ser., vol. 373. Taipei, 1973.

Wei Yuankuang 魏元曠, ed. *Nanchang wenzheng* 南昌文徵. 1935. Reprint, 3 vols. Taipei, 1970.

Wen Bing 文秉. 1609–1669. *Xianbo zhishi* 先撥志始. Reprint, Taipei, 1968.

Wu Changyuan 吳長元. *Chenyuan zhilue* 宸垣識略. 1788. New ed., Beijing, 1983.

Wu Weiye 吳偉業. 1609–1672. *Meicun jiacang gao* 梅村家藏稿. Reprint, 3 vols. Taipei, 1970.

Wu Yingji 吳應箕. 1594–1645. *Qizhen liangchao baofu lu* 啓禎兩朝剝復錄. Reprint, *Beijing tushuguan guji zhenben congkan,* vol. 13. Beijing, 1987.

———, ed. *Donglin shimo* 東林始末. New ed., Taipei, 1964.

Wuyuan xianzhi 婺源縣志. 1693. Reprint, 5 vols. Taipei, 1970.

Xia Xie 夏燮. 1799–ca. 1875. *Xinxiao Ming tongjian* 新校明通鑒. New ed., 6 vols. Taipei, 1967.

Xia Yunyi 夏允彝. 1596–1645. *Xingcun lu* 幸存錄. *Ming Qing shiliao huibian,* 2d ser., vol. 4. Taipei, 1967.

Xiaogan xianzhi 孝感縣志. 1882. Reprint, 5 vols. Taipei, 1975.

Xinchang xianzhi 新昌縣志. 1793. Reprint, *Xijian Zhongguo difangzhi huikan* 稀見中國地方志彙刊, vol. 27. Nanjing?, 1992.

Xincheng xianzhi 新城縣志. 1935. Reprint, 2 vols. Taipei, 1968.

Xiong Kaiyuan 熊開元. 1599–1676. *Yushan shenggao* 魚山剩稿. Reprint, Shanghai, 1979.

Xu Bin 徐賓, ed. *Lidai dangjian* 歷代黨鑑. Reprint, *Shiliao liubian* 史料六編. Taipei, 1974.

Xu Ke 徐珂. 1868–1928. *Qing bai leichao* 清稗類鈔. Reprint, 12 vols. Taipei, 1966.

Xu Qianxue 徐乾學 1631–1694. *Xuben Mingshi liezhuan* 徐本明史列傳. Reprint, *Mingdai zhuanji congkan,* vol. 94. Taipei, 1991.

Xu Shichang 徐世昌, ed. 1858–1939. *Da Qing Jifu xianzhe zhuan* 大清畿輔先哲傳. Reprint, 5 vols. Taipei, 1968.

Xu Zhaotai 徐肇臺. 17th century. *Jiayi jizheng lu. Xubing jizheng lu. Xuding ji-zheng lu* 甲乙、續丙、續丁記政錄. Reprint, *Beijing tushuguan guji zhen-ben congkan,* vol. 9. Beijing, 1987.

Yan Ke 燕客 (pseud.). 17th century. *Tianren hezheng jishi* 天人合徵紀實. In Huang Yu, ed., *Bixue lu,* in Wu yingji, ed., *Donglin shimo.* New ed., Taipei, 1964.

Yang Lian 楊漣. 1571–1625. *Yang Zhonglie gong ji* 楊忠烈公集. Reprint, 2 vols. Taipei, 1968.

Yang Shicong 楊士聰. 1597–1648. *Yutang huiji* 玉堂薈記. Reprint, Taipei, 1977.

Yang Tingshu 楊廷樞. 1595–1647. *Quan Wu jilue* 全吳記略. Reprint, *Ming Qing shiliao huibian,* 3d ser., vol. 4. Taipei, 1968.

Yangzhou fuzhih 揚州府志. 1810. Reprint, 16 vols. Taipei, 1970.

Yao Zongdian 姚宗典 (fl. 1629–1661). *Cunshi lu* 存是錄. *Jieyue shanfang huichao* ed.

Ye Xianggao 業向高. 1562–1627. *Ju bian* 籧編. Reprint, Taipei, 1977.

———. *Lunfei zoucao* 綸扉奏草. Reprint, 7 vols. Taipei, 1977.

Yu Minzhong 于敏中, ed. 1714–1780. *Rixia jiuwen kao* 日下舊聞考. New ed., 8 vols. Beijing, 1981.

Yuxuan Ming chen zouyi 御選明臣奏議. 1781. Reprint, 4 vols. Taipei, 1968.

Yuyao xianzhi 餘姚縣志. 1899. Reprint, 2 vols. Taipei, 1970.

Zhang Chun 張春. 1565–1641. *Zhang Taipu buerge ji* 張太僕不二歌集. Reprint, *Ming Qing zhi ji congshu,* vol. 3. Taipei, 1974.

Zhang Po 張澎. 17th century. *Gengshen jishi* 庚申紀事. *Jieyue shanfang huichao* ed.

Zhang Pu 張溥. 1602–1641. *Qilu zhai shiwen heji* 七錄齋詩文合集. Reprint, 3 vols. Taipei, 1977.

Zhangzhou fuzhi 漳州府志. 1877. Reprint, 3 vols. Taipei, 1965.

Zhao Jishi 趙吉士. 1628–1706. *Jiyuan jisuo ji* 寄園寄所寄. Reprint, *Qingren bailu* 清人稗錄. Shanghai, 1991.

Zhao Nanxing 趙南星. 1550–1627. *Zhao Zhongyi gong wenji* 趙忠毅公文集. Reprint, *Qiankun zhengqi ji,* vols. 18–19. Taipei, ca. 1960.

Zheng Man 鄭鄤. 1594–1638. *Tianshan zixu nianpu* 天山自敘年譜. In *Zheng Man shiji* 鄭鄤事蹟. Reprint, *Guxue huikan* 古學彙刊, vol. 3. Taipei, 1964.

Zheng Zhongkui 鄭仲夔. 17th century. *Er xin* 耳新. New ed., *Congshu jicheng,* 1st ser. Shanghai, 1936.

Zhou Hongmo 周洪謨. 1562–1631+. *Jianyuan qishu* 諫垣七疏. Reprint, *Congshu jicheng,* 3d ser., vol. 19 Taipei, 1996.

Zhou Lianggong 周亮工. 1612–1672. *Laigutang chidu xinchao* 賴古堂尺牘新抄. Reprint, 3 vols. Taipei, 1972.

Zhou Maolan 周茂蘭. 17th century. *Zhou Duanxiao xiansheng xueshu tiehuangce* 周端孝先生血書貼黃冊. *Zhibuzu zhai congshu* ed.

Zhou Shunchang 周順昌. 1584–1626. *Zhou Zhongjie gong jinyu ji* 周忠介公燼餘集. *Jieyue shanfang huichao* ed.

Zhou Zongjian 周宗建. 1582–1626. *Zhou Zhongyi gong zouyi* 周忠毅公奏議. Reprint, *Qiankun zhengqi ji*, vol. 23. Taipei, ca. 1960.

Zhu Changzuo 朱長祚. 17th century. *Yujing xintan* 玉鏡新譚 (1628). New ed., Beijing, 1989.

Zhu Guozhen 朱國禎. 1557–1632. *Yongchuang xiaopin* 湧幢小品 (1622). New ed., *Biji xiaoshuo daguan* 筆記小說大觀, vol. 2. Taipei, 1962.

Zhu Haoling 朱鶴齡. 1606–1683. *Yu'an xiaoji* 愚庵小集. Reprint, 2 vols. Shanghai, 1979.

Zhu Yizun 朱彝尊. 1629–1709. *Pushu ting ji* 曝書亭集. Reprint, *Sibu congkan*. Shanghai, 1919–1936.

Zhu Zuwen 朱祖文. 17th century. *Beixing ripu* 北行日譜. *Zhibuzu zhai congshu* ed.

Zuo Guangdou 左光斗. 1575–1625. *Zuo Zhongyi ji* 左忠毅集. Reprint, *Qiankun zhengqi ji*, vol. 22. Taipei, ca. 1960.

Modern Works

Atwell, William. "The T'ai-ch'ang, T'ien-ch'i, and Ch'ung-chen Reigns." In *Cambridge History of China*, vol. 7, pt. 1, edited by Frederick W. Mote and Denis Twitchett, 585–640. Cambridge, 1988.

Baum, Richard. "The Road to Tiananmen: Chinese Politics in the 1980s." In *The Politics of China, 1949–1989*, edited by Roderick MacFarquhar, 340–472. Cambridge, 1993.

Busch, Heinrich. "The Tung-lin Shu-yuan and Its Political and Philosophical Significance." *Monumenta Serica*, 14 (1949–1955): 1–163.

Carlitz, Katherine. "Style and Suffering in Two Stories by 'Langxian.'" In *Culture and State in Chinese History*, edited by Theodore Huters et al., 207–235. Stanford, Calif., 1997.

Deng Tuo 鄧拓. *Yanshan yehua* 燕山夜話. Beijing, 1981.

Elman, Benjamin. "Imperial Politics and Confucian Societies in Late Imperial China." *Modern China*, 15/4 (October 1989): 379–418.

Esherick, Joseph W., and Jeffrey N. Wasserstrom. "Acting Out Democracy: Political Theater in Modern China." In *Popular Protest and Political Culture in Modern China: Learning from 1989*, edited by Jeffrey N. Wasserstrom and Elizabeth J. Perry, 26–66. Boulder, Colo., 1991.

Feigon, Lee. *China Rising: The Meaning of Tiananmen*. Chicago, 1990.

Goodman, Howard L., and Anthony Grafton. "Ricci, the Chinese, and the Toolkits of Textualists." *Asia Major*, 3d ser., 3/2 (1990): 95–148.

Goodrich, L. Carrington, and Chaoying Fang, eds. *Dictionary of Ming Biography*. 2 vols. New York, 1976.

Han Minzhu (pseud.), ed. *Cries for Democracy: Writings and Speeches from the 1989 Chinese Democracy Movement*. Princeton, N.J., 1990.

Huang, Ray. *1587: A Year of No Significance*. New Haven, Conn., 1981.

———. "The Lung-ch'ing and Wan-li Reigns." In *Cambridge History of China,* vol. 7, pt. 1, edited by Frederick W. Mote and Denis Twitchett, 511–584. Cambridge, 1988.

Hucker, Charles O. "The Tung-lin Movement of the Late Ming Period." In *Chinese Thought and Institutions,* edited by John K. Fairbank, 132–162. Chicago, 1957.

———. *The Censorial System of Ming China.* Stanford, Calif., 1966.

———. "Su-chou and the Agents of Wei Chung-hsien." In *Two Studies in Ming History,* edited by Charles O. Hucker, 41–83. Ann Arbor, Mich., 1971.

Israel, John. "Reflections on 'Reflections on the Modern Chinese Student Movement.'" In *Popular Protest and Political Culture in Modern China: Learning from the Past,* edited by Jeffrey N. Wasserstrom and Elizabeth J. Perry, 85–123. Boulder, Colo., 1991.

Kishimoto Mio 岸本美緒. "'Gojin' jō no seiritsu." 五人像の成立. In *Minmatsu Shincho no shakai to bunka* 明末清初の社会と文化, edited by Ono Kazuko, 503–534. Kyoto, 1996.

———. *Min Shin kyōdai to Kōnan shakai: jūnana seiki Chūgoku no chitsujo mondai* 明清交替と江南社会：17 世紀中国の秩序問題. Tokyo, 1999.

Li, Wai-yee. *Enchantment and Disenchantment: Love and Illusion in Chinese Literature.* Princeton, N.J., 1993.

Li Yan 李棪. *Donglin dangji kao* 東林黨籍考. Beijing, 1957.

Lin Jinshu 林金樹. *Tianqi huangdi dazhuan* 天啓皇帝大傳. Shenyang, 1993.

Link, Perry. *Evening Chats in Beijing: Probing China's Predicament.* New York, 1992.

Mammitsch, Ulrich Hans-Richard. *Wei Chung-hsien (1568–1628): A Reappraisal of the Eunuch and the Factional Strife at the Late Ming Court.* Ph.D. diss., University of Hawai'i, 1968.

Meng Sen 孟森. *Ming Qing lunzhu jikan xubian* 明清論著集刊續編. Beijing, 1987.

Needham, Joseph. *Science and Civilisation in China,* vol. 5, pt. 5. Cambridge, 1983.

Ono Kazuko 小野和子. *Minki tōsha kō—Tōrintō to Fukusha* 明季党社考：東林党と復社. Kyoto, 1996.

Peterson, Willard. "Confucian Learning in Late Ming Thought." In *Cambridge History of China,* vol. 7, pt. 2, edited by Frederick W. Mote and Denis Twitchett, 708–788. Cambridge, 1998.

Tsai, Shih-shan Henry. *The Eunuchs in the Ming Dynasty.* Albany, 1996.

Tsou, Tang. "The Tiananmen Tragedy: The State–Society Relationship, Choices, and Mechanisms in Historical Perspective." In *Contemporary Chinese Politics in Historical Perspective,* edited by Brantly Womack, 265–327. Cambridge, 1991.

Wakeman, Frederic. *The Great Enterprise: The Manchu Reconstruction of Order in Seventeenth-Century China.* 2 vols. Berkeley, 1985.

Wang Tianyou 王天有. *Wan Ming Donglin dangyi* 晚明東林黨議. Shanghai, 1991.

Xie Guozhen 謝國楨. *Ming Qing zhi ji dangshe yundong kao* 明清之際黨社運動考. Taipei, 1967.

———. *Zengding wan Ming shiji kao* 贈訂晚明史籍考. Shanghai, 1981.

Yan Jiaqi. *Toward a Democratic China: The Intellectual Biography of Yan Jiaqi.* Honolulu, 1989.

Zhao Chengzhong 趙承中. "Zhou Shunchang shoudai qian chuanshu Gao Pan-long shi kao." 周順昌受逮前傳書高攀龍事考. *Zhongguoshi yanjiu* 中國史研究, no. 4 (1983): 136.

Index

◀

academies: suppression of, 133–135, 187nn.28, 31, 191n.38. *See also* Donglin

Chongzhen emperor, 146; dismantles Wei Zhongxian regime, 151–155; and the *Ni an* (Treason Case), 156; opposes thorough purge, 159; on partisanship, 163–164; and the *Sanchao yaodian,* 157–159

Cui Chengxiu, 127, 129–130, 146, 148–149, 158; dismissal and suicide, 151–153

Donglin: academy, 134, 160; defined, 1, 192n.51; and Grand Secretariat appointments, 46–48, 58–59; ideas, 124; leadership, 71; and Madame Ke, 41–43; and Manchuria, 50; program for China, 31–32, 160–161; protest compared to Tiananmen, 2–5, 7, 168–169; in retrospect, 164–169; and Shoushan academy, 53–58, 133, 177n.82; sources, 5; and the Three Cases, 20, 27, 29, 58, 73, 83, 131–134, 157–159, 166

Eastern Depot. *See* Wei Zhongxian
Embroidered-uniform Guard, 101

Fang Congzhe (Grand Secretary), 17, 21–22, 25–27, 45, 47, 176n.61
fasi (Censorate, Court of Judicial Review, Ministry of Justice), 51, 53, 97–98, 100, 114, 120
Feng Congwu, 134; and Shoushan academy, 53–57, 177n.82
Feng Quan (Grand Secretary), 126–129, 187n.9

Gao Panlong, 82, 103–104, 129–130, 153, 160–162, 192n.52; suicide, 107–108

Grand Secretariat: appointments to, 46–48, 58–59, 176n.61; decline of, 130; and rescript drafting, 46
Gu Bingqian (Grand Secretary), 58, 82, 90–91, 112, 114, 131–132, 135
Gu Dazhang (Donglin martyr), 52–53, 84, 94, 97–98, 183n.102

Han Kuang (Grand Secretary), 19, 22, 39–40, 76, 78, 80–82
Huang Zongxi, 122, 157, 165, 192nn.55, 58
Huang Zunsu (Donglin martyr), 51, 65, 73–74, 79–80, 103, 130; 173n.40, 180n.32; arrest, 111, 113; imprisonment, 122; posthumous rehabilitation, 157
Hucker, Charles O., 1, 75
Huo Weihua, 34, 146

Jurchens. *See* Manchus

Ke, Madame, 35–37, 44, 75, 89, 145, 151, 174nn.10, 11; death, 155–156; Donglin attack on, 41–43

Li, Lady, 20, 36, 92, 173n.39; as focus of partisan fighting, 26–29; role in the Palace Case, 21–26, 100, 132
Li Shi, 103–104, 157, 184n.13
Li Yingsheng (Donglin martyr), 65, 80–82, 103, 105, 130; arrest, 106–107; imprisonment, 114, 122–123
Liu Duo, 136–138
Liu Zongzhou, 43, 104, 113, 161–162, 164

Manchus, 6, 32, 49–50, 141
Miao Changqi (Donglin martyr), 74, 76–77, 81–82, 106, 126, 179n.4; arrest, 102–103, 105; ideas, 124; imprisonment, 113–114

ABOUT THE AUTHOR

John W. Dardess is a professor of history
at the University of Kansas. He is the
author of *Conquerors and Confucians*
(New York: Columbia University Press,
1973); *Confucianism and Autocracy*
(Berkeley: University of California Press,
1983); and *A Ming Society* (Berkeley:
University of California Press, 1996).